ROUTLEDGE LIBRARY EDITIONS:
EDUCATION

THE BEHAVIOURIST IN THE
CLASSROOM

THE BEHAVIOURIST IN THE CLASSROOM

Edited by
KEVIN WHELDALL

Volume 68

Routledge
Taylor & Francis Group

LONDON AND NEW YORK

First published in 1987

This edition first published in 2012
by Routledge
2 Park Square, Milton Park, Abingdon, Oxfordshire OX14 4RN

Simultaneously published in the USA and Canada
by Routledge
711 Third Avenue, New York, NY 10017

First issued in paperback 2014

Routledge is an imprint of the Taylor and Francis Group, an informa company

British Library Cataloguing in Publication Data
A catalogue record for this book is available from the British Library

ISBN 13: 978-0-415-67846-9 (Volume 68)
ISBN 13: 978-0-415-75057-8   (pbk)

Publisher's Note
The publisher has gone to great lengths to ensure the quality of this reprint but
points out that some imperfections in the original copies may be apparent.

Disclaimer
The publisher has made every effort to trace copyright holders and would
welcome correspondence from those they have been unable to trace.

The Behaviourist in the Classroom

EDITED BY

Kevin Wheldall

London
ALLEN & UNWIN
Boston   Sydney   Wellington

in association with Positive Products

**Allen & Unwin (Publishers) Ltd,
40 Museum Street, London, WC1A 1LU, UK**

Allen & Unwin (Publishers) Ltd,
Park Lane, Hemel Hempstead, Herts HP2 4TE, UK

Allen & Unwin, Inc.,
8 Winchester Place, Winchester, Mass. 01890, USA

Allen & Unwin (Australia) Ltd,
8 Napier Street, North Sydney, NSW 2060, Australia

Allen & Unwin NZ Ltd,
Private Bag, Wellington, NZ

This edition first published in 1987

First edition originally published by Educational Review,
Faculty of Education, University of Birmingham, 1981.

British Library Cataloguing in Publication Data

The Behaviourist in the classroom.—[New ed.]
1. Educational psychology
I. Wheldall, Kevin
371.1′02   B1051
ISBN 0-04-370177-9
ISBN 0-04-370178-7 Pbk

Library of Congress Cataloging-in-Publication Data

The Behaviourist in the classroom.
Bibliography: p.
Includes index.
1. Behavior modification—Great Britain.   2. Classroom
management.   3. School discipline—Great Britain.
I. Wheldall, Kevin.
LB1060.2.B45   1987   371.1′024   86–17261
ISBN 0-04-370177-9
ISBN 0-04-370178-7 (pbk.)

Set in 10 on 11 point Goudy by V & M Graphics Ltd, Aylesbury, Bucks
and printed in Great Britain by Billings & Sons Ltd, London and Worcester

For my son Robin, again

Contents

Preface

In 1981, a first edition of this book was published by *Educational Review*. It consisted largely of the edited proceedings of conferences held in 1979. As such, it was the first book reporting exclusively on behavioural research carried out in British schools. The success of this first edition and its warm reception by reviewers is a tribute to the Editorial Board of *Educational Review*, and not least to the executive editor, Barrie Wade. I would like to take this opportunity of thanking them for their encouragement and for being willing to gamble on publishing a book that might have appealed to no more than a handful of behavioural 'enthusiasts'. Happily, their gamble paid off and this 1981 edition of *The Behaviourist in the Classroom* was reprinted twice. As I had hoped, publication coincided with the upsurge (or resurgence) of interest in behavioural methods that I (among others) had been attempting to help bring about. It is now fair to say that the behavioural approach to teaching is at last beginning to enjoy the growing interest of, and acceptance by, British teachers and educationists.

As a result of this renewed (and increased) interest in behavioural methods it was timely for *The Behaviourist in the Classroom* to be revised and the result is this new edition. Considerable progress has been made in the five years since its first publication and the new edition attempts to reflect these changes and developments. More than half of the material in the second edition is new, and the chapters that have been retained from the first edition have been revised and updated. I believe this collection of chapters to be a true reflection of the current 'state of the art' of the application of behavioural methods in mainstream schools in Britain today. The emphasis remains the same as that for the earlier edition where the chapters are concerned with perspectives on some current issues relating to the application of behavioural methods to (relatively) 'normal' schoolchildren and students, but some work is included with children whose behaviour problems are such as to earn them the label of 'maladjusted' and those whose academic progress is relatively slow. We have deliberately eschewed studies of, or commentary on, more clinically inspired research with severely mentally or physically handicapped children, which already receives extensive coverage.

In the first chapter, I have attempted to consider several important issues underpinning contemporary applications of behaviour analysis in education. In effect, I have tried to develop some of my (still uncertain) conceptualizations of what behaviour analysis in education is really about and to declare where I personally stand on certain issues within the discipline.

The second chapter, written jointly with my colleague and research partner for more than ten years, Dr Frank Merrett, surveys the first part of the programme of research on the behavioural approach to teaching, which we have completed in the Birmingham area. Frank has made a major contribution to both the development and the acceptance of behavioural teaching methods in this country. In this chapter, we pose five questions pertinent to the use of behavioural teaching methods by British teachers and answer them by reference to the various research studies we have completed. The conclusions drawn pave the way for a subsequent chapter on our more recent work on training teachers to use behavioural skills effectively (see Chapter 7).

Most of our previous work has been concerned with primary teachers and classrooms, although we report some studies carried out in secondary schools and this is certainly the focus of much of our current work. Eddie McNamara, however, is a specialist in behavioural approaches in the secondary school and was one of the pioneers of the behavioural movement in education in the early 1970s. In Chapter 3, Eddie reviews some of his important research in this area, and not least the examples of successful behavioural interventions carried out in secondary classrooms in Lancashire by using relatively 'light' (non-intrusive) behavioural methods.

The work of Professor Ted Glynn, first at Auckland and now at Otago University, Dunedin, in New Zealand, has rightly become influential within education during the last ten years or so, and not only within behavioural circles. Ted will be embarassed to read that I regard him as one of my mentors. He has certainly had a profound influence on my thinking in behaviour analysis. Ted's Chapter 4 is one of the few to be retained from the first edition, although he has thoroughly revised it to include much new information about the success of the behavioural methods he has developed with his colleagues by which parents can tutor their own children in important academic skills. The 'pause, prompt and praise' technique for remedial reading, in particular, is now beginning to attract enthusiasts in the UK and it should also be remembered that some of Ted's early work in this area was done during his sabbatical year in the Department of Educational Psychology at the University of Birmingham.

The Teacher-Child Interaction Project (TCIP), described in Chapter 5, was almost certainly the first major project that researched the behavioural approach in British mainstream schools. The project team comprised Dr Michael Berger, Dr William Yule and Ms Veronica Wigley and the research was carried out with the support of the Inner London Education Authority. Pioneers of the behavioural movement in mainstream schools in the UK, the TCIP team present here for the first time in full published form the results of their controlled experimental study of the effectiveness of teaching British teachers to use behavioural methods. Such training can only be properly evaluated in terms of changes in teacher and class behaviour, but this is by no means as straightforward as it might sound. This most welcome chapter provides an illuminating account of behavioural research in the real world of schools, which will act as an all-too-familiar reminder to those who have already experienced this type of work and as a caution to those about to attempt it.

If I mention that Dr Roger Burland has been described as the godfather of behavioural methods in British education, let me quickly add that his influence has been wholly benign and his methods exclusively positive! Roger was primarily responsible for inaugurating the Association for Behaviour Modification with Children (subsequently the Association for Behavioural Approaches with Children) and for carrying it almost single-handedly for many years in its infancy, when it was taking its first faltering footsteps. Equally important, however, has been his success with his behaviourally orientated Chelfham Mill School, a residential school for emotionally disturbed boys in Devon. Chapter 6 is a revised version of Roger's contribution to the earlier edition, bringing up to date his description of the methods and practices of this remarkable, if not unique, educational experiment.

Chapter 7, as mentioned earlier, is also by Frank Merrett and myself and describes the development of our Behavioural Approach to Teaching Package at the Centre for Child Study in the University of Birmingham. The logical concomitant of our programme of research, reported in Chapter 2, was to develop an effective training programme in behavioural methods for teachers. This chapter outlines the theoretical underpinnings of BATPACK and describes its development with special reference to our experimental evaluations of its effectiveness.

This revised edition, then, presents a series of perspectives by different authors on how they have seen and tackled the problems in their own particular field. The aim is to demonstrate the richness and diversity of behavioural methods and applications subsumed under the umbrella term of 'the behavioural approach to teaching'. The last two chapters constitute a critique of the behavioural approach to teaching and focus on ethical and theoretical considerations.

Chapter 8 is a revised version of that contributed by Professor Robert Dearden to the first edition of this book. As one of Britain's leading philosophers of education, Robert needs little introduction here, but what I would like to acknowledge, with gratitude, is the interest he has shown in the behavioural approach to teaching, both in this chapter and in conversation as a colleague in the Faculty of Education at the University of Birmingham. As will be seen, he is certainly not uncritical of aspects of the behavioural approach, but, unlike the usual run of education critics (see Chapter 1), he has taken the trouble to base his criticisms within a clear appreciation and understanding of what the behavioural approach is about and what it is attempting to achieve.

A further critique is provided in the last chapter by Nigel Hastings and Josh Schwieso, this time from within the behavioural 'camp'. Both Nigel and Josh, working from Bulmershe College of Higher Education in Reading, have been active in promoting behavioural methods for many years, not least through their work for the Association for Behavioural Approaches with Children (ABAC), of which Nigel is currently chairman and Josh is treasurer. Committee meetings are rarely rewarding, but my regular attendance at ABAC's meetings must certainly have been maintained by the subsequent wide-ranging and thought-provoking informal seminars with Josh and Nigel, usually held in Indian restaurants! In Chapter 9 they explore, with their usual clarity and insight, various conceptual problems within the behavioural approach to teaching. Although based on their original contribution to the first edition, this chapter is so thoroughly revised as to be almost completely new.

This book is written for teachers: all teachers – student teachers, probationer teachers, teachers scale one to scale four, heads of department, head teachers and their deputies, and college and university teachers. It will also prove useful and informative to educational psychologists, LEA advisers and inspectors, Her Majesty's Inspectorate and, not least, Secretaries of State for Education! More specifically, it will be of particular value to those who have read *Positive Teaching: The Behavioural Approach* (an introductory text by my colleague Frank Merrett and myself), because it provides readings in 'positive teaching' for all those who want to follow up their studies in greater depth and detail. Similarly, tutors who have been trained to teach our Behavioural Approach to Teaching Package and our Positive Teaching Package will find in this revised edition details of the background research they will need in order to teach their courses successfully, and much more of interest besides. I would also like to take this opportunity of drawing the attention of all readers to the Association for Behavioural Approaches with Children, which exists to promote the use of positive, behavioural methods with children in all aspects of their lives.

Finally, in editing this collection of papers I have received help and support from many individuals, but I would like to single out two for special thanks. First, I would like to express my sincere appreciation to Brenda Cox for her preparation of this manuscript. Her secretarial brilliance and skill on the word processor are matched only by her unfailing charm and ready wit. Secondly, I would like to thank Frank Merrett, my colleague, research partner and greatly valued friend, for his careful reading of successive versions of this manuscript, his many helpful suggestions and, especially, for his generosity in compiling the extremely professional index for me.

Kevin Wheldall, 1986

1

The Behaviourist in the Classroom: Revisited

KEVIN WHELDALL

Five years ago one could write with confidence that few British teachers really knew what the behavioural approach to teaching entailed, but this is no longer strictly true. Many more of the teachers I meet these days have some passing acquaintance with, or superficial appreciation of, behavioural methods and growing numbers are going out of their way to find out more about their use in the classroom. Of course, this is partly the result of an increasing awareness of what the behavioural approach is *not*. Once British teachers and educationists were disabused of the notion that behavioural methods were necessarily dependent upon the apparent penchants of American behaviourists for electric shocks and Smarties, many rapidly began to take notice. (We will return to this point later.) They realized that the behavioural approach was, quite simply, good teaching practice systematized into a clear and coherent framework. Knowing a good thing when they saw one, many British teachers quickly came to see that positive, non-punitive behavioural methods were preferable to aversive methods of classroom control. Some of these aversive methods, in any case, were being outlawed as schools and LEAs (and Parliament) attempted to grapple with the implications of the European Court's ruling against the use of corporal punishment in school.

During the last five years we have seen major changes in the fortunes of the 'behavioural movement', especially within educational psychology. Probably the majority of practising professional psychologists working in School Psychological Services (or similar organizations) would today characterize their approach as essentially 'behavioural', if rather eclectic. (Pearson and Tweddle (1985) would go further, criticising some of their professional colleagues as 'those whose eclectic repertoire of skills and approaches is drawn from bewildering combinations of incompatible psychological and educational models'!) Their behavioural orientation is less firmly rooted in applied behaviour analysis *per se*, however, and finds its origins more deeply entrenched in the field of behavioural objectives and instructional technology. This is operationalized as attempts at behavioural curriculum design and development (see Pearson and Tweddle again for an example). (I am tempted to add 'at least in the West Midlands' to qualify these statements, but my understanding is that this is a fairly general picture of current professional practice).

In this introductory chapter to the revised edition I would like to examine some of the implications of these developments for behavioural practice in British schools, to reiterate some of the points I raised in the 1981 edition of *The Behaviourist in the Classroom* and to relate all of this to developments in my own conceptualization of what the behavioural approach is all about or, rather, should be about. Hence, 'The Behaviourist in the Classroom: Revisited'.

ABA in education or behavioural pedagogy

I have sometimes used the term 'behavioural pedagogy' (Wheldall, 1982) as a shorthand term for referring to what we have learned, and are learning, about teaching from applied behaviour analysis (ABA). It may be simply defined as 'the behavioural science of teaching' and is an attempt to go beyond the concept of teachers as 'Smartie dispensers', by emphasising antecedents as well as consequences in the teaching, acquisition and maintenance of behaviour. It includes within its remit a concern with teacher variables, curriculum material as antecedent stimuli, teacher–child interactions as setting events and aspects of the physical geography of the classroom as relevant ecological variables. In short, it reflects accurately the true nature of ABA rather than the commonly accepted 'received wisdom' of what constitutes 'behaviour modification'. Since the origins and fortunes of ABA are inextricably entwined with the *Journal of Applied Behavior Analysis*, it is not unreasonable to return to this journal for a reminder of what ABA is all about. Barlow (1981), the then editor of JABA, wrote:

In 1968 JABA followed its sister publication, the *Journal of the Experimental Analysis of Behavior* into print as an outlet in the applied area for an approach and methodology that were not always welcome in other publications ... Conceptually, JABA published approaches to problems that reflected some of the philosophical foundations of behaviourism. These foundations and a methodology emphasising detailed analysis of individual behavior were puzzling to some and heretical to others.

But it was in the very first issue of JABA in 1968 that the defining characteristics of applied behaviour analysis were first explicitly laid out by Baer, Wolf and Risley (1968) in their article 'Some current dimensions of applied behavior analysis'. Wahler and Fox (1981) recently summarized these criteria succinctly:

Seven dimensions or criteria for applied behavior analysis were described. Briefly, ABA was to concern itself only with the actual behaviors of an individual, behaviors that were both socially important and objectively measured. Changes in these specific behaviors were to be related to deliberate and specifically described changes in social and non-social environmental events through experimental analyses. Behavioral techniques were effective if they produced 'large enough effects to have practical value' (Baer *et al.*, 1968), and more so if the effects were durable or generalised. Finally, behavioral procedures were to be related to a particular model or set of general principles. Though this requirement was simply that ABA be conceptually systematic to avoid collecting a grab bag of tricks and no particular model was explicitly called for, there seemed to be an implication that the model of preference was an operant one.

Wahler and Fox then go on to point out that, since 1968, there have been several proposals to expand the scope of inquiry, and make a plea themselves for a greater consideration of the role of setting events. These points are reiterated here as a reminder of what behaviour analysis is supposed to be about and of the scope of its methodology compared with the sometimes narrow and limited perspective of its application in educational settings, at least in the UK.

Anti-behavioural prejudice

In the 1981 edition of this book, I wrote:

Some of the initial reaction to recent books advocating behavioural approaches suggests that anti-behaviourist bias is still alive and well. A reviewer accused one book of being 'nakedly behaviourist' as if behaviour modification was something which should only be carried out by consenting adults in private! (Wheldall, 1981a).

It would be unwise to pretend that we now live in more enlightened times in education and that the behavioural approach is now widely accepted without question, but there are definite, noticeable signs of a thaw in the frosty reception that behaviourism has hitherto received among educationists.

This is only partly due to the efforts of behaviourists. One is tempted, in fact, to write 'almost in spite of the efforts of some behaviourists', since we have all been guilty, from time to time, of 'going over the top' in our rhapsodies about the behavioural approach as a universal panacea for all educational ills. In my own case, older if not wiser, I can now see that evidence is not enough and never was. The presentation of ideas is almost equally as important as content, not least in our use of terminology and examples (a point to which I shall return in a later section). Certainly, I believe still (as I pointed out in 1981(a and b) and 1982) that there are dangers in what I have termed 'behavioural overkill':

the employment of unnecessarily 'heavy' behavioural technology to control behaviour, with concomitant, predictable 'by-products' including poor generalisation towards control by more naturally occurring reinforcers.

The behavioural movement in education has been perhaps better served by more circumspect, less involved and more senior figures in British educational psychology, who have highlighted the benefits to be enjoyed from behavioural approaches. For example, Professor Dennis Child, in his inaugural address on taking up the chair of education at Leeds commented in 1981:

Against the trend of thinking in educational psychology at present, I happen to believe that the influence of Applied Behavioural Analysis (the new term for behaviour modification) will become substantial. The principles involved in designing software had their origins in behaviourism. But a second line of development is the treatment of disruptive children in normal classrooms, and I feel confident that any useful advice on this subject would be gratefully received by the teaching profession (Child, 1984).

Similarly, in the context of special education, Professor Peter Mittler (1981) has written:

The success of behavioural methods of teaching undoubtedly constitutes one of the major developments of the last decade.

But he goes on to warn:

Some people still associate this approach with the continuous dispensing of edible reinforcers or with the use of aversive methods, restriction of liberties or even electric shock. Even those who are better informed may have only a schematic grasp of the general principles.

There are still, certainly, many educationists who, almost wilfully, seem determined to misunderstand what the behavioural approach is about. Perhaps sympathy for behavioural methods would be unlikely to come from an educational sociologist, but the following quite from Martyn Denscombe's recent book *Classroom Control: A Sociological Perspective* is breathtaking:

One example of how pupils' thinking can be moulded to fit the [teachers'] needs for control can be found in the work of educational psychologists who, faced with 'problem' pupils, argue that bringing pupils into line can be achieved in a Skinnerian fashion through a process of stimulus–response learning (for example, O'Leary and O'Leary, 1977). Such *behaviour modification* in class can use fear, guilt, embarrassment or inconvenience as methods for negatively reinforcing types of misbehaviour by pupils and effectively working as aversion therapy to prevent the recurrence of behaviour the teachers regard as undesirable. As a strategy for control this continues to be rather heavy-handed because is still relies on teachers handing out 'deterrents' that pupils, against their wishes, feel compelled to suffer. The co-operation that gets elicited, as a result, might expect to be less than wholehearted. (Denscombe, 1985).

Thankfully, there have been those who, while not themselves being particularly behaviourally orientated, have nevertheless been supportive of the achievements of behavioural research in education. David Fontana springs immediately to mind as a (not uncritical) supporter of recent behavioural research in classrooms. In his review of the 1981 edition of this book he wrote:

It effectively answers those critics who say that behaviour modification cannot be used to much purpose in open communities such as the normal school ... They (the papers in the first edition) prove that psychological research does, after all, have something very definite to say about the practicalities of teacher-child interaction. (Fontana, 1982).

Fontana (1984) has subsequently edited a valuable collection of papers entitled *Behaviourism and Learning Theory in Education*.

Professor Ted Wragg, another influential commentator on educational practice, gives fair-minded, if rather dated, mention of behavioural methods.

More persistent has been the use of behaviourist learning theory in behaviour modification techniques, especially with maladjusted or badly behaved children. The techniques and philosophy involved have been well documented by writers such as Poteet (1974) and O'Leary and O'Leary (1977). They usually consist of a number of basic steps. Initially the teacher clarifies ground rules in behavioural terms and then baseline data are collected using classroom observation of individual children to see which rules are infringed. Teachers subsequently ignore rule breaches and deliberately and systematically reinforce rule compliance with extrinsic rewards such as tokens which can be exchanged for goods, or what the behaviour modifiers call intrinsic rewards such as privileges, but which in some cases seem every bit as extrinsic as tokens. Eventually fresh observation data are collected and behaviour change is evaluated. Behaviour modification attracts odium because in some American experiments hyperactive children were sedated and because many teachers regard the techniques as mechanistic. More recent contract forms of behaviour modification, however, where pupils negotiate their desired behaviour with teachers (Thacker, 1983) seem less objectionable. (Wragg, 1985).

Apart from the reference to Thacker in passing, it is a pity that references are given only to rather outmoded American practices, ignoring the more recent, exciting and relevant research carried out in the UK and in New Zealand, for example. Equally unfortunate is his (unsupported) reference to children being sedated in some behaviour modification experiments, since behavioural methods in the early years were often employed in large part in reaction to the medical model that advocated drug therapy.

Bennett and Desforges (1985), leading educational researchers, argue that behavioural approaches clearly demonstrate practical outcomes,

but with a disregard for an understanding of how classrooms work. Nevertheless the approach holds promise for providing explanations of classroom behaviour. Currently the assumption appears to be that children are the passive recipients of teachers' managerial reinforcers, but other contributions make clear that this is not so even when teachers appear to be getting what they ask for. Additionally, the behavioural approach appears not to concern itself with such central questions as what sort of relationship should pertain between teachers and taught in relation to particular tasks or learning objectives. Should these issues be taken seriously by researchers in this tradition it would seem likely that behavioural theory could make significant contributions to the wider understanding of classroom dynamics. Doyle's (1983) ecological approach to the explanation of classroom behaviour, for example, contains behavioural principles. He suggests that children read the subtle reinforcement procedures in classrooms and perform to maximise their return on effort. Since it is easier to follow these processes when tangible rewards are available for tangible behaviours the natural process of adaptation to the classroom militate against less tangible cognitive objectives. It may thus be that the contribution of behavioural research could be enhanced by encouraging the associationist element of the theory at the expense of the peripheralist element since this would allow the assumption that human beings interpret contiguous events. (Bennett and Desforges, 1985).

More cautious, but generally positive, support is offered here, with a leaning (if the rather opaque final sentence is interpreted correctly) to the so-called cognitive behaviour modification (Meichenbaum, 1976) currently seducing not a few behaviourally orientated clinicians (see, for example, the journal *Behavioural Psychotherapy* for recent years).

To end this section on a less optimistic note, it should not be forgotten that there are still influential figures in educational psychology who are less than sympathetic to the behavioural approach. Not always publicly 'up front' in their distaste for behavioural research, they choose instead to pretend that it does not exist, to the extent of excluding any mention of behavioural approaches.

What's in a name?

At least part of the prejudice referred to above is related to the language of the behavioural approach, and some readers may have been wondering why I have avoided using the most common term for behavioural intervention, i.e. behaviour modification. An anecdote related to me by a visiting Australian behaviour analyst working in education, Peter Sharpe, will serve to illustrate this. Peter regularly attracted 15 to 20 student teachers to his course, 'Learning principles and classroom behaviour', which covered, in essence, the behavioural approach to teaching. A few years ago he decided to re-title it, using a more accurate description, and offered the same course as 'Behaviour modification in the classroom'. That year he attracted two students. In subsequent years he reverted to his original course title and started to attract 15 to 20 students again.

This story will not surprise those who have read Woolfolk, Woolfolk and Wilson's (1977) study entitled 'A rose by any other name'. Schwieso and Hastings (1981) summarized this study neatly in their contribution to the 1981 edition of this book when discussing the 'terminology of behaviourism as an "aversive stimulus"', and drew the logical conclusions.

Briefly, a videotape showing a teacher operating a token economy in a classroom was introduced to teachers either in behaviourist terminology or as an example of, and in the terminology of, humanistic psychology. Both the teacher and the approach were rated as more effective by the group receiving the 'humanistic' commentary. The experimenters' conclusion was that the terminology used in the two conditions had created the difference. However, this and other studies have not found teachers to be hostile to B. M. procedures as observed. Responses to the 'behaviouristic' commentary were in fact positive, though significantly less so than responses under the 'humanistic' condition. This finding is compatible with those of surveys conducted with teachers in America by Musgrove (1974) and in Britain by Wheldall and Congreve (1980) which found that knowledge of B. M. procedures is associated with a positive attitude towards them. B. M. procedures, it would seem, are attractive to teachers; more so when they are not described in the terminology that derives from and is shared with Behaviourism. (Schwieso and Hastings, 1981).

It is for these reasons that the term behaviour modification is now avoided by many behaviour analysts working in education. In my own earlier writings I used the term, along with almost everyone else at the time, but it became increasingly apparent that to do so was to invite criticism. In spite of its broad definition it tended to be associated with therapy and clinical practice rather than with teaching. Moreover, whatever the rights or wrongs of the legitimacy of the term and its precise meaning within ABA, the media continually used the term to include a wide variety of non-behavioural interventional methods. The practice continues with brain surgery, electro-convulsive therapy and drug therapy, all freely and frequently described as behaviour modification. (In the sense that all of these methods will modify behaviour it cannot even be claimed that such usage is unreasonable.) In fact, the media definition for behaviour modification appears roughly to be 'anything unpleasant professionals inflict on their clients in order to change their behaviour, usually against their will and often involving electricity'. Given the false (and disturbing) impression created by use of such a term, it is scarcely surprising that, at its annual conference in 1981, the Association for Behaviour Modification with Children decided to change its name to the Association for Behavioural Approaches with Children. This was not a unanimous decision, but it was certainly greeted with relief by those of us who were weary of working with this unnecessary and counterproductive term.

It was at about this time that we began using the phrase 'the behavioural approach to teaching' which we feel is less threatening to teachers. More recently, we have also used the term 'positive teaching' (Wheldall and Merrett, 1984). Both of these terms serve to re-direct the emphasis to where it belongs, to teaching. In our earlier enthusiasm we were seeking to show how behavioural psychology could be applied to teaching. Our new orientation is subtly but significantly different, with teaching being the focus and behaviour analysis being the chosen methodology and technology by which to investigate and develop the teaching process. The term 'positive teaching' also reflects both a determination to change for the better and the non-punitive nature of the behavioural approach.

Individual differences and the behavioural approach to teaching

Another misconception commong among critics of behavioural methods in the educational world is a belief that 'individual differences' are dirty words in ABA circles. Certainly, many educational psychologists with a behavioural orientation are scornfully dismissive of anything to do with traditional psychological testing (which purports to pick up individual differences whether cognitive or affective) and of anything suggesting that there may be influences on attainment other than problems of teaching and/or learning. Coupled with this is the view that behaviourists do not believe in heredity and inherited 'mental' differences. Not only is this belief held by non-behaviourists critical of behaviourism, but it is also held by many would-be behaviourists who think they *ought* to believe this, in spite of the ever-present evidence to the contrary. As Skinner said in *Walden Two*:

Everyone knows that talents and abilities don't develop at the same rate in different children. (Skinner, 1948).

First, we shall consider the origins of the view that behaviourists believe that nothing is inherited but all is learned. This misconception dates back to Watson and his deliberately provocative and exaggerated claims. Watson was so personally convinced of the importance of learning at the expense of hypothesized, but unproven, innate processes that he made several 'over the top' and now widely quoted statements (see, for example, Watson 1913 and 1928), which have been seized on as evidence for this distorted view of what behaviourists are supposed to believe.

Few of even the most fervent behaviourists would argue so extreme an environmentalist case today, since it has been convincingly demonstrated that heredity exerts a powerful influence, which effectively sets the limits on an individual's potential. Even Watson admitted that he was exaggerating when he made his claims, and Skinner has subsequently said in interviews, 'I have never known any behaviourist, with one exception, who has denied the very considerable role of genetic endowment' (see below). Moreover, as Huxley (1964) has powerfully declared, extreme environmentalists 'forget that even the capacity to learn, to learn at all, to learn only at a definite stage of development, to learn one thing rather than another, to learn more or less quickly, must have some genetic basis'.

In *About Behaviourism*, Skinner considers the view that behaviourism 'neglects innate endowment and argues that all behaviour is acquired during the lifetime of the individual'. His argument refuting it is worth presenting in detail:

It is hard to understand why it is so often said that behaviorism neglects innate endowment. Watson's careless remark that he could take any healthy infant and convert him into a doctor, lawyer, artist, merchant-chief and yes, even beggar-man or thief can scarcely be responsible, because Watson himself repeatedly referred to the 'hereditary and habit equipment' of people. A few behaviorists, particularly J. R. Kantor, have minimized if not denied a genetic contribution, and in their enthusiasm for what may be done through the environment, others have no doubt acted as if a genetic endowment were unimportant, but few would contend that behavior is 'endlessly malleable' ...

The view that little or nothing is due to the environment has been influential in education. Students are classified essentially as those who do not need to be taught and those who cannot be, and the doctrine of universal education is challenged on the grounds that some children are essentially unteachable. But the roles of heredity and environment are to be discovered through observation, not assigned in conformity with political beliefs. Species differ in the speeds with which they can be conditioned, and in the nature and size of the repertoires they can maintain, and it is probable that people show similar inherited differences. Nevertheless, the topography or form of behaviour is only rarely affected. To say that intelligence or some other ability or trait is twenty percent a matter of the environment and eighty percent a matter of genetics is not to say that twenty percent of a person's behaviour is due to contingencies of reinforcement and eighty percent to genetic endowment. Raise one identical twin in China and the other in France and their verbal behaviour will be completely different ... (Skinner, 1974).

In his novel, *Walden Two*, Skinner had made his position crystal clear on individual differences in 'intelligence'. One of Frazier's guests at Walden Two, Skinner's behavioural Utopia, asks:

'What do you do about differences among your children in intellect and talent? And what do you do to avoid producing a lot of completely standardized young people?'

Another guest, Burris, attempts to predict Frazier's answer.

'My guess is that differences are due to environmental and cultural factors and that Mr. Frazier has no great problem to solve. Give all your children the excellent care we have just been witnessing and your differences will be negligible.'

'No, you're wrong, Burris,' said Frazier. 'That's one question we have answered to our satisfaction. Our ten-year-olds have all had the same environment since birth, but the range of their IQs is almost as great as in the population at large. This seems to be true of other abilities and skills as well.' (Skinner, 1948)

What clearer statement could we have from the archetypal behaviourist that, in his view, individual differences are genetically based?

Few applied behaviour analysts work in the field of individual differences and few workers on individual differences employ the methodology of ABA. And yet it is apparent that while human beings learn behaviours by the same general processes, the speed at which they do so and their responsiveness to subtle changes in the learning process yield individual differences in performance and style. Those working in the field of individual differences would certainly benefit from ABA methodology to test out their hypotheses regarding differences in learning rate and method between differing personality types, for example. Similarly, behaviour analysts must accept that, although the reasons for this may still be in doubt and may eventually be at least partially explained behaviourally, individuals may differ in their susceptibility to different intervention strategies. On a purely pragmatic level, *if* a much despised personality test really could sort out which children are more likely to respond to behavioural technique A than to behavioural technique B, then this would be worth knowing. *If* such methods were to exist, then not only would it be arrogant to ignore the relevant findings of non-behaviourally orientated psychologists, not only would there be a danger of throwing babies out with the bathwater, but also, more seriously, it would be grossly unprofessional to ignore such knowledge, which might improve the service we provide to client groups.

Acknowledging the role of heredity and genetic endowment, however, does not necessarily mean accepting that, for example, 'intelligence' (whatever that is) is inherited – what is inherited may be something much more basic, such as responsiveness to different forms of reward and/or punishment. Nor is accepting the role of heredity to deny for one moment the essential plasticity of human behaviour, which allows considerable and continual remoulding by the environment. So-called 'low' or 'poor' intelligence in a child, which may in part be (in some as yet unknown way) genetically determined, may possibly prevent the Watsons of today turning out 'doctors or lawyers', but this restriction is only at the upper end of a range of complex skilled behaviours that still allows considerable scope for changing the child's behaviour. In fact, it is probably true to say that relatively few children are prevented from achieving their goals by genetic limitations, since their potential is so rarely maximized by efficient manipulations of their environment to optimize appropriate learning. As Skinner says, again in *Walden Two* (op. cit.), 'How close have we ever got to making the most of our genes?'

Concluding comments

Schwieso (1985) has recently provided a brief, clear and accessible account of how applied behaviour analysts assess the outcomes of interventions and contrasts this with the traditional group designs favoured by educational researchers. Educational researchers, however much they may question behaviourism and operant psychology, could learn a lot from behavioural researchers in terms of an improved model for evaluating change and effectiveness. Note that Wahler and Fox (1981) in their summary of the defining characteristics of applied behaviour analysis, quoted earlier, commented:

Though this requirement was simply that ABA be conceptually systematic to avoid collecting a grab bag of tricks and no particular model was explicitly called for, there seemed to be an implication that the model of preference was an operant one.

The implication of this is that ABA methodology *per se* is not wedded to an operant orientation; it is simply a powerful tool for evaluating change, however that change has been brought about.

There is evidence that single subject methodology, pioneered by behaviour analysts, is becoming more generally accepted as a means by which practitioners in the field can assess the effectiveness of their work. In some field settings, it is certainly difficult, if not impossible, to run fully randomized control group designs with large sample sizes. On the other hand, using the single subject as his or her own control, by means of reversal and/or multiple baseline designs, allows rigorous evaluation of treatment effectiveness for a wide range of educational innovations. The manifest major disadvantage of such methods, weak generalizability, is (at least partially) overcome by the accumulation of clear replications of the effect over a number of subjects. It is important not to over-emphasize, however, the applicability of single case methodology; it is neither feasible nor appropriate for all experimental studies.

It is obvious from what has gone before and from my other writings in this area that my own preference and bias is behavioural and that I believe this to be the only model combining explanatory power and predictability with experimental rigour. What I am arguing here is that educational researchers could, with profit and without buying the whole behavioural package, borrow an extremely effective methodology to evaluate the effectiveness of change and innovation, irrespective of its theoretical origins, providing that there is commitment to conceptual rigour coupled with a reluctance to talk about 'benefits which cannot be measured'. If they do want to talk about unmeasurable benefits they may as well save themselves the trouble of carrying out research in the first place, and to discuss them *ex post facto*, when the evidence has not gone your way, is quite simply dishonest.

As the subsequent chapters of this book demonstrate, the behavioural approach offers a powerful technology for bringing about dramatic changes in classroom behaviour. There is no doubt that behavioural methods can be used to reduce disruptive and off-task behaviours and to increase appropriate behaviour and work output of pupils. A question many ethical behaviourists working in education then have to ask themselves is 'How far am I justified in doing this? Am I not in danger of using my behavioural knowledge and skills to support an educational system which I am not sure I believe in?' Obviously questions such as these are personal ones, which we each must answer for ourselves. For my own part, I have been concerned that by helping teachers to develop more positive and more effective classroom management skills, I might also be helping merely to prop up weak or lazy teachers. One does not have to be a Marxist to view disruptive behaviour as a legitimate reaction to uninspired teaching and dull lessons. However, there is little doubt that for effective teaching to take place, good classroom discipline is essential. Classroom management of children's social behaviours, in the sense of increasing the amount of time children spend academically engaged in relevant learning tasks, is a necessary (but not sufficient) condition for academic progress. To put it more simply, the quality of lesson content may be irrelevant if the children are not attending or, even worse, if they are disruptive.

However, it is equally important to emphasize that behaviour analysis can offer far more than just effective classroom management. It can also help us to determine ways of teaching that encourage not only the learning of relevant skills and material in classroom settings but also their generalization to the real world. As we have said elsewhere, 'the more artificial the teaching context, the less likely the behaviour is to generalize to the natural environment' (Colmar and Wheldall, 1985).

This issue is also addressed by Ted Glynn in his inaugural lecture, 'Contexts for independent learning', at the University of Otago.

If we are genuinely concerned about aims of autonomy and independence in learning, then we need to discover and analyse those characteristics of responsive environments which support and promote independent learning. (Glynn, 1985).

Glynn then goes on to specify four characteristics of a truly responsive learning context:

(i)   It should promote initiations by the learner.
(ii)   It should encourage shared activity by the learner with a more skilled performer.
(iii) It should foster reciprocity and mutual influence between the less skilled party and the more skilled party.
(iv)   It should provide the appropriate amount and type of feedback for a learner's initiations.

It is immediately obvious that the form of educational context Glynn is attempting to specify is not only radically different from the commonly held view of what a 'behaviourist' classroom must be like (the 'clockwork classroom') but is also totally at odds with those who would seek to devise a programmed behavioural curriculum, built on behavioural objectives and supported by endless behavioural check lists. In some respects, Glynn's model may be seen as an attempt to operationalize child-centred discovery learning within a behaviour analytic framework. He ends this paper provocatively:

The next challenge will be to convince teachers and instructors that the more they relinquish control, the more their learners will utilise opportunities for independent learning. (Glynn, 1985, p. 13).

This is a very different picture from that painted by Denscombe as noted earlier; it goes a long way towards answering Bennett and Desforges's criticisms; it may even be regarded by some as one of Pearson and Tweddle's 'bewildering combinations of incompatible psychological and educational models'. It is also a fresh, radical perspective within behavioural pedagogy that goes a long way towards laying the ghost of Winett and Winkler's (1972) classic criticism: 'Current behavior miodification in the classroom: be still, be quiet, be docile.'

Reactions have been mixed to our own recent writings on, for example, antecedent control (Wheldall, 1981b), 'behavioural overkill' (Wheldall, 1982) and behavioural language training

(Colmar and Wheldall, 1985), which are critical of some current behavioural applications in education. In discussion, we have come across those who share a similar contemporary behaviour analytic perspective and are appreciative. In addition, we meet those who are not behaviourally oriented but who can feel some sympathy with this wider perspective. Some of these, however, have suggested that this is no longer 'real' behaviourism and have reacted with alarm, the argument running something like this: 'I agree with what you are saying, but I am not a behaviourist and, therefore, you are not either.' Similarly, some behaviourally oriented psychologists seem to believe that criticism of behavioural practice signifies a weakening of resolve, of selling out or perhaps just of getting old. In reply to this we can only point out that behaviour analysis does not stand still, it is a developing discipline. It is no disrespect to the original behavioural theorists and their accomplishments to seek to clarify and to improve our models of behaviour. Behaviour analysis has certainly moved on from the 1950s, and it has come a long way since the 1970s. In the 1980s, both our theory and our practice should reflect these new developments in conceptualization and experimental research. As behaviour analysts we must be seen to be, in Glynn's (1983) phrase, 'responsive to data.'

References

Baer, D. M., Wolf, M. M. and Risley, T. R. (1968), Some current dimensions of applied behavior analysis, *Journal of Applied Behavior Analysis*, vol. 1, pp. 91–7.

Barlow, D. H. (1981), Editorial, *Journal of Applied Behavior Analysis*, vol. 14, pp. 1–2.

Bennett, N. and Desforges, C. (1985), 'Conclusion', in Bennett, N. and Desforges, C. (eds,) *Recent Advances in Classroom Research* (Edinburgh: Scottish Academic Press).

Child, D. (1984), 'Educational psychology: past, present and future', in Entwhistle, N. (ed.), *New Directions in Educational Psychology. Volume 1: Learning and Teaching* (London: The Falmer Press).

Colmar, S. and Wheldall, K. (1985), 'Behavioural language teaching: using the natural language environment', *Child Language Teaching and Therapy*, vol. 1, pp. 199–216. Also in *Behavioural Approaches with Children*, vol. 8, pp. 92–110 (1984).

Denscombe, M. (1985), *Classroom Control: A Sociological Perspective* (London: Allen & Unwin).

Doyle, W. (1983), 'Academic work', *Review of Educational Research*, vol. 53, pp. 159–200.

Fontana, D. (1982), Review of *The Behaviourist in the Classroom: Aspects* of Applied Behavioural Analysis in British Educational Contexts, British Psychological Society Education Section Review, vol. 6, no. 1, pp. 55–6.

Fontana, D. (ed.) (1984), Behaviourism and Learning Theory in Education (Edinburgh: Scottish Academic Press).

Glynn, T. (1983), 'Building an effective teaching environment', in Wheldall, K. and Riding, R. (eds) Psychological Aspects of Learning and Teaching (London: Croom Helm).

Glynn, T. (1985), 'Contexts for independent learning', Educational Psychology, vol. 5, pp. 5–15.

Huxley, A. (1964), Essays of a Humanist (New York: Harper & Row).

Meichenbaum, D. (1976), 'Cognitive behavior modification', in Spence, J. T., Carson, R. C., Thibaut, J. W. and Bandura, A. (eds) Behavioural Approaches to Therapy (Morristown, NJ: General Learning Press).

Mittler, P. (1981), foreword to McBrien, J. and Foxen, T. Training Staff in Behavioural Methods: the EDY In-Service Course for Mental Handicap Practitioners (Instructor's Handbook) (Manchester: Manchester University Press).

Musgrove, W. (1974), 'A scale to measure attitudes toward behavior modification', Psychology in the Schools, vol. 11, pp. 392–6.

O'Leary, K. D. and O'Leary, S. G. (eds) (1977), Classroom Management: The Successful Use of Behaviour Modification (2nd edition) (New York: Pergamon).

Pearson, L. and Tweddle, D. (1984), 'The formulation and use of behavioural objectives', in Fontana, D. (ed.) Behaviourism and Learning Theory in Education (Edinburgh: Scottish Academic Press).

Poteet, J. A. (1974), Behaviour Modification: A Practical Guide for Teachers (London: University of London Press).

Schwieso J. (1985), 'Baselines and basics: some issues in the assessment of behavioural interventions in education', Educational Psychology, vol. 5, pp. 159–70.

Schwieso, J. and Hastings, N. (1981), 'The role of theory in the teaching of behaviour modification to teachers', in Wheldall, K. (ed.) The Behaviourist in the Classroom: Aspects of Applied Behavioural Analysis in British Educational Contexts (Birmingham: Educational Review Publications).

Skinner, B. F. (1948), Walden Two (New York: Macmillan).

Skinner, B. F. (1974), About Behaviourism (London: Jonathan Cape).

Thacker, V. J. (1983), Steps to Success (London: NFER–Nelson).

Wahler, R. G. and Fox J. J. (1981), 'Setting events in applied behavior analysis: towards a conceptual and methodological expansion', Journal of Applied Behavior Analysis, vol. 14, pp. 327–38.

Watson, J. B. (1913), 'Psychology as the behaviorist views it', Psychological Review, vol. 20, pp. 158–77.

Watson, J. B. (1928), The Psychological Care of Infant and Child (London: Allen & Unwin).

Wheldall, K. (1981a), 'The behaviourist in the classroom', in Wheldall, K. (ed.), The Behaviourist in the Classroom: Aspects of Applied Behav-

ioural Analysis in British Educational Contexts (Birmingham: Educational Review Publications).

Wheldall, K. (1981b), 'A before C or the use of behavioural ecology in the classroom', in Gurney, P. (ed.), *Behaviour Modification in Education, Perspectives No. 5* (Exeter: School of Education, University of Exeter). Also published in: Wheldall, K. (ed.), *The Behaviourist in the Classroom: Aspects of Applied Behavioural Analysis in British Educational Contexts* (Birmingham: Educational Review Publications, 1981) and in Entwhistle, N. (ed.), *New Directions in Educational Psychology. Volume 1. Learning and Teaching* (London: The Falmer Press, 1985).

Wheldall, K. (1982), 'Behavioural pedagogy or behavioural overkill', *Educational Psychology*, vol. 2, pp. 181-4.

Wheldall, K. and Congreve, S. (1980), 'The attitudes of British teachers towards behaviour modification', *Educational Review*, vol. 32, pp. 53-65.

Wheldall, K. and Merrett, F. (1984), *Positive Teaching: The Behavioural Approach* (London: Allen & Unwin).

Winett, R. A. and Winkler, R. C. (1972), 'Current behavior modification in the classroom: be still, be quiet, be docile', *Journal of Applied Behavior Analysis*, vol. 5, pp. 499-504.

Woolfolk, A. E., Woolfolk, R. L. and Wilson, G. J. (1977), 'A rose by any other name: labelling bias and attitudes towards behavior modification, *Journal of Counselling and Clinical Psychology*, vol. 45, pp. 184-91.

Wragg, T. (1985), 'Theory into practice', in Bennett, N. and Desforges, C. (eds) *Recent Advances in Classroom Research* (Edinburgh: Scottish Academic Press).

2

British Teachers and the Behavioural Approach to Teaching

FRANK MERRETT and KEVIN WHELDALL

The behavioural approach to teaching is now beginning to offer an important contribution to current educational practice in Britain. Since the early 1970s, inspired by the pioneering work of North Americans such as Becker and Madsen, British educational psychologists (both 'pure' and 'applied') have been researching and developing appropriate behavioural methods for use in mainstream British schools. Among the early 'enthusiasts' were Presland, first in the West Midlands and later in Wiltshire, Berger and Yule in London, Ward in Manchester, Harrop and McNamara in the North West and our own 'Birmingham Group' (Wheldall, Merrett and associated students) in the West Midlands. Since much of the earlier work was carried out in special schools for client groups with manifest handicaps, it is not perhaps surprising that initial attempts to use behavioural methods in mainstream schools were often characterized by the use of rather intrusive intervention strategies, cheerfully referred to as 'behaviour mod'.

Latterly, however, some British researchers and practitioners, including ourselves, have tended to play down the clinical angle and have adopted a perspective that might more properly be referred to as applied behaviour analysis in education. By this we mean a methodology that seeks to identify effective teaching methods based on behavioural principles. In many respects this 'behavioural approach to teaching' may be seen as an approach which merely formalizes and enhances, within a behavioural methodology and technology, the natural learning processes of the everyday world. We have also referred to the behavioural approach to teaching as 'positive teaching' (Wheldall and Merrett, 1984) and have defined it in terms of five basic principles:

1. We are to be concerned with the observable, i.e. behaviour.
2. For practical purposes we assume that behaviour is learned.
3. Learning involves change in behaviour.
4. Changes in behaviour depend mainly upon consequences.
5. Behaviours are also governed by the contexts in which they occur.

Of particular importance, we believe, is our emphasis on antecedents (principle 5), since much other current British behavioural practice has been concerned almost obsessively with consequences and consequence management strategies. Wheldall (1981, 1982) has warned of the dangers of 'behavioural overkill', which he sees, in part, as the result of an over-emphasis on (usually rather intrusive) consequence management strategies and the relative neglect of antecedents. Our concern with antecedents (especially setting events) reflects the influence of Ted Glynn's work in New Zealand (see for example, Glynn 1982, 1985).

In this chapter our aim is to consider a series of five questions about British teachers in relation to the behavioural approach to teaching, with particular reference to classroom management of troublesome social behaviour. We would like to outline the research of the 'Birmingham Group' in this area during the last ten years, in an attempt to answer these questions.

Our first question concerns the degree to which troublesome classroom behaviour is a problem for British teachers and, if it is, which particular classroom behaviours are regarded as most troublesome. We present the results from our surveys in answer to this question. Secondly, we ask whether there is any evidence that behavioural methods employed by British teachers are effective in British classrooms. In reply we provide a brief literature review of critical references and give details of four of our demonstration studies. Next we ask, to what extent do British teachers already employ behavioural methods 'naturally' in their everyday teaching? The results of a long-term programme of teacher observations are reported in response to this question. Then we turn to teacher attitudes, asking what British teachers think of the behavioural approach and report the results of a large-scale attitude survey and smaller-scale studies of attitude change. Finally, we anticipate the concern of Chapter 7 in this book and begin to explore the question of how best to teach teachers to use behavioural techniques. It was the empirical answer to this question that inspired our subsequent programme of research on the effective training of teachers in behavioural skills for classroom management.

Question 1: To what extent is troublesome classroom behaviour a major problem for British teachers and what forms does it take?

Children with behaviour problems are a common type of referral to educational psychologists and teachers frequently cite classroom behaviour problems as one of their major difficulties. We have recently carried out several surveys enquiring into the frequency and nature of troublesome behaviour experienced by primary and secondary schoolteachers in their classrooms. Our first, small-scale survey, as reported in Merrett and Wheldall (1984), was a preliminary investigation into troublesome behaviour in primary classrooms. This helped us to identify critical problem behaviours and the experience gained influenced our subsequent survey based on a much larger, random sample. Since the findings of the two studies are very similar, we shall detail only the second study here.

In brief, the survey involved a 25 per cent random sample (32 schools) of the infant, junior and junior infant schools in a West Midlands LEA. Sufficient survey forms were sent to each of these schools for each full-time class teacher (excluding nursery classes) to complete the questionnaire. Replies were received from all 32 schools involved, resulting in a very high overall return of 93 per cent. Of the 198 teachers replying, 73 per cent were women; 22 per cent of respondents were in their twenties, 40 per cent in their thirties, 22 per cent in their forties and 16 per cent were in their fifties. The sample was distributed fairly evenly over the range of ages taught from five to eleven years, with the majority of men teaching the older children.

Half of our sample (51 per cent) responded affirmatively to the question 'Do you think that you spend more time on problems of order and control than you ought?' (in the earlier survey it had been more than 60 per cent. Equal percentages of men and women responded in this way and there were no differences between the responses of younger and older teachers or between teachers of younger and older pupils.

The average class size was 27, of whom, on average, 4.3 children were regarded as troublesome and three of these were boys. Asked to pick out the two most troublesome individual children in the classes, boys were picked as the most troublesome by 76 per cent and as the next most troublesome by 77 per cent. This supports the anecdotal view that boys tend to be more troublesome than girls.

What was it that these children did that was troublesome? As we said earlier, it was the type and frequency of troublesome behaviours in which we were particularly interested. We offered ten alternative behaviour categories, based on our pilot inquiries. When asked to pick out the most troublesome behaviours 46 per cent of teachers cited 'talking out of turn' (TOOT) and 25 per cent cited 'hindering other children' (HOC). None of the other categories reached more than 10 per cent. This was confirmed by the results for the next most troublesome behaviour in which 31 per cent opted for HOC and 17 per cent for TOOT. The findings for the most *frequent* troublesome behaviours gave a very similar picture, and when we went on to ask about the troublesome behaviours of individual children again we got the same response, TOOT followed by HOC. These two behaviours are not particularly serious misbehaviours, in the sense that they are hardly crimes, but they are irritating, time-wasting, exhausting and stressful for teachers in that they give rise to a great deal of 'nagging' and other negative responses. It is interesting to note that this sort of classroom problem behaviour has been shown to be particularly amenable to resolution by behavioural methods.

We now have the results of a survey of the opinions of secondary school teachers in the West Midlands carried out with one of our students (Houghton) using a very similar questionnaire. The survey was based upon a stratified random sample (approximately 30 per cent) of the secondary schools in the same West Midlands LEA as before. Replies were received from all six schools approached, yielding a return of 62 per cent. Of Houghton's sample of 251 secondary teachers responding, 55 per cent admitted to spending more time on problems of order and control than they ought. Once again TOOT (50 per cent) and HOC (17 per cent) were readily identified as by far the most frequent and troublesome classroom misbehaviours. As at the primary level, boys were picked as the most troublesome by the majority of teachers. McNamara (see Chapter 3), following up our earlier work and using much the same procedures, obtained similar findings from his sample of secondary schoolteachers from the North-West.

What may we conclude from these results? We would appear to be safe in assuming that the classroom behaviour problems experienced by most primary and secondary schoolteachers are not dissimilar. TOOT and HOC appear to be the two misbehaviours that teachers generally identify as causing them the most trouble and as occurring most often. This is not to say that serious incidents do not occur occasionally in some schools, but they are certainly not as frequent as the media would have us believe.

Physical violence appears to be a problem encountered (thankfully) by relatively few teachers, but many, if not most, teachers have their job made more stressful by the petty misbehaviours which we have identified and which, as we have said, are readily amenable to amelioration by behavioural methods.

Question 2: Do behavioural methods work for British teachers?

The ways of maintaining control in an unruly classroom are many and various, but the key principle is basically to praise the good while trying to ignore the bad. This central tenet was elucidated in classic, original studies carried out in the United States by Becker, Madsen, Arnold and Thomas (1967) and Madsen, Becker and Thomas (1968) using 'rules, praise and ignoring' (RPI) strategies. These studies were replicated many times in north America and behavioural approaches to classroom management were subsequently refined and elaborated. Since the late 1960s a vast literature has accumulated (mainly North American), which we shall not attempt to review here. Our concern is rather to examine the impact of this research, here, in Britain.

In this section an attempt is made to review briefly some of the experimental studies of the use of behavioural methods in the classrooms of 'ordinary' schools in Britain. No attempt is made here to consider case-study reports and we have concentrated on published experimental work. A fuller account may be found in Merrett (1981).

One of the earliest British researchers was Barcroft (1970) who carried out a straightforward replication of the American study of Becker, Madsen, Arnold and Thomas (1967), which used contingent teacher attention and praise in reducing classroom behaviour problems in a class of 10-year-olds. The results were positive, but Barcroft referred to the difficulties experienced in the freer organizational climate of English schools and expressed doubts about the usefulness of 'praise and ignore' techniques with the whole class. Two studies by Ward (1971, 1973) subsequently attempted replications of the Becker *et al.* RPI techniques. Generally, his results were ambiguous and Ward suggested that the chief problem in studies of this sort is the communication of advice.

Harrop and Critchley (1972) and Peake (1972) also attempted to demonstrate improvement in the classroom behaviour of primary schoolchildren following increased social reinforcement from their teachers. Both studies were considered by their authors to have been successful, but both admitted to methodological weaknesses. It was not until the studies by Tsoi and Yule (1976) and Merrett and Wheldall (1978) were published that firm evidence could be presented for the success in British contexts of behavioural methods of classroom management. Both these studies were well-designed and well-controlled and the results were unequivocal.

Tsoi and Yule attempted to investigate the effects of group reinforcement in two junior classes, using extra break time as a back-up reinforcer.

The results suggested that group reinforcement produced desirable changes in the behaviour of the school children. Two types of group reinforcement strategies, one using the behaviour of a single child as the basis for reinforcement and the other using changes in group behaviour as the criterion, both proved to be effective (Tsoi and Yule, 1976 p. 137).

They suggested that the cost in terms of the school programme and in teacher's time was low. 'Above all, this study has provided teachers with another effective management technique which involves the participation of the whole group' (p. 138). In this study, which involved the whole class, observation of the teacher's behaviours was included and inter-observer agreement was measured. Similarly, Merrett and Wheldall (1978), in a study that will be reported later, demonstrated clearly that RPI within the context of a 'timer game' was extremely effective in increasing time on-task and the work output of a junior school class. Rennie (1980) subsequently employed similar 'game' strategies with success. But, as with the 'game' in the Merrett and Wheldall (1978) study, generalization was a problem.

Studies employing strategies other than consequence management (i.e. by antecedent control) have been infrequent. Studies by Wheldall, Morris, Vaughan and Ng (1981) on manipulating seating arrangements in junior school classes are reported later in this chapter.

Far fewer studies have been carried out in secondary schools. Davie's (1975) study, although not truly experimental, underlined the first and major difficulty associated with interventions in secondary schools (which have subject specialization), namely, that classes are constantly changing teachers. Davie also comments that, 'Talking, which accounted for almost half of all recorded misbehaviour, was the most chronic form of inappropriate behaviour' (p. 121). This comment is in accord with the results of our surveys reported earlier in this chapter.

McNamara (1979) investigated the effectiveness of self-recording with older pupils in a comprehensive school, using three observers and three teachers. In each of three classes, two pupils, matched for production of inappropriate verbal behaviour, were observed. After baseline observations were complete, one was instructed in self-recording techniques while the other acted as a control. In one of the rooms results were clear cut, the experimental child showing marked improvement in response rates, but in the other two they were equivocal. McNamara's subsequent experimental research and his surveys of troublesome behaviour in secondary schools (McNamara 1984, 1985) are reported by him in the next chapter of this book. Merrett and Blundell (1982) have also successfully demonstrated the use of self-recording in the secondary school, while Wheldall and Austin (1980) have shown that simple RPI and the manipulation of antecedents can be effective with secondary classes. Both studies are detailed later in this chapter.

To sum up, the early studies like those of Barcroft (1970), Ward (1971, 1973) and Harrop and Critchley (1972) were seen to have serious methodological weaknesses. By degrees, however, later researchers paid attention to more careful definition and observation, to inter-observer agreement and to more rigorous design methods. Studies such as those of Tsoi and Yule (1976), Merrett and Wheldall (1978), Wheldall and Austin (1980), Merrett and Blundell (1982) and McNamara (1984) provide strong evidence that behavioural methods can be applied to a variety of problems at both primary and secondary levels in 'ordinary' schools. One positive outcome of many of the studies reported is that the children involved have enjoyed taking part. Note that the studies reported have been almost exclusively concerned with consequence management strategies. An exception has been Wheldall's work in changing the work demands in secondary maths lessons (Wheldall and Austin, 1980) and in manipulating seating arrangements in junior classrooms (Wheldall et al., 1981).

It can be seen that the effectiveness of the behavioural approach to teaching in the normal classroom has been demonstrated in a variety of experimental studies. Our own studies carried out in local schools have demonstrated how to bring about changes in the problem behaviour of single children, small groups and even whole classes of children from a wide range of educational populations. At the extreme ends of educational provision, we have shown how nursery-aged children can be encouraged in more appropriate eating behaviours (Wheldall and Wheldall, 1981) and how poorly motivated higher education students can benefit from behavioural techniques using the Keller Plan or Personalised

System of Instruction (Pickthorne and Wheldall, 1982). In addition, we have shown teachers how to encourage and increase the kinds of behaviour they want to see children in their classes engaged in and which are of educational benefit to them. Our work with teachers shows how such simple and straightforward strategies can dramatically improve the classroom atmosphere and the quantity and quality of work produced. Moreover, methods like these yield a more satisfying and rewarding classroom experience for both teachers and children. Further demonstration studies of this sort are provided in our book (Wheldall and Merrett, 1984), which is an introduction to the behavioural approach to teaching, and in Merrett (1985), a collection of intervention studies carried out by teachers.

We now turn to a more detailed description of four of our demonstration studies of behaviour management carried out in British schools. Before doing so, however, we wish to digress briefly in order to explain why we felt it necessary to provide such demonstration studies when there was already a wealth of North American evidence testifying to the effectiveness of the behavioural approach to classroom management. In our experience, British teachers are not impressed by American research. They do not share our admiration for the quantity, quality and rigour of the research carried out by behaviour analysts in schools in the United States. Quite simply, North American studies travel badly in that British teachers find it difficult to relate their experience to the examples given. They are wary of importing techniques directly since there are many cultural differences and the education systems are dissimilar. For example, a study which one of us once recounted to a large group of teachers (as reported anecdotally by Skinner himself) concerned a token economy in which a classroom teacher operated, in effect, a simple lottery. The teachers listened with interest until it was disclosed that the prizes to be awarded were transistor radio sets and Hallowe'en outfits. At this point all credibility was lost in a gale of protest and scornful laughter. Apparent recommendations to use such expensive rewards for good behaviour rang hollow in the ears of British teachers struggling to provide the bare essentials, such as paper and pencils, on a meagre budget. In our view, British teachers needed to be convinced by appropriate demonstration studies that behavioural techniques do work in British schools and that expensive rewards and equipment are an unnecessary luxury. The four studies that follow are examples of such demonstrations.

Playing the game

'Playing the game' was one of the first interventions we attempted and constituted an elaboration of RPI in the context of a 'timer' game. The original study was carried out in 1976 (Merrett and Wheldall, 1978). In retrospect, it was rather intrusive but has subsequently proved to be remarkably robust. It was carried out in a primary school situated in the centre of a large council housing estate in the West Midlands. The teacher was a young woman who had just successfully completed her probationary year. The headmaster was more than pleased with her work but, in her own estimation, she was having a lot of trouble in controlling her class of thirty intellectually below-average 10–11 year-olds. Classroom seating was arranged around four groups of tables and it was decided to make use of this very common arrangement in the intervention strategy.

A cassette-tape was prepared to give a clear 'ping' on a variable interval schedule of sixty seconds, i.e. the signal occurred at irregular intervals but on average once per minute. On hearing the sound, the teacher would look at one of the four tables of children, indicated in random order on a prepared sheet, and note the behaviour of the target child for that table by ticking the appropriate column. The target child was chosen afresh for each observation session on a random basis and thus all children in the class were observed during the study. Every time she heard the 'ping' the teacher had to glance at the schedule to see which table was next and record the behaviour of the target child by ticking the appropriate code. She could do this while working at her desk and, with experience, while walking around the room still advising individuals and commenting on their work. After several weeks of practice, 'baseline' data were collected. The reliability of the teacher's results was checked from time to time by an observer using an identical record sheet and the same target children. There was found to be very high inter-observer agreement of around 90 per cent.

The teacher who had no prior knowledge of behavioural methods, was then given some basic instruction in the behavioural approach and was helped to choose an intervention which appealed to her and which she felt she could cope with. Briefly, the children were told the rules of a 'game' which were:

(a)   we stay in our seats while working;
(b)   we get on quietly with our work;
(c)   we try not to interrupt.

These rules were to be clearly displayed in the classroom. While the game was in progress, the cassette would be switched on and every time the 'ping' sounded the teacher would look at one of the tables. If everyone on the table was keeping the rules, then each child on the table would score a house point. (They were assured that all tables would get an equal number of turns, but that the order would be random.) Each time team points were given, the fact was announced publicly and was accompanied by verbal praise. This procedure lasted for five weeks, when an amendment was announced. In future, points were to be awarded on only 50 per cent of the signals (pings), again on a random basis. The pings continued to serve the teacher as a signal for observing and recording the behaviour of the target children as well as a signal for reinforcement.

The results were remarkable and immediate and are shown in graph form in Figure 2.1. From the baseline average of only 44 per cent, on-task behaviour rose to 77 per cent following the intervention. Moreover, when the amendment to a 'leaner' schedule of reinforcement was made, after five weeks, the on-task behaviour rose even higher, to more than 85 per cent. It is of interest that the quality of off-task behaviour also changed. Whereas, before the intervention, disruptiveness was shown mainly in loud talking and quite a lot of movement around the

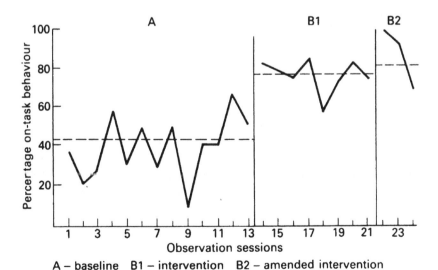

A – baseline   B1 – intervention   B2 – amended intervention

Figure 2.1 Percentage on-task behaviour of the class over the three phases.

room, afterwards, off-task behaviour consisted chiefly of passive inattention, daydreaming, watching other children and so on. A purely subjective judgement of the classroom after the intervention was that great improvement had taken place in terms of orderliness and quiet during classroom work periods.

An attempt was also made to measure academic output both before and after intervention. Samples of written work taken from the class during the collection of baseline data showed a mean output of approximately five written words per minute. During one of the first intervention sessions this had improved to a mean of approximately 13 written words. However, the number of spelling errors, despite the big increase in output, had hardly changed. This finding is important, because it supports a simple and straightforward relationship between on-task behaviour and the quantity and quality of academic work completed. Others have questioned the necessity of this relationship (e.g. Winter, 1982; Glynn, 1983), whereas our findings have been unequivocal in consistently supporting it.

The teacher found the recording of baseline data 'tedious and time-consuming' at first, but it became easier and less distracting after practice. She said she 'felt silly' about putting up the wall chart of rules, but agreed that the intervention was immediate and proved to be very effective. She indicated that she would continue using behavioural techniques, especially in providing positive reinforcement for good behaviour. Almost all the children liked the 'game' and commented upon the fact that the quietness that prevailed enabled them to concentrate and get on with their work without interruption. It had been supposed initially that some stronger back-up reinforcement might be needed to make the game effective, but the house points proved to be sufficient on their own.

We have found 'Playing the game' to be very robust and almost immediately effective with many age groups and in numerous situations. It has been replicated many times by our students and has never been known to fail (Wheldall and Merrett, 1984). The great problem is one of generalization, which calls for skilful use of praise and encouragement while the game is in operation and a careful passing out of the use of the 'game' itself so that behaviour comes under the control of more natural social reinforcement. However, as noted above, it is intrusive, and not suitable for all lessons. No teacher would want to use such a device often, or for long periods, but it remains a very useful strategy for gaining, or regaining, control of a group of children who display difficult and/ or disruptive behaviour.

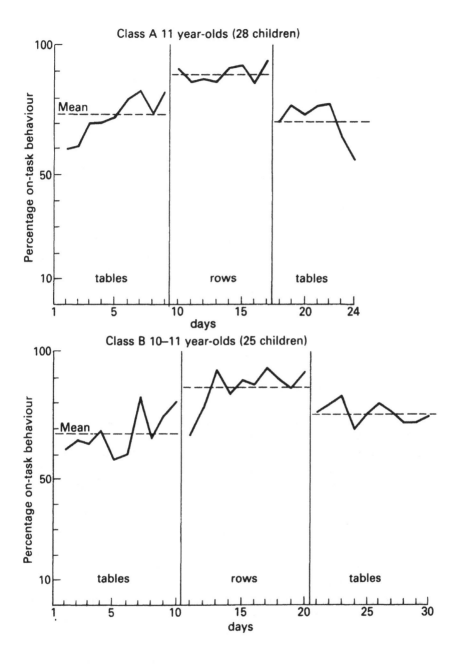

Figure 2.2 Percentage on-task behaviour of the two classes over the three phases.

Rows versus tables

We referred earlier to the paucity of reported interventions in which antecedents were manipulated. One of the few such studies in the UK was our research looking at the effects of different classroom seating arrangements. Two parallel studies, comparing 'tables' and 'rows' type seating arrangements, were carried out with the fourth year classes in two junior schools. One class consisted of 28 mixed ability children and the other comprised 25 similar children. In both classrooms children were normally seated around tables in groups of four, five or six.

Both classes were initially observed for two weeks in their normal seating arrangements around tables, using an observation schedule based on a time sampling procedure to obtain estimates of on-task behaviour. This was defined, by the teachers, as doing what the teacher instructed, i.e. looking at and listening to her when she was talking to them, looking at their books or work cards when they were required to complete set work, being out of seat only with the teacher's permission, etc. The observation schedule required each child to be observed twice per lesson in random order for 30 seconds. This yielded an estimate of the percentage on-task behaviour for each child for each lesson, which, when averaged, gave an estimate of on-task behaviour for the whole class.

After observing the class for two weeks sitting around tables (baseline data), the desks/tables were moved into rows without comment from the teacher and the children were observed for a further two weeks. Finally, the tables were returned to their original positions (again without comment) for a further two weeks of observation. This time there were a few complaints from the children, because they said that they preferred sitting in rows.

Mean on-task behaviour for both classes was higher when the children were placed in rows than when they were seated around tables. Mean on-task behaviour in class A was 72 per cent under 'tables 1', 88 per cent under 'rows' and 69 per cent under 'tables 2'. Similarly, for Class B, mean on-task behaviour was 67 per cent under 'tables 1', 84 per cent under 'rows' and 72 per cent under 'tables 2'(see Figure 2.2). As might be expected, the effect was less in the case of children with high initial on-task behaviour. However, when we looked at children whose initial on-task behaviour was very low (less than 60 per cent) the effect was considerable (increases of 30 per cent being not uncommon).

This study clearly shows that children's on-task behaviour may be controlled by the simple manipulation of antecedents, in this case seating arrangements, especially with children whose initial on-task behaviour is low. Manipulating antecedents in this way may prove to be a more immediate means of gaining control over children's classroom behaviour than changing the consequences. It may also prove to be a useful bridge while other behavioural teaching skills are learned and could serve to increase instances of desired behaviour for the teacher to reinforce.

The reasons for these findings would appear to be straightforward. The tables-based seating arrangement is geared towards enhancing social interaction. It facilitates eye contact, a prime means of initiating a social encounter and provides a setting for increased participation in such interactions by involving the whole group. Moreover, tables provide ideal cover for covert aggression or teasing by means of kicking or pinching under the table, thereby increasing disruption. Rows formations, on the other hand, minimize either form of social contact, allowing fewer occasions for the teacher to comment adversely and more instances of desirable behaviour for him or her to comment upon favourably. In short, it could be argued that it amounts to little short of cruelty to place children in manifestly social contexts and then to expect them to work independently. The 'Oracle' research (Galton, Simon and Croll, 1980) suggests that, while the 'tables' formation is the commonest in junior schools, individual tasks are the norm there. It is also interesting to note that the research of Bennett (Bennett, Desforges, Cockburn and Wilkinson, 1984) and others has suggested that a quite low proportion of the social interaction engaged in by children sitting in the 'tables' formation is work-related.

It must immediately be emphasized, however, that a return to rows for all work is not being advocated. It is offered only as a possible strategy to encourage academic work which requires the child to concentrate on the specific task in hand without distractions. Rows would be totally inappropriate, for example, for small group discussions or group topic work, where table arrangements might prove more effective.

This study is fully reported in Wheldall, Morris, Vaughan and Ng (1981) and the findings have subsequently been replicated several times. For example, it has been shown that changing the seating arrangements in this way also influences teacher behaviour (see Wheldall, 1981), and Bennett and Blundell (1983) have shown that the 'rows' formation led to improved quantity and quality of academic output. The latter finding has been supported by another study carried out with one of our students (Croft), and our work with another student (Olds) has demonstrated that mixed-sex seating arrangements yield higher trends of on-task behaviour than same-sex seating arrangements (Wheldall and Olds, in preparation).

Self-recording in the secondary school

Our research has also included work with secondary-aged pupils who can sometimes be directly involved in the interventions. We have completed several studies in self-recording, for example. One such study involved a boy in the remedial department of a large modern comprehensive school. Timothy was rather small and under weight for a thirteen-year-old and his work was well below that expected for his age. He made a great deal of fuss before settling to work and took any opportunity to stop, setting himself up as a 'funny man' to gain attention and approval from his peer group. He became very anxious if asked to work alone and would soon begin to interact with others, usually to their annoyance or detriment. His behaviour became disruptive if he encountered the slightest difficulty and if the teacher was not immediately available.

The teacher allowed three weeks of the new term to pass, as a settling-in period, before collecting baseline data. The operational definitions of behaviour for this purpose were:

(i)   getting out of seat and moving two paces or more to touch another child's work;
(ii) unrequested verbalizations, which could be heard over a distance of two metres.

A sampling technique was employed for observation, so that the teacher could get on with her job of teaching for most of the time. A tape cassette was played, which gave an audible cue thirty times during a half-hour period but at variable intervals. Every time she heard the signal the teacher would look at Timothy and tally his behaviour as on-task or one of the categories of deviance, as defined above. On-task behaviour was defined as 'getting on with whatever he had been given to do'. Baseline data were collected on five successive days for thirty minutes during the time set aside for English, which occurred at a different period on each day.

During this phase the records indicated that most of Timothy's time was taken up with what had been defined as deviant behaviour. He was very shocked when he saw a graphical representation of these data. He had not realized that he 'wasted so much time', as he put it and asked, 'What are *we* going to do about it?' Because of his obvious concern and his relative maturity, it was decided that he should be involved in the monitoring of the intervention, by self-recording. The intervention programme was aimed at increasing on-task behaviours, using the Premack principle. Timothy was very fond of using a Doodle Art sketch pad to colour in a cartoon picture and this was made contingent upon on-task behaviour. The boy was accordingly given the opportunity to tally his on-task behaviour with an observation schedule like his teacher's and using the same signal. He knew that the teacher would be recording at the same time and understood that only those tally marks for on-task behaviour that were agreed between them would count. Ten such agreed tally marks could be exchanged for two minutes of the reinforcing activity, i.e. colouring in the Doodle Art picture. During weeks seven and eight the teacher arranged a return to baseline conditions so that Timothy did not record his on-task behaviour and was not told his 'score' until the end of the week. He continued to earn time for the reinforcing activity, however. During weeks nine and ten, Timothy once again recorded his on-task behaviour every time the signal was heard.

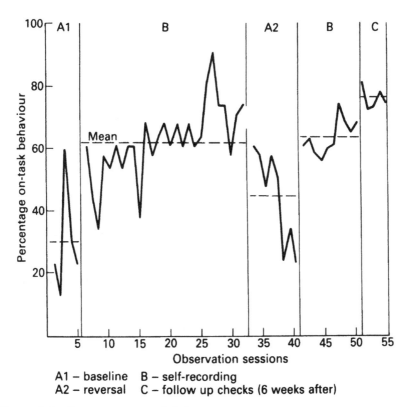

A1 – baseline   B – self-recording
A2 – reversal   C – follow up checks (6 weeks after)

Figure 2.3 Percentage on-task behaviour over the five phases.

As can be seen from Figure 2.3, on-task behaviour rose from a mean level of approximately 30 per cent to more than 60 per cent during the first intervention period. For the two weeks when the boy ceased to record his own on-task behaviour this level fell to a mean of 40 per cent, rising again to a mean level of 61 per cent for the last two weeks when the programme was reintroduced. When the boy first began to record his own behaviour, the level of agreement between his results and those of his teacher was just over 90 per cent. Subsequently, the level of agreement never fell below 93 per cent, which is very satisfactory.

The end of the programme coincided with the end of the term. The next term, Timothy agreed to try to maintain his on-task behaviour without the aid of self-recording, although the teacher maintained her social reinforcement in response to his efforts. After six weeks, she carried out base-line observations just as she had done at the beginning, using an ear-piece with the recorder so that Timothy would not be aware of what was going on. The graph shows that there is good evidence that his rate of on-task behaviour was being maintained at a high level. One of the chief effects of this intervention was that, for the first time, Timothy began to receive positive reinforcement from his teacher for well-defined acceptable behaviour instead of peer reinforcement for 'clowning' and other avoidance behaviours. It would seem that, in this case at least, teenage children are not too sophisticated to respond to a simple intervention. It appealed to his peers as well as to Timothy himself. This study is reported fully in Merrett and Blundell (1982).

Using RPI in secondary maths lessons

Our fourth example of a successful demonstration study was also concerned with secondary-aged pupils and demonstrated how simple RPI and manipulation of antecedents could yield dramatic results. The study was undertaken in a large, split-site, multicultural comprehensive school with a group of twenty-five academically below-average 14–15 year-old boys and girls during their maths periods. They were being taught by the headmaster of the school, a highly skilled teacher who had a good working relationship with the children. The class gave trouble to most teachers who attempted to teach them and even the headmaster admitted that they could be troublesome. Baseline data were collected during eleven lessons, in which on-task behaviour was observed and recorded. All twenty-five children were observed for at least two 30-second periods during each lesson, in random order. The amount of time within each 30-second period spent by the child in on-task behaviour was recorded on a cumulative stopwatch and percentage on-task behaviour per lesson was calculated. A second observer was also present on six occasions during the baseline and subsequent phases to provide estimates of inter-observer agreement, which were consistently more than 90 per cent.

The observations indicated that a large proportion of off-task behaviour occurred when some of the class (the quicker children) had finished the task set for them, usually consisting of a number of examples written on the blackboard. It was at this time (chiefly) that they would indulge in off-task behaviours themselves and disrupt the work of others. It was suggested to the teacher that he should manipulate antecedents for on-task behaviour by putting up extra problems on the blackboard for the quicker children to get on with until all the class had finished the basic set. Following this first intervention, observation continued for a further seven sessions.

It was decided that on-task behaviour could be improved still more and a multi-element or alternating conditions design was agreed upon. On the first, and thereafter on every other day, a simple 'rules, praise and ignore' strategy was employed. The rules for this were:

1 When the teacher is talking to us we look at him.
2 We get on with our work quietly.
3 We try not to stop others from working.
4 We try to pay attention to our work and try not to daydream.

These were printed on card, read out at the beginning of every lesson and also, on occasion, referred to during the lesson, but were not contingent upon infractions of the rules. Infringements of the rules were to be ignored unless serious or dangerous disruptions occurred. On the other hand, the teacher was instructed to look out continually for pupils keeping the rules, individually or collectively, and to emphatically praise those pupils, e.g. 'It's good to see Errol, David and Patrick getting on with their work'; 'Susan is working well'; 'This is good, I can see you are all working well'

In addition to this, on the alternate days, a 'timer game' was introduced, where points for on-task behaviour were awarded. Basically, a cassette was played, which emitted a chime on a variable interval, averaging two minutes. The chimes were a signal to the teacher to look up to see if the pupils were observing the rules. If they were, he awarded a point and praised the class. Each point was worth one minute's free time during the last maths lesson of the week on Friday afternoon. Scoring twenty-five points would win the whole lesson off. During the free period, the children could chat quietly but freely, or play games such as draughts or cards, which were supplied. This multi-element design was implemented and observations continued for a further fifteen lessons.

As the graph (Figure 2.4) clearly shows, average percentage on-task behaviour for the class during the baseline phase was fairly stable over the eleven lessons at around 55 per cent. After the extra sums were put on the blackboard, average on-task behaviour rose by nearly 15 per cent to an average of 69 per cent. The multi-element design clearly showed the relative effectiveness of the two subsequent procedures, which improved on-task behaviour still further. On the odd days when the RPI strategy alone was employed, on-task behaviour increased to more than 80 per cent, and by yet another 10 per cent on even days when the 'timer game'

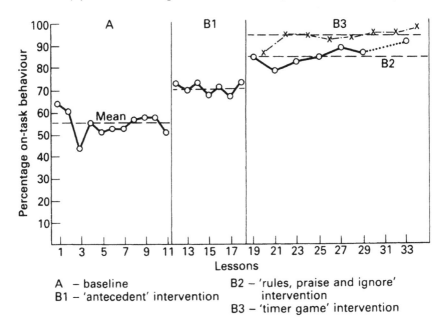

A – baseline   B2 – 'rules, praise and ignore'
B1 – 'antecedent' intervention   intervention
                                  B3 – 'timer game' intervention

Figure 2.4   Percentage on-task behaviour of the class over the four phases.

was played. It should be noted, however, that, after twelve lessons, the rates for the two conditions merged at around 95 per cent average on-task behaviour.

This study gives a firm indication that relatively 'light' behavioural strategies, such as the manipulation of antecedents and RPI, can be very effective at the secondary level, although the teacher found that ignoring some behaviours was quite difficult. Doubt is thus cast on the 'common-sense' view that overt teacher praise may be counter-productive with adolescents (see, for example Ward, 1976). Another aspect of this study that may call for comment is the use of 'free time' as a reinforcer. It was the opinion of the headteacher who took part in this study that more work was done in the four lessons for which the intervention was in operation that in the five lessons occupied by maths previously. This study is reported fully in Wheldall and Austin (1980). A subsequent study carried out with another of our students (Kane) has demonstrated that simple RPI strategies were effective in reducing noise levels and increasing rates of on-task behaviour in home economics lessons in a secondary school.

To sum up this section, the answer to our question is unequivocal. Behavioural methods have clearly been shown to be effective in British classrooms. Moreover, this is true of both primary and secondary schools where non-intrusive 'light' interventions have demonstrated their efficiency in bringing about good working conditions in the classroom.

Question 3: Do British teachers use behavioural methods naturally?

Many of the techniques we advocate in the behavioural approach to teaching are those that are used by successful parents and teachers the world over. Consequently, one of the commonest reactions of teachers when they first hear about them is to say, 'That's nothing new. We do that sort of thing already.' One of the main objectives of the research discussed here was to discover the extent to which teachers make use of social reinforcement in terms of their use of approval and disapproval of children's behaviour. It must be remembered, of course, that approval is not necessarily positively reinforcing and that unless it occurs contingently, it is unlikely to be effective. Nevertheless, teachers are, at least potentially, powerful mediators of social reinforcement and this operates chiefly through their approval and disapproval of children's behaviour.

Work in this area is slim and appears to have been pioneered in the United States by White (1975), who attempted to measure rates of teacher (verbal) approval over grades. Under her guidance sixteen observational studies were carried out. In brief, she found that, over all, teachers' disapproval of children's behaviour outweighed their approval. They expressed more approval than disapproval for academic behaviour, but, for social behaviour, although teacher disapproval was common, teacher approval was almost non-existent.

Russell and Lin (1977), in South Australia, subsequently carried out related research, observing and recording the behaviours of the ten children classed by their teacher as worst-behaved and the ten children classed as best-behaved, noting their teacher's negative and positive responses to them. Teacher responses overall were directed at a higher rate to the worst-behaved group. Negative teacher responses, in particular, were directed to the worst-behaved group at a much higher rate than to the best-behaved group. This was also true for positive teacher responses but these differences were not so marked. The authors suggest that there was no evidence that high rates of appropriate behaviour were being maintained by teacher attention, but that, in fact, teacher attention probably maintained the rate of inappropriate behaviour in the worst-behaved group. They point to the differences in the two types of behaviour. Getting on with work is unobtrusive and calls for no comment: it is maintained by longer-term, perhaps intrinsic, rewarding, and on very lean, intermittent schedules. Much inappropriate behaviour, on the other hand, is brief but overt, intrusive and disruptive – almost demanding a response from the teacher. No attempt was made in this study to separate types of teacher behaviour into responses to academic and social behaviours. Russell and Lin suggest that improvements could best be brought about by a great increase in teacher attention to appropriate behaviour, or a great decrease in teacher attention to inappropriate behaviour, or both.

Thomas, Presland, Grant and Glynn (1978) also followed up White's work, looking at natural rates of teacher verbal approval and disapproval in some schools in New Zealand. Although the observational techniques used and the cultural and ethnic groups were different from those of White, their results were similar to hers; most teachers displayed rates of disapproval that were higher than their approval rates. The work of Thomas and his co-workers was, however, restricted to one grade level (Grade VII, i.e. ages 11.6 to 13.6 years) and to ten teachers.

To our knowledge, no comparable body of data had been collected on the classroom behaviour of British teachers, and so we decided to examine this sort of behaviour, using carefully designed, objective measures of teacher behaviour and of the behaviour of the classes they taught. Data were obtained by a number of observers, using specially prepared schedules, on 128 teachers in primary schools in the West Midlands area. In all cases, each teacher and class was observed for at least three sessions, each of thirty minutes.

The observation schedule employed is known as OPTIC (Observing Pupils and Teachers In Classrooms) and has been developed by the authors over the last ten years in the Centre for Child Study at the University of Birmingham. The earliest version was loosely based on a schedule devised by Persons, Brassell and Rollins (1976). OPTIC allows the observer to look systematically at and sample two main aspects of classroom behaviour. In Section A, the observer is concerned with positive and negative teacher responses to children's academic and social behaviours. Instructional language is ignored. Section B is concerned with estimating children's on-task behaviour. The observer alternates between the two sections at three-minute intervals. Studies carried out by our students working in pairs have shown the schedule to be both reliable and valid. Inter-observer agreement figures for both sections of the observation schedule have averaged over 90 per cent and the schedule has been shown to compare very favourably, in terms of validity, with others that pick up much more data but are more time-consuming. A full account of OPTIC and its development is to be found in Merrett and Wheldall (1986a).

In brief, we found that British primary schoolteachers gave out more approval than disapproval overall. For academic behaviour alone, rates of approval were three times higher than disapproval rates, whereas for social behaviour disapproval was five times higher than approval (as Table 2.1 shows). Approval is seldom given for social behaviour despite the fact that disapproval occurs at a fairly high rate.

Table 2.1 Rates of approval and disapproval of social and academic behaviours by a sample of British teachers.

Behaviour	Approval		Disapproval		Total	
	Mean	(%)	Mean	(%)	Mean	(%)
Academic	37.3	(50)	12.3	(16)	49.6	(66)
Social	4.3	(6)	21.3	(28)	25.6	(34)
Total	41.6	(56)	33.6	(44)	75.2	(100)

Our finding that teachers tended to approve over all slightly more than they disapprove conflicts with the results of the other studies already referred to. This may be due to differences in style between

British teachers and those in America, Australia and New Zealand. In all other important aspects, however, our findings concurred with those of other studies, in particular with White's assertion that, 'Teacher approval for managerial (social) behaviour was almost non-existent'. (White, 1975) The children were expected to behave well and were reprimanded if they did not. Our main conclusion is that most British teachers do not use approval nearly as much as they think they do and that few use it systematically. To this extent, then, the answer to our question is that few British teachers are using behavioural methods 'naturally'. This study is reported fully in Merrett and Wheldall (1986b). So far, we have little evidence regarding the behaviour of secondary teachers in Britain. We are currently collecting similar observational data on teachers in secondary schools. Preliminary results suggest that secondary schoolteachers use very similar rates of both positive and negative responses than their primary colleagues.

Question 4: What do British teachers think of behavioural methods?

To our knowledge, there is little empirical evidence regarding the attitudes of British teachers towards the behavioural approach to teaching, but a purely subjective estimate is of widespread ignorance and/or antipathy based upon misconceptions of what it might entail. This may, in part, be due to the attitudes and practices of those responsible for the training of teachers. Consequently, in 1977, we carried out a small survey to investigate the attitudes of British teachers towards behavioural methods, as no evidence was then available. It was important to know (a) if teachers' general attitudes were favourable or unfavourable and (b) if their attitudes became more favourable once they knew more about the behavioural approach. Musgrove's (1974) scale provided a ready-made and suitable instrument for attempting to provide such data.

Musgrove, working in the University of South Florida, constructed a scale (based on the Likert model) to measure teachers' attitudes towards 'behaviour modification'. His aim was to evaluate the attitudes of teachers in normal schools regarding their acceptance of behavioural theory and its application in educational settings. His scale used five points (strongly agree, agree, neutral, disagree, strongly disagree) and the scores 1–5 were numerically weighted so that the higher the score, the more positive the attitude towards 'behaviour modification'. The final version of the scale consisted of 20 items, comprising 13 positively and 7 negatively worded statements, the order having been randomly determined. The absolute range of scores on the scale runs from 20, signifying a strong rejection of 'behaviour modification' to 100, signifying extremely positive attitudes, with a mid-score of 60, representing a neutral or undecided attitude. Examples of attitude statements include:

1 The benefits of behaviour modification have been exaggerated.
5 The extra time involved in dispensing rewards is worth the improvement seen as a result of using behaviour modification.
7 Behaviour modification helps a child to learn how to cope with his environment.
15 Behaviour modification is just another name for tyranny.

Musgrove's original (random) sample of 280 Florida elementary schoolteachers yielded a mean scale score of about 65, which indicates a slightly positive attitude towards 'behaviour modification' overall.

Using the same scale, Throll and Ryan (1976) examined a sample of 92 New Zealand primary school teachers 'to see if certain subject variables were related to a behavioural approach to dealing with classroom behaviour problems'. The overall mean score in their study was 69, higher than that obtained by Musgrove. Their analyses revealed no significant relationships between test score and age, length of teaching experience or sex. A highly significant difference was found, however, between those who had had previous exposure to behavioural methods and those who had not. Vane (1972), Frey (1974) and Ryan (1976) have also looked at attitudes towards 'behaviour modification', but not, however, using Musgrove's scale. These studies are reviewed in Wheldall and Congreve (1980), in which a full report of our own research may be found.

In our study, 116 experienced British teachers, following advanced courses in education, anonymously completed Musgrove's scale and another sheet giving details of school experience and knowledge of behavioural techniques. Their overall mean score was about 64, which suggested a general ambivalence of attitude in line with Musgrove and Throll and Ryan. More important, however, was the evidence suggesting a strong positive relationship between prior knowledge of behaviour modification by study or practical experience and attitude scores. Teachers who had prior experience or knowledge of behavioural methods scored significantly higher than those who had not, i.e. they were very much more favourable. Moreover, this finding was supported by a retest study. Forty-four teachers from the original sample were retested after completing one of our courses on the behavioural approach to teaching. Following the course of lectures their scores had improved significantly by an average of seven points (from 63 to 70). Of the 44 retest subjects, 31 showed increased scores and only 13 showed retest scores that remained the same or lower.

What, then, do our results tell us in answer to our question? Primarily, they suggest that if teachers hold negative or neutral views about the behavioural approach as a result of ignorance or incomplete or factually incorrect knowledge, then once they are educated or corrected about what behavioural methods really entail, they will express a more positive attitude toward its use. The evidence for attitude change as a result of greater knowledge consists of both the retest study and the fact that those who have previously taken a course or who have had practical experience express more positive attitudes. We have subsequently replicated these findings. In the study described in the following section, teacher attitudes (as measured on the Musgrove scale) were again shown to improve significantly following a course of instruction in behavioural methods (Merrett and Wheldall, 1982). Similarly, studies evaluating the effectiveness of the Behavioural Approach to Teaching Package (BATPACK; see Chapter 7) have shown teacher attitudes becoming significantly more favourable after BATPACK training. We feel that such findings are important evidence for providing courses about the behavioural approach in the initial training of teachers. The more teachers know about the behavioural approach the more positive they become about its use in schools and the more receptive they are likely to become to the idea of applying behavioural methods in their own classrooms. We shall return to this point in the next section.

Question 5: Does telling teachers about behavioural methods improve their classroom behaviour?

As we have said, many studies have demonstrated the effectiveness of training teachers in the use of classroom management techniques derived from applied behaviour analysis. Moreover, as we have shown, teachers' attitudes towards the behavioural approach are certainly influenced by increased knowledge of it. The question remains, however, whether learning more *about* the behavioural approach, compared with being trained in the techniques, leads to improved classroom performance.

There seem to be no detailed reports of attempts to teach behavioural techniques in initial training courses or subsequent attempts at evaluations of effectiveness. A survey by Schwieso and Hastings (1981), based on a questionnaire sent to colleges of education, universities, polytechnics and colleges of higher education that were engaged in teacher education, was an attempt to obtain information regarding teaching about behavioural methods in initial training. These authors suggest that their figures refer to about two-thirds of the 45,000 students in initial training in Britain and that, of these, about half get some information about behaviour modification. It tends, on the whole, to be information about the method rather than the opportunity to put it into practice. Moreover, this may be an optimistic estimate since their figures are based on the courses for which replies were received. (This is likely to be a biased sample, given that courses that did include coverage were more likely to have replied to a survey into behaviour modification.)

We carried out a study that attempted to evaluate the effectiveness of teaching student teachers about the behavioural approach in terms of their subsequent classroom performance on teaching practice. The subjects were 110 mature students, all preparing for primary work, who were in their third year and about to embark on their final teaching practice. All the supervisory tutors on the college staff (thirty-four in all) helped in the assessment. Of the 110 students beginning their third year, twenty-five chose psychology as an option course, which included a taught element on the subject of 'behaviour modification'. The twenty-five students in this option group were considered to be the experimental group and the remainder, who had made other choices for their third-year work in education, constituted the control group.

The experimental group attended a short course on 'behaviour modification', which was mainly concerned with pin-pointing, defining, observing and recording behaviour. It also included the opportunity for observation work in classrooms, using schedules the students had devised themselves. There was not much time for a close study of possible interventions, but reference was made to the importance of positive reinforcement and especially of social reinforcers at junior school level. The Musgrove (1974) scale was completed by the students in the experimental group before the course in behaviour modification began and again after the completion of the experiment.

Since a large number of supervisory tutors was to be employed in observing and reporting, a rating scale was devised with a view to using their existing skills. This scale asked tutors to rate their students, using five literal grades for eight aspects of classroom performance. It was suggested that in grading students on the scale tutors should attempt to use the whole of the scale from A to E.

Two aspects of performance were of particular interest: item 3 'Control of classroom situation – discipline' and item 5 'Ability to respond to children in terms of encouragement, praise, etc.'. It was argued that students who had some knowledge of 'behaviour modification' would be able to cope better with their final teaching practice than those who had not, especially in regard to items 3 and 5, since the course would have alerted them to the importance of social reinforcement in control of the classroom situation. The other items on the scale were there simply as a cover for these key questions.

When the gradings for the experimental and control groups were compared item by item, those for the experimental group were found to be superior. Comparison of the means for the experimental and control groups for each of the items 1 to 8 showed the experimental group to be higher in each case, but none of these differences was statistically significant except for item 8, overall rating. Either the students in the experimental group were not much more successful in their controlling tactics and in their use of positive reinforcement than the control group, or their tutors failed to notice any differences that were present. The results of the two testings on the Musgrove scale, however, showed that a highly significant change in opinion had taken place (from a mean score of 66 to 73). Students' attitudes changed positively in favour of 'behaviour modification', presumably as a result of the course.

Thus we had no firm evidence to suggest that teaching teachers about behavioural methods manifestly improved their teaching performance in the classroom, but we did find evidence for improved attitudes. From this, we concluded that teaching teachers about the behavioural approach is undoubtedly useful, if not essential, because, although not directly improving classroom practice it did make teachers more amenable to its use. In other words, the seeds were sown for future in-service work in which training in *how*, rather than teaching *about*, might be given. Such in-service courses are far more likely to yield improved classroom practice. It is probably expecting too much at this stage in British education for practical training in the behavioural approach to be given in initial training courses, in view of the lack of expertise or even of interest of college lecturers, but we feel that we must press strongly for the inclusion, at the very least, of courses that are *about* the behavioural approach.

Conclusions

In summary, the following conclusions may be drawn from our ten-year programme of research in schools:

1 At least half of British teachers are prepared to admit that they spend more time on problems of order and control than they ought. The behaviours that they find troublesome in class are not serious in the sense that they are violent or destructive, but they are, nevertheless, time-consuming and disruptive. The two main problem behaviours are 'talking out of turn' and 'hindering other children'.
2 Behavioural methods have been shown to be highly successful in bringing these sorts of problem behaviour under control in both primary and secondary classrooms.
3 Contrary to self-reports, British teachers do not generally apply behavioural principles 'naturally'. In fact, praise for appropriate social behaviour is relatively rare in British classrooms and reprimands are common.
4 British teachers become more favourably disposed towards the use of behavioural methods once they know more about what the behavioural approach entails.
5 Teaching teachers *about* behavioural methods has not been shown to yield clearly discernible changes in their classroom behaviour.

In our view, these conclusions have clear implications for practice and they have influenced our subsequent programme of research into the effective training of teachers in behavioural methods of classroom management (see Chapter 7). In order for effective teaching to be possible, good classroom discipline is an essential prerequisite. Our research and our experience indicate that teachers are only too aware of the fact that having to deal continually with troublesome behaviour is stressful and prevents them from getting on with what they see as their proper job. Many have commented that classroom management was barely mentioned in their initial training courses. The current phasing-out of corporal punishment has encouraged teachers to look for non-punitive positive methods of achieving good classroom discipline. They are certainly relieved to be disabused of the notion that teaching is an inborn natural talent, and become enthusiastic about the possibilities of the behavioural approach once they know more about it. The multitude of clear demonstrations soon convinces them that there is a body of useful skills to be learned, which are based upon a firm rigorous model that has clear implications for practice. Unfortunately, 'teaching is not telling' and merely lecturing teachers about the behavioural approach and citing examples of its use by others does not, by itself, improve their performance in the classroom.

We concluded that it is important for British teachers to be knowledgeable about and practised in the behavioural skills of classroom management. To this end we have written books and articles and run courses in order to inform them. In addition, we have tried to make skills-training in behavioural techniques available to them, mainly through the Behavioural Approach to Teaching Package (BATPACK). The nature of this package and details of its development are described in Chapter 7 of this book. By training teachers to use behavioural methods (using BAT-PACK), we have successfully demonstrated major changes in teacher behaviour so that teachers become much more positive in their interactions with pupils. As a result, teachers have found that their pupils subsequently spend more time getting on with their work and, hence, teachers experience far less troublesome behaviour in their classrooms.

References

Barcroft, J. (1970), 'Behaviour modification in the school', unpublished M. Phil thesis, University of London.

Becker, W. C., Madsen, C., Arnold, C. R. and Thomas, D. (1967), 'The contingent use of teacher attention and praise in reducing classroom behaviour problems', *Journal of Special Education*, vol. 1, pp. 287–307.

Bennett, N. S., Desforges, C. W., Cockburn, A. D. and Wilkinson, B. (1984), *The Quality of Pupil Learning Experience* (London: Lawrence Erlbaum Associates).

Bennett, N. and Blundell, D. (1983), 'Quantity and quality of work in rows and classroom groups', *Educational Psychology*, vol. 3, pp. 93–105.

Davie, C. A. M. (1975), 'Classroom management: a theoretical and observational study', unpublished PhD thesis, University of Dundee.

Frey, S. H. (1974), 'Teachers and behavior modification', *Phi Delta Kappan*, vol. 55, pp. 634–636.

Galton, M., Simon, B. and Croll, P. (1980), *Inside the Primary School* (London: Routledge & Kegan Paul).

Glynn, T. (1982), 'Antecedent control of behaviour in educational contexts', *Educational Psychology*, vol. 2, pp. 215–29.

Glynn, T. (1983), 'Building an effective teaching environment', in Wheldall, K. and Riding, R. (eds) *Psychological Aspects of Learning and Teaching* (London: Croom Helm).

Glynn, T. (1985), 'Contexts for independent learning', *Educational Psychology*, vol. 5, pp. 5–15.

Harrop, L. A. and Critchley, C. (1972), 'Classroom management and deviant behaviour', *Behaviour Modification*, vol. 3, pp. 6-10.

McNamara, E. (1979), 'The use of self-recording in behaviour modification in the secondary school', *Behavioural Psychotherapy*, vol. 7, pp. 57-66.

McNamara, E. (1984), 'Behaviour modification in the secondary school: issues and outcomes', *Educational Psychology*, vol. 4, pp. 103-23.

McNamara, E. (1985), 'Are the techniques of behaviour modification relevant to problems of concern to teachers in secondary schools?, *Behavioural Approaches with Children*, vol. 9, pp. 34-45.

Madsen, C. H., Becker, W. C. and Thomas, D. R. (1986), 'Rules, praise, and ignoring – elements of elementary classroom control', *Journal of Applied Behavior Analysis*, vol. 1, pp. 139-50.

Merrett, F. E. (1981), 'Studies in behaviour modification in British educational settings', *Educational Psychology*, vol. 1, pp. 13-38.

Merrett, F. E. (1985), *Encouragement Works Better Than Punishment* (Birmingham: Positive Products).

Merrett, F. E. and Blundell, D. (1982), 'Self-recording as a means of improving behaviour in the secondary school', *Educational Psychology*, vol. 2, pp. 147-57.

Merrett, F. and Wheldall, K. (1978), 'Playing the game: a behavioural approach to classroom management', *Educational Review*, vol. 30, pp. 41-50.

Merrett, F. E. and Wheldall, K. (1982), Does teaching student teachers about behaviour modification techniques improve their teaching performance in the classroom?', *Journal of Education for Teaching*, vol. 8, pp. 67-75.

Merrett, F. E. and Wheldall, K. (1984), 'Classroom behaviour problems which Junior school teachers find most troublesome', *Educational Studies*, vol. 10, pp. 87-92.

Merrett, F. E. and Wheldall, K. (1986a), 'Observing Pupils and Teachers in Classrooms (OPTIC): a behavioural observation schedule for use in schools', *Educational Psychology* (in press).

Merrett, F. E. and Wheldall, K. (1986b), 'Natural rates of teacher approval and disapproval in British primary and middle school classrooms', *British Journal of Educational Psychology* (in press).

Musgrove, W. (1974), 'A scale to measure attitudes towards behaviour modification', *Psychology in the Schools*, 11, 392-396. vol. 11, pp. 392-6.

Peake, A. (1972), 'A study of the techniques of behaviour modification in a junior school', *Behaviour Modification*, vol. 3, pp. 11-14.

Persons, W. S., Brassell, W. R. and Rollins, H. A. (1976), 'A practical observation procedure for monitoring four behaviours relevant to classroom management', *Psychology in the Schools*, vol. 13, pp. 64-71.

Pickthorne, B. and Wheldall, K. (1982), 'A behavioural approach, to teaching subsidiary physics to engineering students', *Educational Psychology*, vol. 2, pp. 79-85.

Rennie, E. N. F. (1980), 'Good behaviour games with a whole class', *Remedial Education*, vol. 15, pp. 187-90.

Russell, A. and Lin, L. G. (1977), 'Teacher attention and classroom behaviour', *The Exceptional Child*, vol. 24, pp. 148–55.

Ryan, B. A. (1976), 'Teacher attitudes toward behaviour modification one year after an in-service training programme', *Behaviour Therapy*, vol. 7, pp. 264–5.

Schwieso, J. and Hastings, N. (1981), 'The role of theory in the teaching of behaviour modification to teachers', in Wheldall, K. (ed.) *The Behaviourist in the Classroom: Aspects of Applied Behavioural Analysis in British Educational Contexts* (Birmingham: Educational Review Publications).

Thomas J. D., Presland, I. E., Grant, M. D. and Glynn, E. L. (1978), 'Natural rates of teacher approval and disapproval in Grade VII classrooms', *Journal of Applied Behavior Analysis*, vol. II, pp. 91–4.

Throll, D. and Ryan, B. A. (1976), 'Teacher attitudes toward behaviour modification', *New Zealand Journal of Educational Studies*, vol. 2, pp. 68–71.

Tsoi, M. M. and Yule, W. (1976), 'The effects of group reinforcement in classroom behaviour modification, *Educational Studies*, vol. 2, pp. 129–40.

Vane, J. (1972), ' A school behaviour modification programme: teacher attitudes a year later', *Behaviour Therapy*, vol. 3, pp. 41–4.

Ward, J. (1971), 'Modification of children's deviant behaviour', *British Journal of Educational Psychology*, vol. 41, pp. 304–13.

Ward, J. (1973), 'The use of teacher attention and praise as control techniques in the classroom', *Educational Review*, vol. 26, pp. 39–55.

Ward, J. (1976), 'Behaviour modification in education – an overview and model for programme implementation', *Bulletin of the British Psychological Society*, vol. 28, pp. 259 – 68.

Wheldall, K. (1981), 'A before, C or the use of behavioural ecology in classroom management, in Gurney, P. (ed.) *Behaviour Modification in Education* (Exeter: School of Education, University of Exeter).

Wheldall, K. (1982), 'Behavioural pedagogy or behavioural overkill?', *Educational Psychology*, 2, 181–184.

Wheldall, K. and Austin, R. (1980), 'Successful behaviour modification in the secondary school: a reply to McNamara and Harrop', *Occasional Papers of the Division of Education and Child Psychology of the British Psychological Society*, vol. 4, pp. 3–9.

Wheldall, K. and Congreve, S. (1980), 'The attitudes of British teachers towards behaviour modification', *Educational Review*, vol. 32, pp. 53–65.

Wheldall, K and Merrett, F. (1984), *Positive Teaching: The Behavioural Approach* (London: Allen & Unwin).

Wheldall, K., Morris, B., Vaughan, P. and Ng, Y. Y. (1981), 'Rows versus tables: an example of the use of behavioural ecology in two classes of eleven-year-old children', *Educational Psychology*, vol. 1, pp. 171–84.

Wheldall, K. and Wheldall, D. (1981), 'School meals, praise and contingent dessert: an attempt to improve eating behaviour in the nursery class, *Behavioural Approaches with Children*, vol. 5, no. 2, pp. 30–46.

White, M. A. (1975), 'Natural rates of teacher approval and disapproval in the classroom', *Journal of Applied Behavior Analysis*, vol. 8, pp. 367–72.

Winter, S. (1982), 'Classroom disruptive behaviour: a plea for balance', *Behavioural Approaches with Children*, vol. 6, no. 2, pp. 20–2.

3

Behavioural Approaches in the Secondary School

EDDIE MCNAMARA

The application of behavioural methods in the primary school sector has passed through a number of readily identifiable phases, but the same claim cannot yet be made for developments in secondary schools. The first phase of development in the primary sector consisted of replications of North American 'demonstration' research studies in British primary classrooms (see Chapter 2). The second phase consisted of teachers being taught the principles underlying such research and then applying these principles themselves, i.e. the teachers acted as both observers and contingency managers. Such studies had design shortcomings, but were at least a step away from relatively 'pure' experimental research and a step towards applying the principles in naturalistic settings. Since such work was reported (e.g. Harrop and McNamara, 1979), a further phase of development can be identified. This involves the development of packages for use with the staff of schools as a form of In-Service Education of Teachers (INSET). An obvious example is the package known as BATPACK (Behavioural Approach to Teaching Package) described in Chapter 7. It is a skills-based package, developed by Wheldall and Merrett, the main aim of which is to help teachers to acquire teaching strategies based on behavioural principles; strategies which would subsequently be assimilated into the teachers' repertoires. Consequently, such acquired skills could be used all the time and not just to deal with a 'problem child'. Work in secondary schools has not yet proceeded far enough for any similar pattern to appear, but the beginnings of a similar trend are slowly emerging.

In 1969, McAllister, Stachowiack, Baer and Conderman published a paper in the United States which indicated that the inappropriate classroom behaviour of a group of 16–19 year-olds could be substantially reduced by using 'light' behavioural interventions, i.e. praise, reproof and an evaluative statement. However, the lack of replication of these findings provide grounds for questioning their generalizability. Such caution is supported when the absence of replication is viewed in conjunction with the findings of McCullough (1972). McCullough's research on the effect of social reinforcement on the behaviour of 14–18 year-olds produced outcomes diametrically opposed to those of McAllister et al. (1969), namely that when student oral participation in English lessons was specifically 'reinforced' by teacher praise and attention the result was a *reduction* in student oral contributions to the lessons. When teacher recognition and praise were withdrawn, student oral participation increased. Thus, teacher praise in this instance acted as punishment and inhibited student verbal participation in lessons. Further, many of the students reported that they viewed these teacher strategies as childish and ineffective.

McCullough's findings were consistent across five of six experimental classes of students aged between 14 and 18 years, in which two teachers were involved. Consequently, there are grounds for claiming some generalizability of findings. Indeed, the observation that secondary-aged pupils do not respond to public teacher praise often finds support among teachers attending workshops run by the writer and has also been suggested in the literature by, for example, Ward (1976).

There is, then, a need to determine whether the techniques of behaviour modification can effect change in the classroom behaviour of pupils in British secondary schools. However, such research would be irrelevant if the type of pupil behaviour amenable to change by such techniques is of little concern to teachers in secondary schools.

Nature and incidence of problem behaviours

The types of inappropriate behaviour evidenced by pupils may vary along a continuum from minimal (for example, quiet but inappropriate talking) to maximal disruptive behaviour (for example, public defiance of the teacher). However, a second important variable needs to be considered in addition to type of behaviour, when assessing the influence of the pupils' behaviour on the teachers' assessment of disruptiveness, namely, *frequency*. The reasons for this are twofold. First, extremely disruptive, violent pupil behaviour is of low frequency (Laslett, 1977); yet such behaviour none the less produces consequences far in excess of what its frequency of occurrence might indicate (Lawrence,

Steed and Young, 1978). Secondly, mildly disruptive behaviour can produce problems far in excess of what might be predicted from the type of behaviour – if the *frequency* of occurrence is high.

The use of 'light' classroom contingency management procedures is judged by the writer to be maximally effective in situations in which the inappropriate pupil behaviours are of the less seriously disruptive type. Such behaviours (for example, not paying attention, distracting others) need to occur at a relatively high frequency if they are to be judged as disruptive by teachers. An isolated incident of any of these behaviours during a lesson would probably go unnoticed, or at least unattended to, by the teacher. Indeed, this may be regarded as 'normal' pupil behaviour. When such behaviour occurs very frequently, then appropriate pupil behaviour must occur at a relatively low frequency. There is thus considerable room for improvement, and a contingency management programme that is successful in increasing appropriate behaviours must, necessarily, reduce the level of inappropriate behaviour. However, such strategies will be of use to secondary schoolteachers only if they regard such mildly disruptive behaviours as a problem.

This led the writer to enquire into whether this, in fact, was the case. The aim of the enquiry was to assess teachers' perceptions of the incidence and type of problem behaviour occurring in the secondary school, and especially to identify which categories of problem behaviour were perceived to be *most disruptive* and which were *most frequent*. Details of the research methodology are described fully in McNamara (1985a). Briefly, the survey sample consisted of a selective, i.e. non-random, sample of secondary schools. The teachers' views regarding frequency and nature of disruptive behaviour were elicited. The schools involved were ten of the eleven comprehensive schools in an education district. The teachers were asked for their views on the behaviour of the class of pupils taught during the last teaching session of Wednesday morning. It was recognized that for an individual teacher this lesson might not be representative of the lessons taught in the course of a week; it was, none the less, hoped that, given a sufficiently high rate of questionnaire return from the sample as a whole, the overall picture obtained would be representative of the teachers' views on the nature and incidence of problem behaviour. In order to substantiate this, the teachers were asked for their responses to the *same questions* in relation to the *range of classes* taught in the course of a week.

The questionnaire consisted of a modified form of that previously employed by Merrett and Wheldall (1984; see also

Chapter 2). The first and third questions were related to a specific class while the second and fourth were related to the range of classes taught by the teachers. Questions 1 and 2 were about behaviours found to be most disruptive and questions 3 and 4 referred to the most frequent disruptive behaviours.

Teachers were presented with an array of behavioural categories from which to choose. The array was based on those categories of behaviour listed by Becker, Madsen, Arnold and Thomas (1967). In addition, a further category was added, that of 'disobeying'. This was intended to be sensitive to disruptive pupil behaviour involving active pupil refusal to follow the teacher's directions and publicly flouting the teacher's authority. The categories were:

A	Orientating behaviour	F	Making a noise
B	Motor behaviours (while seated)	G	Non-attending
C	Gross motor behaviour (not at desk)	H	Disobeying
D	Disturbing others (including aggression)	I	Others
E	Talking	J	No problem

The teachers were directed to respond 'none' if no problem pupil behaviour occurred in the class in question. The teachers were also requested to rank-order the categories of problem behaviour; this ranking was quantified by ascribing a score of 3, 2 and 1 respectively to the categories of behaviour ranked first, second and third. Thus, if all 200 teachers who returned the questionnaire rated the same category of behaviour as rank order 1, that category would receive a score of 600. Consequently the range of scores possible for each category of behaviour was from 0–600. The return rate for questionnaires was 56 per cent.

'Inappropriate talking' was rated most frequently as the most disruptive behaviour. This behaviour accumulated a score of 293. The next two highest rated categories of behaviour for disruptiveness were 'orientating behaviours' (i.e. turning round in seat) (120) and 'non-attending' (112). The remaining six behavioural categories all obtained ratings of less than 60. Of particular significance is the fact that a large number of teachers chose not to rank three behaviours as disruptive – indeed the 'none' category accumulated a score of 192, the second highest.

The three categories of 'most disruptive' behaviour reported as occurring most frequently (i.e. talking, orientating behaviours and non-attending) are the least disruptive behaviours of the array offered to the teachers to choose from. The most disruptive categories of behaviour (for example, motor behaviours – at desk and out of seat, disturbing others and making a noise) were infrequently chosen and the most disruptive category, disobeying, was chosen least of all. Thus, in terms of the two variables relevant to problem behaviour referred to earlier, i.e. type and frequency, there is evidence that the teachers' main concern is with high frequency mildly disruptive behaviour, rather than low frequency highly disruptive behaviour. Consequently, the very behaviours that classroom contingency management procedures are particularly effective in changing are the ones of most concern to the secondary schoolteachers surveyed.

When the same question was raised in relation to the *range* of classes taught during the week several interesting points emerged. 'Inappropriate talking' was again ranked highest of the 'most disruptive' problem behaviours but received a much higher score than the same question did when referring to a specific class (377). 'Orientating behaviours' and 'non-attending' respectively were the second and third 'most disruptive' problem behaviours. Although the order of ranking was reversed, the actual scores obtained by both were substantially similar for specific classes and the range of classes. The category 'none' was used substantially less when the range of classes taught was considered as opposed to a specific class; the equivalent of 64 teachers ranked 'none' first with reference to a specific class, but only 25 when the range of classes taught was considered. Finally, all the other categories of behaviour except one (gross motor behaviour) showed small increases in frequency of occurrence when classes taught generally were considered as opposed to a specific class.

Questions 1 and 2 were concerned with pupil problem behaviour which the teachers report as 'most disruptive'. Perhaps surprisingly, some behaviours that might seem to be relatively innocuous were in fact assessed as being most disruptive. The writer's *post hoc* hypothesis was that such behaviours were ranked as most disruptive because of the frequency of their occurrence. This hypothesis could be tested because of the inclusion of questions 3 and 4 in the questionnaire. These asked the teachers to rank the *most common* disruptive behaviours both in the selected class and generally. The results for the selected class, supported this hypothesis. Inappropriate talking, non-attending and orientating behaviours, ranked most disruptive by the teachers, were ranked 1, 4 and 3 respectively as most common in the selected class. Category J, 'no problem', was interposed at rank-order 2. When the teachers' ranking of most common disruptive behaviour is assessed with respect to the range of classes taught, the similarity to that for the most disruptive behaviours was even closer. Talking, non-attending and orientating behaviours were ranked 1, 2 and 3 respectively. The above considerations indicate a high degree of similarity between the teachers' ranking of pupil behaviours which were judged to be *most disruptive* and those judged to be *most common*. The data on the teachers' perception of the most commonly occurring problem behaviours underline the earlier conclusion drawn that the very problems most amenable to amelioration by using classroom contingency management procedures are those of most concern to secondary schoolteachers. In addition to generating this conclusion, the data lent support to the view that seriously disruptive and violent pupil behaviour may not be as prevalent as the media seem to imply.

Classroom management research in secondary schools

Although there has been far less research in secondary than in primary school classrooms, for reasons which have been discussed elsewhere (McNamara and Harrop, 1979), some studies have been reported, particularly in educational settings in the USA. This research has been catalogued by Presland (1980). A feature of the research listed is the preponderance of 'heavy' and/or intrusive behavioural interventions. 'Heavy' in this context is used to refer to any teacher management strategy other than social reinforcement, reproof or other teacher verbal behaviour – these exceptions being considered 'light' (Wheldall and Austin, 1980). 'Intrusive' is the term used to indicate any intervention strategy that involves great change in teacher behaviour: the greater change required, the more intrusive is the intervention. An exception to this is pupil self-recording, which is not intrusive from the teacher's perspective but may be so in relation to pupil behaviour. Thus, the terms 'heavy' and 'intrusive' are used to refer to initiated management practices that call for changes in classroom routine, usually directly on the part of the teacher, but occasionally on the part of the pupil.

Lobitz and Burns (1977), in a consideration of the intrusiveness of interventions, suggest that the optimal intervention strategy for teachers is to begin with the least intrusive method and add more powerful procedures only if needed. They express the view that behaviour modification techniques are not readily accepted by some teachers because they are disruptive of normal classroom procedures or are too time-consuming.

Those studies listed by Presland (1980) included the use of (i) tokens (Main and Munro, 1977); (ii) time-out (Webster, 1976); (iii) self-determined reinforcement (Glynn, 1970); (iv) daily report card (Schumaker, Hovell and Sherman, 1977); (v) self-recording (Broden, Hall and Mitts, 1971); (vi) peer reinforcement (Solomon and Wahler, 1973); (vii) tokens plus teams (White-Blackburn, Semb and Semb, 1977).

Examination of the less extensive research carried out in British secondary school settings reveals a similar preponderance of 'heavy' behavioural procedures, e.g. token points with an individual pupil (Presland, 1980) or classes of children (Lane, 1978); plastic tokens (Merrett, 1982); contracts (Lane and Millar, 1977); self-recording (McNamara, 1979; Merrett and Blundell, 1982).

The work of McAllister, Stachowiack, Baer and Conderman (1969) is a much-quoted exception to the 'heavy' interventions. This study reported how, in a high school in the USA, a three component 'light' behavioural intervention substantially reduced the occurrence of two categories of unwanted behaviour in a class of 16–19 year-olds. The target behaviours were inappropriate talking and turning around. Unlike most intervention packages utilized with younger children, that of McAllister *et al.* did not contain an 'ignore inappropriate behaviour' element. Teacher disapproval was a component and it was both personalized and explicit, e.g. 'Johnny, stop talking'. This negative control technique was coupled with teacher praise of appropriate behaviour and an evaluative statement to the whole class at the end of the lesson.

In the UK, Wheldall and Austin (1980) report the effective use of teacher praise and attention coupled with ignoring inappropriate behaviour. In their investigation the pupils involved were 14–15 year-olds and were described as being below average academically. This study is detailed in Chapter 2.

These two studies provide evidence that 'light' behavioural strategies can be used to change the behaviour of secondary-aged pupils – but without further research (and bearing in mind McCullough's (1972) findings) they are an inadequate basis from which to claim generality of findings. By this is meant that one single-case experimental design outcome does not constitute sufficient evidence to suggest that, in similar circumstances, there is a reasonable probability that the same intervention will result in an analogous outcome. However, if researches demonstrating a similar outcome are reported regularly, the power of the demonstration of the effect, and hence the grounds for claiming generalizability of findings, are progressively strengthened.

The need for repeated replication to justify the claim for generalizability of findings is not necessarily met by the publication of a number of successful single-case design studies. Journals selectively publish successful outcome research and, therefore, the accumulation of a number of such successful outcome researches is not necessarily evidence of generalizability of findings. This is because the number of unsuccessful interventions attempted is unpublished and therefore unknown. An example of such a situation is to be found in the literature on behavioural contracting. A number of case-studies exist that report successful outcomes for this method of intervention (e.g. Bristol and Sloan, 1974; Cantrell, Cantrell, Huddleston and Woolridge, 1969, and White-Blackburn, Semb, and Semb, 1977). Such evidence could be used to claim generalizability of findings relating to the effectiveness of behavioural contracting, yet larger-scale research, (e.g. Weathers and Liberman, 1975; Stuart, Tripodi, Jayaratnes and Camburn, 1976) gives grounds for less optimistic conclusions to be drawn. It can be seen from this discussion that single case studies need to be repeated, and equally that there is a need for the results of such investigations to be published, whether they support or do not support the original findings.

Several such studies have been reported (McNamara, 1984). The implementation problems encountered (see McNamara, 1982) lead the writer to believe that such difficulties, leading to lack of research *per se*, rather than negative outcomes, account for the paucity of research reported in the literature. None of the six case studies reported (McNamara, 1984) yielded outcomes supporting the conclusion of McCullough that 'singling out of the individual High School student and praising him in front of his peers functions is a punishing consequence and will not constructively modify classroom behaviour'. Indeed, the opposite was the case. Two case studies strongly supported the view that light behavioural interventions could significantly change the behaviour of pupils in a positive direction. These two cases are briefly described below.

Case 1

This study was carried out with a fifth-year class of twenty-six 15–16 year-old pupils following a GCE English course. The teacher was a 30 year-old graduate with nine years' teaching experience. He described the class as noisy and talkative. He did not describe them as disruptive, but indicated that the pupils' application was significantly poorer than O-level English groups of previous years. The intervention consisted of (i) commending individual pupils, groups of pupils and the class as a whole when on-task; (ii) naming pupils who were off-task and specifying the nature of the inappropriate behaviour; (iii) making an evaluative statement at the end of the lesson.

As the graph (Figure 3.1) shows, on-task behaviour increased from a baseline level of 60 per cent to a level of 84 per cent. When the intervention was discontinued, on-task behaviour dropped to 66 per cent. This represented a significant demonstration that pupil behaviour was under the experimental control of teacher behaviour and could be changed in predicted directions. Graphically there appears to be a significant change; the increase in level of on-task behaviour of 24 per cent from baseline levels represents an average increase of approximately 10 minutes of on-task behaviour in a 45-minute lesson. Of equal importance was the class teacher's observation that the class were more biddable and industrious during the intervention phase. He declared his intention to continue using the intervention strategies.

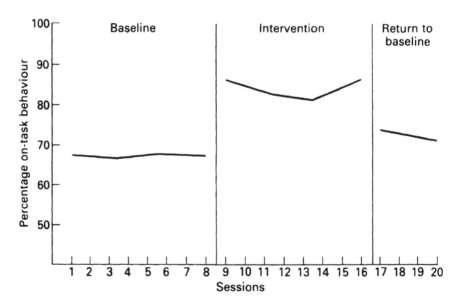

Figure 3.1 Changes in percentage on-task behaviour on introduction and withdrawal of intervention.

Although this case was demonstrably of benefit both to the pupils and to the class teacher, it would not be credible to suggest that the target class, a fifth-year examination group, was typical or representative of the classes of pupils that secondary teachers identify as problem classes. The next example is perhaps more representative of the type of class some teachers see as posing a management problem.

Case 2

This study was carried out with a fifth-year class of eighteen 15–16 year-old pupils, half of whom were following a CSE history course and half of whom were termed 'non-examination'. The teacher was a 27 year-old male graduate, who had four years' teaching experience. The group were described as disruptive. Disruption took the form of calling out, talking across the teacher, non-completion of written work and lack of response to teacher direction. The intervention consisted of (i) praising individuals, groups and the whole class when on-task and (ii) making an evaluative statement regarding work and behaviour to the class as a whole at the end of the lesson.

As the graph (Figure 3.2) shows, on-task behaviour rose from a baseline level of 67 per cent to an intervention level of 84 per cent – an increase of 17 per cent in on-task behaviour. This represented an average increase in on-task behaviour of between 6 and 7 minutes in a 45-minute lesson. The level of on-task behaviour dropped to an average of 72 per cent once the intervention procedures were discontinued. Again, this demonstrated that pupil behaviour had been brought under the experimental control of teacher behaviour.

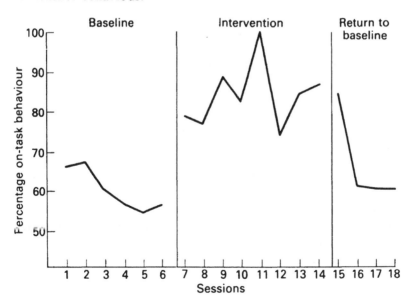

Figure 3.2 Changes in percentage on-task behaviour on introduction and withdrawal of intervention.

These two cases, then, support the thesis that teacher behaviour can influence the behaviour of pupils in positive directions. However, such findings need to be replicated if convincing evidence is to be established. The writer is currently engaged in such replication studies, and the evidence to date is providing support for the work of McAllister *et al.* Two such cases are described before moving on to other considerations.

The first study (Case 3) employed an alternative design to the ABA design of the two previous studies. A multiple baseline (Kazdin, 1983) across classes design was used, which avoided a return to baseline phase. The two classes concerned were reasonably representative of the classes of pupils that teachers find difficult to manage. The study is therefore considered in some detail.

Case 3

This study was carried out in a comprehensive school catering for pupils aged 11 years to 16 years. The catchment area served was a mixed middle-class and working-class community. Within the school pupils were set by ability, with eight sets in each year-group. The lowest set comprised pupils with learning difficulties and some of these also presented problem behaviour. The bottom set of each year-group was known as the remedial class.

Experimental Class 1 comprised the second year remedial class, who were being taught mathematics during the lessons observed for the present research. The topics covered by the use of work-cards and textbooks included fractions (equivalent fractions, cancelling mixed numbers and improper fractions), shapes and rectangles, and percentages. There were 17 pupils in the class, aged 12 to 13 years; 9 boys and 8 girls. It was observed that they came into the classroom noisily, jostled each other for places, sitting where and with whom they wished. Sometimes tables were pushed together without the teacher's permission being sought. Many pupils arrived at the lesson without equipment (pencils and rulers). A prompt start to the lesson proved impossible as these pupils pestered the teacher for equipment. During the lesson the pupils got up out of their places without hesitation and chattered to each other.

Experimental Class 2 was similar to Experimental Class 1, but was a third-year group receiving remedial mathematics. The topics covered by the use of work-cards and textbooks included length, mass, capacity, scale drawing, area and work involving calculators. There were 15 pupils in the class aged 13 to 14 years; 10 boys and

5 girls. The pupils were noisy and disruptive at the start of each lesson. They sat where they wished, shouted out and walked about the classroom. Both classes were taught by the same young female teacher, who was relatively inexperienced.

The frequency and severity of problems in those two classes was such that a multi-component intervention strategy was utilized:

(i)   Classroom seating arrangements were altered so that tables were set in rows and the pupils sat two to a table. Previously, the tables were scattered about the room and were occasionally pushed together by pupils.

(ii) The 'rules of the classroom' were displayed on a flip-chart in a prominent position at the front of the classroom. Copies of the rules were given to each pupil on a printed sheet. The rules were read over and commented on by the teacher at the beginning, middle and end of the lesson. The rules were: (a) arrive on time; (b) have the correct equipment; (c) no shouting out; (d) work quietly; (e) don't prevent others working.

(iii) The teacher was encouraged to make evaluative statements about the work and behaviour of the pupils after commenting on the rules at the end of the lesson.

(iv) If the teacher evaluated the pupils' behaviour positively, the last ten minutes of the lesson could be spent doing puzzles, as a reward. These consisted of, for example, messages in number codes. The pupils found these puzzles interesting and enjoyable.

(v)   Self-assessment involved the rules of the classroom, which were distributed at the beginning of the lesson. The pupils were instructed to give themselves a mark on a 0 to 5 scale for rule compliance (for each rule). The teacher indicated that she would scrutinize their self-assessments.

As the graph (Figure 3.3) shows, on-task behaviour in both cases substantially increased: in the case of Class 1 from 49 per cent during baseline to 75 per cent during the intervention, and in Class 2 from 54 per cent during baseline to 69 per cent during intervention. These represent average increases in on-task behaviour of 12 minutes and 7 minutes, respectively, per 45-minute lesson. That the behaviour of the class came under teacher control is confirmed by a closer analysis of the intervention data for Class 1. Lessons 7 and 12 represent 'troughs' in the elevated levels of pupil on-task behaviour. Examination of the implementation data (see McNamara 1986a) revealed that in both these lessons only

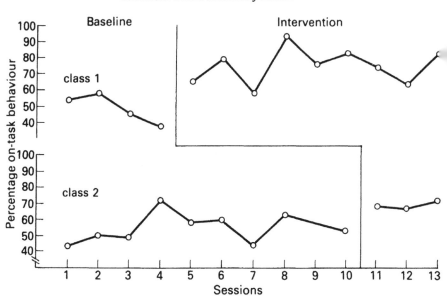

Figure 3.3　Changes in percentage on-task behaviour of two classes of disruptive pupils.

one of the five intervention components was actually implemented.

This case study involved multi-component interventions, in which antecedents (seating arrangements) were manipulated and an element of pupil self-management was involved, in that self-assessment procedures were used. It may well be that with particularly difficult classes no single intervention will suffice but rather many complementary strategies might be a better approach. With classes presenting lesser problems than those described above, much less dramatic interventions may improve pupil behaviour. Such was the case in the following study.

Case 4

This study was carried out with a first-year mixed ability geography class. The teacher, a 33 year-old male with 12 years' teaching experience, considered the class quite amenable to discipline, but reported that some of the pupils were over-talkative. However, general concern among the teaching staff regarding the behaviour of the class was such that the class as a whole was 'on report': a school-based monitoring programme. The class was on report for the duration of the study. The intervention in this case involved reading the rules of the classroom at the beginning of the lesson and making an evaluative statement on pupils' work and behaviour at the end of each lesson.

As the graph shows (see Figure 3.4), the already high level of on-task behaviour (77 per cent) was further increased to 89 per cent. Withdrawal of the intervention resulted in a fall in on-task behaviour to near pre-intervention level (79 per cent).

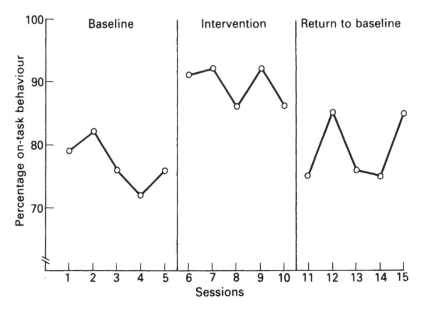

Figure 3.4 Changes in percentage on-task behaviour on introduction and withdrawal of intervention.

The outcomes of the behavioural interventions used in the four cases described all lend support to the view that the behaviour of secondary pupils can be changed in a predicted direction by changes in teacher behaviour. Although teacher praise was a component of the intervention strategies in Cases 1 and 2, the adverse reaction reported by McCullough was not replicated. In addition, Cases 3 and 4 indicated that teacher praise may not be a necessary component of teacher-determined management strategies.

Concluding comments

Applied behaviour analysis comprises an analysis of behaviour not only in terms of its consequences but also in terms of its antecedents. This ABC model (Antecedents – Behaviour – Consequences) underpins the behaviour modification movement. In mainstream primary school settings, behaviour modification has continually emphasized the 'C' component of the ABC model, i.e. changing pupil behaviour by manipulation of consequences. Some attention has been given to antecedents (for example, by Wheldall, Morris, Vaughan and Ng (1981), who investigated the influence of seating arrangements on pupil behaviour) but, generally, the study of antecedents has been ignored, at least in the UK. A similar situation obtains in the secondary school. Yet, intuitively, it seems reasonable to suggest that antecedent control may be even more influential with the behaviour of secondary school pupils than with that of primary- aged children. For example, the movement of pupils and teachers between lessons will influence the time they arrive at lessons and, therefore, how effectively the lesson starts. The influence of the many school organizational factors that may influence secondary pupils' behaviour is beyond the scope of this chapter, but secondary schools do differ markedly from primary schools in many aspects of organization. An important example is the sanction and incentive systems existing at the organizational level. Consideration of behavioural approaches in secondary schools should also include a consideration of the structure of such systems, as the author has argued elsewhere (see McNamara, 1985b; 1986b).

Behavioural approaches in the secondary school have a much shorter history than in other educational sectors. This can probably be attributed to the complexity of the organization: a complexity that can often produce forces that militate against either the implementation or success of behavioural interventions. Wahler and Graves (1983) have recently drawn attention to the influence of environmental events that, although removed in time from stimulus–response interactions, none the less influence the functional relationships of such interactions. Although Wahler and Graves focused on family situations, there is no doubt that research into what the authors termed 'setting events' will also pay dividends in the secondary school situation.

The emphasis of this chapter has been concerned with extrapolations of contingency management into the secondary school sector, yet an examination of the interventions used in the four case studies described earlier reveals that other teacher behaviours (e.g. the statement of rules and the issuing of evaluative statements) are perhaps very significant influences on pupil behaviour. Consequently, the study and innovation of the psychology of instruction (e.g. Becker and Engelmann, 1977) and the psychology of feedback (e.g. Van Houten, 1984) may ultimately be more influential than contingency management theory and practice. Further, contingency management practices sometimes detract from a consideration of the antecedents of behaviour, the most important of which in an educational setting is the curriculum. A consideration of pupil classroom behaviour that ignores the curriculum is seriously at fault. In addition to the *content* of the curriculum, *organization* is also a potentially powerful determinant of pupil behaviour. Curiculum negotiation, negotiated learning (short, medium and long-term objectives) are all compatible with the current trend towards a modular curriculum, which would facilitate pupils' self-regulation of behaviour. There have been some attempts to use behavioural methods to enhance academic behaviours (e.g. creative writing, Harrop and McCann, 1984), and a focus on academic product as opposed to on-task behaviour is to be welcomed.

Perhaps the most glaring omission in this chapter has been the absence of a consideration of behaviour contracting and pupil self-management. These are important areas of concern, but an in-depth consideration is beyond the remit of this chapter. Self-management skills are helpful to pupils who wish to change their behaviour (see McNamara, 1986c). Brigham, Happer, Hill, Armas and Newsom (1985) have recently published an article on the theme of self-management. Included in it is a reference to curriculum materials, which may have applicability in UK school situations. All too often, however, there is an absence of commitment to change from disruptive pupils. In such cases, commitment to change has to be negotiated, the product of the negotiation being an agreement that structures positive reciprocal interactions between the two parties (Stuart, 1971). Again, consideration of this important area is beyond the scope of this chapter.

It would appear that, although contingency management undoubtedly has a place in any behavioural approach in the secondary school, other elements of the behavioural approach, e.g. setting events, self-management, curriculum organization, content and delivery, may ultimately prove even more appropriate and fruitful to pursue.

References

Becker, W. and Engelman, S. (1977), 'Systems for basic instuction: theory and applications', in Catania, A. C. and Brigham, T. A. (eds) *The Handbook of Applied Behavior Analysis* (New York: Irvington).

Becker, W. C., Madsen, C. H., Arnold, C. R. and Thomas, D. R. (1967), 'The contingent use of teacher attention and praise in reducing classroom behaviour problems', *Journal of Special Education*, vol. 1, pp. 287–307.

Brigham, T. A., Happer, C., Hill, B., Armas, A. and Newsom, P. (1985), 'A self-management program for disruptive adolescents in the school: a clinical replication analysis', *Behavior Therapy*, vol. 16, pp. 99–115.

Bristol, M. M. and Sloan, H. N. (1974), 'Effects of contingency contracting on study rate and test performance', *Journal of Applied Behavior Analysis*, vol. 7, pp. 271–80.

Broden, M., Hall, R. V. and Mitts, B. (1971), 'The effects of self-recording on the classroom behavior of two eighth grade students', *Journal of Applied Behavior Analysis*, vol. 4, pp. 191–200.

Cantrell, R. P., Cantrell, M. L., Huddleston, M. C. and Woolridge, R. L. (1969), 'Contingency contracting with school problems', *Journal of Applied Behavior Analysis*, vol. 2, pp. 215–22.

Glynn, E. L. (1970), 'Classroom applications of self-determined reinforcement', *Journal of Applied Behavior Analysis*, vol. 3, pp. 123–32.

Harrop, A. and McCann, C. (1984), 'Modifying creative writing in the classroom', *British Journal of Educational Psychology*, vol. 54, pp. 62–72.

Harrop, L. A. and McNamara, E. (1979), 'The behavioural workshop for classroom problems: a reappraisal, *British Journal of In-Service Education*, vol. 5, pp. 32–8.

Kazdin, A. E. (1983), *Single-Case research designs: Methods for Clinical and Applied Settings* (Oxford: Oxford University Press).

Lane, D. (1978), *The Impossible Child*, Vol. 2 (London: ILEA Publications).

Lane, D. A. and Millar, R. R. (1977), 'Dealing with behaviour problems in school: a new development', *Community Health*, vol. 8, pp. 155–9.

Laslett, R. B. (1977), 'Disruptive and violent pupils: the facts and the fallacies', *Educational Review*, vol. 29, pp. 152–62.

Lawrence, J., Steed, D. and Young, P. E. (1978), 'Monitoring incidents of disruptive behaviour in a secondary school', *Durham and Newcastle Research Review*, vol. 41, pp. 39–43.

Lobitz, W. C. and Burns, W. J. (1977), 'The least intrusive intervention strategy for behavior change procedures: the use of public and private feed-back in school classrooms', *Psychology in the Schools*, vol. 14, pp. 89–94.

McAllister, L. W., Stachowiak, J. G., Baer, D. M. and Conderman, L. (1969), 'The application of operant conditioning techniques in a secondary school classroom', *Journal of Applied Behavior Analysis*, vol. 2, pp. 277–85.

McCullough, J. P. (1972), 'An investigation of the effects of model group size upon response facilitation in the high school classroom, *Behavior Therapy*, vol. 3, pp. 561–6.

McNamara, E. (1979), 'The use of self-recording in behaviour modification in a secondary school', *Behavioural Psychotherapy*, vol. 7, pp. 57–66.

McNamara, E. (1982), 'Reality problems in classroom research', *Occasional Papers of the Division of Educational and Child Psychology of the British Psychological Society*, vol. 6, pp. 50–3.

McNamara, E. (1984), 'Behaviour modification in the secondary school: issues and outcomes', *Educational Psychology*, vol. 4, pp. 41–61.

McNamara, E. (1985a), 'Are the techniques of behaviour modification relevant to problems of concern to teachers in secondary schools?', *Behavioural Approaches with Children*, vol. 9, pp. 34–45.

McNamara, E. (1985b), 'Sanction and incentive systems in the secondary school – a survey enquiry', *Durham and Newcastle Research Review* (in press).

McNamara, E. (1986a), 'The reduction of disruptive behaviour in two secondary school classes'. Unpublished manuscript. Preston: Schools' Psychological Service.

McNamara, E. (1986b), 'Incentive and sanction systems used in secondary schools: a behavioural analysis, *Durham and Newcastle Research Review* (in press).

McNamara, E. (1986c), 'Self-management and pupil behaviour'. Unpublished manuscript. Preston: Schools' Psychological Service.

McNamara, E. and Harrop, L. A. (1979), Behaviour modification in the secondary school: a cautionary tale', *Occasional Papers of the Division of Educational and Child Psychology of the British Psychological Society*, vol. 3, pp. 38–41.

Main, G. C. and Munro, B. C. (1977), 'A token reinforcement program in a public junior high school', *Journal of Applied Behavior Analysis*, vol. 10, pp. 94–4.

Merrett, F. (1982), 'Encouragement works better than punishment: an in-service behavioural workshop for teachers', *Behavioural Approaches with Children*, vol. 6, no. 2, pp. 27–33.

Merrett, F. and Blundell, D. (1982), 'Self-recording as a means of improving classroom behaviour in the secondary school', *Educational Psychology*, vol. 2, pp. 147–57.

Merrett, F. and Wheldall, K. (1984), 'Classroom behaviour problems which junior school teachers find most disruptive', *Educational Studies*, vol. 10, pp. 87–92.

Presland, J. (1980), 'Behaviour modification and secondary schools', in Upton, G. and Gobell, A. (eds) *Behaviour Problems in the Comprehensive School* (Cardiff: Faculty of Education, University College of Wales)

Schumaker, J. B., Hovell, M. F. and Sherman, J. A. (1977), 'An analysis of daily report cards and parent managed privileges in the improvement of adolescents' classroom performance', *Journal of Applied Behavior Analysis*, vol. 10, pp. 449–64.

Solomon, R. W. and Wahler, R. G. (1973), 'Peer reinforcement control of classroom problem behavior', *Journal of Applied Behavior Analysis*, vol. 6, pp. 49–56.

Stuart, R. B. (1971), 'Behavioral contracting within the families of delinquents', *Journal of Behavior Therapy and Experimental Psychiatry*, vol. 2, pp. 1–11.

Stuart, R. B., Tripodi, I., Jayaratnes, S. and Camburn, D. (1976), 'An experiment in social engineering in serving the families of pre-delinquents', *Journal of Abnormal Child Psychology*, vol. 4, pp. 243–61.

Van Houten, R. (1984), 'Setting up performance feedback systems in the classroom', in Heward, W. L., Heron, T. E., Hill, D. S. and Trap-Porter, J. (eds) *Focus on Behavior Analysis in Education* (Columbus, Ohio: Charles E. Merrill).

Wahler, R. C. and Graves, M. (1983), 'Setting events in social networks: ally or enemy of child behavior therapy?, *Behavior Therapy*, vol. 14, pp. 19–36.

Ward, J. (1976), 'Behaviour modification in education: an overview and a model for programme implementation', *Bulletin of the British Psychological Society*, vol. 29, pp. 257–68.

Weathers, L. and Liberman, R. P. (1975), 'Contingency contracting with families of delinquent adolescents', *Behavior Therapy*, vol. 6, pp. 356–66.

Webster, R. E. (1976), 'A time-out procedure in a public school setting', *Psychology in the Schools*, vol. 13, pp. 72–6.

Wheldall, K. and Austin, R. (1980), 'Successful behavior modification in the secondary school: a reply to McNamara and Harrop', *Occasional Papers of the Division of Educational and Child Psychology of the British Psychological Society*, vol. 4, no. 3, pp. 3–8.

Wheldall, K., Morris, B., Vaughan, P. and Ng, Y. Y. (1981), 'Rows versus tables: an example of the use of behavioural ecology in two classes of eleven year-old children', *Educational Psychology*, vol. 1, pp. 171–84.

White-Blackburn, G., Semb, S. and Semb, G. (1977), 'The effects of a good-behavior contract on the classroom behaviors of VIth grade students', *Journal of Applied Behavior Analysis*, vol. 10, p. 312.

4

More Power to the Parents: Behavioural Approaches to Remedial Tutoring at Home

TED GLYNN

In Western societies, children around the age of five live most of their lives in two major settings, home and school. They alternate between these two settings five days a week for about forty weeks every year. Few would dispute that home and school play complementary roles in children's learning. Since parents and teacher share overlapping areas of interest and responsibility for the same children, with whom they interact in different settings, two things might reasonably be expected. First, a co-operative partnership between parent and teacher in helping children to learn should be both feasible and effective. Secondly, the study of children's acquisition of academic skills in one setting and the utilization of these skills in the other setting should be a major focus for applied behavioural research. Surprisingly, progress in *either* of these directions has been somewhat limited. It is interesting just how much the home and the school settings remain isolated one from the other.

Young and McGeeney (1968) noted that, in the UK, the tradition of *in loco parentis* and the extreme autonomy of the teaching profession have led to teachers operating to the virtual exclusion of the parents. In the United States, parents are reported to be losing influence over their children as schools assume roles once reserved for parents (Woodward, 1978). Bronfenbrenner (1979) views with alarm the growing separation of home, school, workplace and community, which progressively isolates the family from other social contexts, so that parents are becoming increasingly powerless to influence the behaviour and development of their own children in settings over which they have little control.

Tizard and Tizard (1979) report a major lack of communication between parent and teacher, with neither party knowing much about how the child functions in the other's setting. All too often parent–teacher contact is a one-way process, with teachers talking to, rather than listening to, parents; this usually takes place at school, rather than in the home. For many parents, the only contact with teachers occurs when the school considers something is wrong. Moreover, the purpose of much parent–teacher contact is frequently limited to teachers soliciting parental support as fund raisers or teacher aides (Blackstone, 1979).

This very infrequent and circumscribed contact between the two settings prevents the parent from knowing on a day-to-day basis which specific behaviours children are currently acquiring at school. Hence, parents are unable to monitor for the possible occurrence of these at home. Lacking this specific information, parents can neither reinforce these skills when they occur, nor re-arrange their home setting in order to support the occurrence and maintenance of skills learned at school. Further, in the absence of specific information about what behaviours children are acquiring at school, parents may, unwittingly, cue and reinforce skills that are counter-productive. This is particularly evident in the areas of reading, mathematics, and written expression. In these areas, parents may cue and reinforce behaviours appropriate to the curriculum that was operative when they themselves were school-children and may even punish behaviours that differ from these. There is a real danger that children might learn to discriminate between settings in performing skills, rather than to generalize the use of skills across both settings. The danger is not that children might acquire two different sets of skills, for the two may even be complementary, but rather that skills reinforced in one setting may be ignored or even punished in the other.

Children's discrimination in skill use between settings could lead to parents and teachers each undervaluing the contribution of the other. As a result, each may deprive the other of an important source of support and reinforcement for their efforts with a particular child. Moreover, parents may be deprived of powerful reinforcers resulting from contributing to their children's growth in competence in academic skills. It is as if the natural contingencies are all operating to ensure the isolation of children's performance at home and school.

A further problem arises from the isolation between home and school. This is seen when children fail to make expected progress in learning academic skills. Schools frequently invoke a deficit model to explain this failure (Bronfenbrenner, 1979). In this model, failures at school are attributed to deficits in individuals, their families or their ethnic group. In fact, failures at school may also be due to deficits in the programmes at school. Hence, intervention to remedy failure is not simply a process of discovering and correcting deficits in the children or in their homes. Instead, parents and teachers should work together to introduce appropriate remedial programmes that call upon the resources of both home and school. Clearly, there must be an improvement in the amount and quality of parent–teacher contact. Existing behavioural studies can point the way to more efficient mechanisms of contact, and these studies will be discussed later. First, it is important to note the evidence which establishes that parents are indeed competent teachers.

The competence of parents in helping their children with academic tasks is well illustrated in the literature on pre-school enrichment programmes. Reviews by Bronfenbrenner (1974), Chilman (1976), and Donachy (1979) conclude that those programmes producing lasting effects on school performance were those in which a trained home visitor had altered the pattern of parent–child interaction, so that both parent and child gained new skills as a result of the training programmes. Indeed, pre-school educators frequently see their role as working in partnership with parents. Blackstone (1979) considers the pre-school as a model for change throughout the educational system.

These pre-school enrichment studies demonstrate important academic gains resulting from parental participation in home-based educational programmes. However, these studies do not provide data on what parents do when implementing these programmes. They lack data particularly on what parents do in the absence of the home visitors. The usual experimental design assesses the impact of home intervention prior to school entry and does not directly address the question of a generalization across settings once children have started school.

It is not argued from the pre-school enrichment studies that all parents are automatically competent teachers, rather, that they are potentially so. However, they have always been exceptional examples of individual parents taking total responsibility for the education of their own children, for example, Deakin (1973).

What is more, there are many other parents who recognize that they do not have the skills to teach their own children, but who nevertheless are concerned at their children's lack of progress at school and are willing to devote time to learning these skills. Young and McGeeney (1968) record the 'passionate but impotent' interest of the parents in an inner London school, who very much wanted to help their children succeed, but did not know how to go about it. A survey in New Zealand by Nicholson (1979) reports this same theme echoed in the answers of parents who had responded to a series of radio programmes on children learning to read. McNaughton, Glynn and Robinson (1981) reported that parents who participated in a remedial reading tutoring programme for their own older low-progress readers were all concerned at their children's lack of progress, but did not know what they could do to help. From a behavioural perspective, this general concern seems to indicate a skills deficit rather than a motivational deficit.

Behaviour therapists have long recognised the advantages of involving parents as co-therapists (Yule, 1975). There is abundant evidence that parents can be trained in the skills needed to modify social behaviour in their own children (Berkowitz and Graziano, 1977; Johnston and Katz, 1973; O'Dell, 1974; Graziano, 1977; Gath, 1979; Sanders and Glynn, 1981).

Behavioural studies that involve parents in modifying academic behaviour, rather than social behaviour, in their own school-age children have been relatively few. This is not surprising, given the lack of contact between home and school. However, Atkeson and Forehand (1979) reviewed 21 studies in which home-based reinforcement programmes were used to modify either social or academic behaviour at school. In these programmes the teacher is responsible for specifying classroom rules, for determining rule violation and for communicating these to parents via some kind of written information. The parent is responsible for dispensing rewards or sanctions based on the teacher report. These programmes have been consistently effective in altering both disruptive and academic behaviour at school.

Atkeson and Forehand, however, make a number of methodological criticisms. Although the majority of studies had adequate experimental control built into their research design, the majority did not carry out a component analysis of treatment variables, nor did they take multiple outcome measures (such as some measures of parent or teacher behaviour in addition to child behaviour). Very few studies took any rigorous follow-up assessment to measure temporal generality of treatment effects. None of the studies reviewed monitored programme implementation in both home and school settings. Moreover, it is not known whether there are different effects attributable either to the frequency or to the degree of specificity of written communications.

Two further points can be made. First, parental dispensing of rewards or sanctions imposed by teachers can be seen as demeaning to the role of parents. The approach does not involve the parents in the more rewarding engagement in instructional or teaching behaviours, nor is it likely to improve their competence in helping their children with academic problems. Dispensing sanctions at home may prove unpleasant for some parents. This is like the school principal called upon by a class teacher to punish a child with whom he has himself a very positive relationship. Secondly, criteria for rewarding academic behaviour have been simplistic, for example the number of maths problems correct. Such criteria may be inadequate for conveying important information about changes that can occur in children's academic learning, for example self-corrections in oral reading. Better quality information is needed if parents are to learn how to help their children with academic problems.

Two studies did involve parents in a simple instructional role, with academic skills, in addition to that of dispensing reinforcement. However, reinforcement was contingent on children's performance on academic tasks in the home setting. These studies, by Ryback and Staats (1970) and Fry (1977), successfully trained parents to use praise and tokens to increase children's basic sight-reading vocabularies. However, they do not present data on programme implementation and the measure taken, word recognition, is an ineffective measure of proficient reading. Further, training children in word recognition is unlikely to provide parents with sufficient information to improve their competence as reading instructors.

Home-based remedial reading

Recent research has focused more sharply on the instructional role of parents in the home settings, particularly in tutoring their own children who need remedial reading. Unfortunately, when children fail to make expected progress in reading at school, they are typically given less, rather than more, opportunities to read from text material (Allington, 1983). Children are frequently withdrawn from a regular reading programme and given remedial help of a kind that restricts the sources of information available to them in their reading (e.g. specific training in subskills assumed to be prerequisites to reading from texts). Furthermore, in the oral reading situation, the teacher may behave in a way that prevents children with difficulties from learning to use context or syntactic cues and may even deny them the opportunity to self-correct. Self-correction of errors in oral reading is known to be strongly predictive of subsequent reading progress (Clay, 1979).

Morgan and Lyon (1979) devised a procedure that trained parents to tutor their own children at home by using increased opportunities for oral reading from texts. Parents were trained to perform two sets of tutoring responses, simultaneous reading (or participant modelling) and independent reading, in which particular attention is paid to praise for spontaneously corrected errors and for correct reading of words recently encountered in simultaneous reading. In their study, Morgan and Lyon provide detailed data on gains in parental reinforcement under baseline and tuition conditions (i.e. before and after training by the authors). All four children progressed in both reading accuracy and comprehension as measured by standardized tests.

Other research (Glynn and McNaughton, 1975; McNaughton and Delquadri, 1978; McNaughton and Glynn, 1981) has suggested several additional tutoring behaviours as important in the oral reading situation. These tutoring behaviours are:

1   Delaying the timing of tutor attention to errors.
2   Providing contextual or graphophonic prompts, rather than simply modelling or 'telling' the child the correct word.
3   Providing praise contingent on (a) correct performance (e.g. sentences or pages read correctly), (b) self-correction of errors and (c) error-correction following a prompt.

More simply these procedures may be summarized as 'pause, prompt and praise'.

The Mangere Home and School Project (McNaughton, Glynn and Robinson, 1981) introduced a home remedial reading tutoring programme to parents of eight 8–12 year-old boys with reading deficits of two to five years. This programme trained parents in their own homes to carry out eight tutoring procedures in accord with the above research. These were introduced by means of a small booklet for each parent (Glynn, McNaughton, Robinson and Quinn, 1979). The tutoring procedures (which are shown in Figure 4.1) were designed to provide a supportive learning context, in which parents implemented both reinforcement and error-correction procedures that encouraged children to acquire independent problem-solving skills while reading from text material. Paradoxically, the procedures require parents to learn to interrupt children's reading as little as possible, but to do so in such a way that children can learn to use all sources of information available in a text passage to solve unknown words.

All parent tutoring sessions were tape-recorded at home by the parents, both under baseline and trained tutoring conditions. The study had five aims. These were to determine baseline levels of

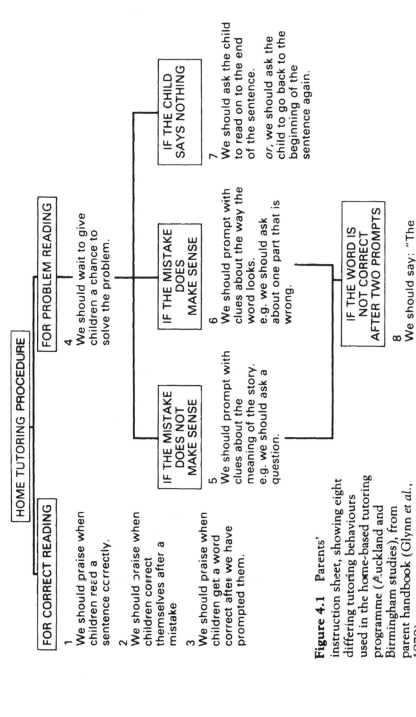

HOME TUTORING PROCEDURE

FOR CORRECT READING

1
We should praise when children read a sentence correctly.

2
We should praise when children correct themselves after a mistake

3
We should praise when children get a word correct after we have prompted them.

FOR PROBLEM READING

4
We should wait to give children a chance to solve the problem.

IF THE MISTAKE DOES NOT MAKE SENSE

5
We should prompt with clues about the meaning of the story. e.g. we should ask a question.

IF THE MISTAKE DOES MAKE SENSE

6
We should prompt with clues about the way the word looks. e.g. we should ask about one part that is wrong.

IF THE WORD IS NOT CORRECT AFTER TWO PROMPTS

8
We should say: "The word is ----,"

IF THE CHILD SAYS NOTHING

7
We should ask the child to read on to the end of the sentence.

or, we should ask the child to go back to the beginning of the sentence again.

Figure 4.1 Parents' instruction sheet, showing eight differing tutoring behaviours used in the home-based tutoring programme (Auckland and Birmingham studies), from parent handbook (Glynn *et al.*, 1979).

programme behaviours displayed by parents in the home setting, to demonstrate that the tutoring programme produced gains in these behaviours, to demonstrate that parents can maintain these behaviours without continued therapist support, to demonstrate gains in children's reading at home and to determine whether these gains could occur at school under conditions that provided less instructional support than that available to children at home. Independent measures of children's accuracy in reading text material at school were taken by graduate student observers. The procedure involved two components:

1   A *written instruction sheet*. A simple diagram was supplied to parents containing statements on what to do to assist a reader learning to read, as in Figure 4.1.
2   *Weekly sessions*. In addition to the weekly training session, a researcher visited the home to conduct a further detailed feedback session. This session was based on her analysis of one of the tapes of tutoring sessions conducted in the absence of any researcher.

Figure 4.2 summarizes some of the detailed session-by-session data. Parents clearly showed increases from baseline to training conditions in delaying their response to errors, in responding to errors with prompts rather than modelling the correct word and in contingent praise statements. All eight parents maintained their training gains on all tutoring behaviours during weekly sessions conducted in the absence of the therapist and all children reached a criterion of 90 per cent accuracy on several successive book levels in their reading at home. Children averaged gains of 1.4 months in book level read at home over the one-month home baseline and 6.5 months over approximately 2.5 months of trained tutoring.

Achievement of the last aim, generalization to school reading of gains in skill to contexts involving less support than provided at home, was limited. For five children, attending intermediate schools, there were almost no opportunities at school for one-to-one oral reading with a supportive tutor. Also, when written exercises related to reading were scheduled, these children, being considered non-readers, were occupied with 'filler' activities. Some children, both at primary and intermediate schools, were withdrawn for individual reading instruction, but this instruction stressed letter–sound information and word identification skills and not reading from texts. Hence, student observers had to be employed to hear children read at school under conditions similar to home baseline (i.e. prior to trained tutoring by parents), in

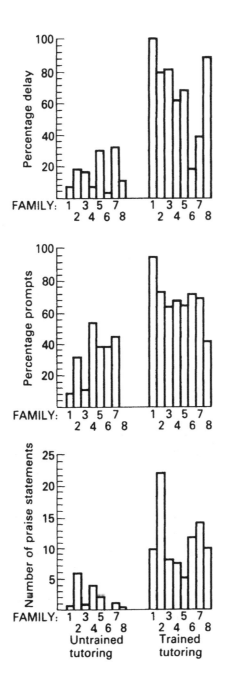

Figure 4.2 Changes in parent tutoring behaviours across untrained (baseline) and trained tutoring conditions for eight families (Auckland study).

order to obtain measures that were capable of showing generalization to a less supportive context.

Using this condition, it was found that rapid gains within the
graded series used to measure school reading occurred without
continued support of the tutoring procedures for only two of the
eight children. The supportive tutoring procedures were then
introduced into the school setting for five of the remaining six
children. With the support of the tutoring procedures in both
settings, four of these five children gained an additional three to
nine months at school in level of book read to criterion.

Since 1980, a further ten small-scale intensive studies have been
reported, in which the Mangere Home and School Procedures
have been employed successfully with children experiencing
reading difficulties. These studies have been reviewed by Glynn
and McNaughton (1985). Six of these studies also involved
parents as tutors of their own children. As well as reporting the
replication of gains in tutoring behaviours by parents and matched
reading gains by children, Glynn and McNaughton noted that two
further studies reviewed provide evidence that children can
generalize reading gains from a supportive context provided by a
trained parent-tutor to the context of school reading without tutor
support (Ritchie, 1984; Love and Van Biervliet, 1984). However,
it should be noted that these studies involved children with reading
deficits that were less severe than those of the children in the
original project.

In the study carried out in the UK (Glynn, 1980) the identical
remedial reading tutoring programme was introduced to parents of
four 10 year-old boys in an inner-city Birmingham school. These
boys had reading deficits of between 2 years 2 months and 2 years
10 months. In the Birmingham school, unlike in the Auckland
schools, all children had a classroom reading programme that
included opportunities to read to their teacher from a graded text
once or twice a week. However, additional measurement sessions
were included, because of difficulties in scheduling visits to
coincide with individual children's reading.

Figure 4.3 presents summary data from each parent–child pair
for baseline and training conditions. In this study, separate data
were not analysed for researcher absent conditions. However,
changes in data analysis procedures allowed parent praise for
prompted corrections and self-corrections to be examined
separately.

Changes in parent tutoring behaviours were very similar to
those in the Auckland study. Delayed attention to errors and use
of prompts occurred at low levels during baseline tutoring, except

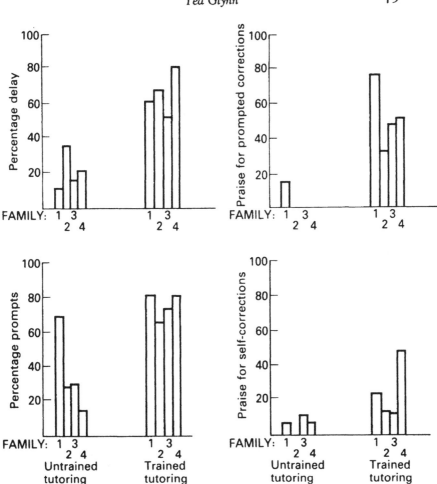

Figure 4.3 Changes in parent tutoring behaviours across untrained (baseline) and trained tutoring conditions for four families (Birmingham study).

for the parent of the first subject, whose use of prompts was close to 70 per cent under baseline conditions. All four parents increased their level of delayed attention and use of prompts with the introduction of the training programme. As was the case with the Auckland parents, the Birmingham parents displayed very low levels of praise under baseline conditions. Three parents did not praise any instances of children's corrections following a prompt. Praise for prompted corrections increased substantially with the tutoring programme and praise for self-correction also increased, though not as substantially.

An additional analysis of the data from the Birmingham parents showed that changes occurred in the effectiveness of prompting. Of those errors where parents responded by offering prompts, S1 corrected 60 per cent at baseline, S2 corrected 4 per cent, S3 corrected 2 per cent and S4 corrected 27 per cent (mean 24 per cent). The corresponding figures for errors corrected following prompts during the programme were 78 per cent, 64 per cent, 57 per cent and 72 per cent respectively (mean 67 per cent). The exceptional example here was the parent of S1 who already at baseline used a high rate of prompts following child errors.

As in the Auckland study, all children showed marked improvement in their reading at home. During three months of home tutoring, two children reached the criterion of 90 per cent accuracy on four different books, one reached criterion on three different books and the fourth child on two different books. In this study, books used at home were selected by the children and so did not always form part of the graded series. This procedure was suggested by Morgan and Lyon (1979). During baseline conditions, the percentage of children's errors that were self-corrected were 3 per cent, 10 per cent, 16 per cent and 8 per cent (mean 12 per cent). Corresponding percentages during the parent training programme were 11 per cent, 21 per cent, 24 per cent and 55 per cent (mean 25 per cent).

Generalization to school reading with less tutor support was more clear-cut than in the Auckland study. During the three months of home tutoring, one child reached criterion of 90 per cent accuracy at school on seven successive books (from the graded series used by the teacher), one child reached criterion on five successive books and the remaining two children reached criterion on two successive books. A standardized test of reading accuracy (Neale, 1966) showed that during the three month period of home tutoring the four children made reading accuracy gains of four, six, seven and eight months (mean 6.25 months).

Results consistent with research in pre-school enrichment, as mentioned earlier, were yielded by these two studies. Trained home visitors successfully altered parent–child interaction during one-to-one oral reading, so that both parent and child gained new skills. The exercise of these skills in the one-to-one context is likely to have been mutually reinforcing. Several parents in Auckland and Birmingham later tutored other children, either siblings of their own child or children of other parents who approached them.

These studies met some but not all of the criticisms of Atkeson and Forehand (1979). Data were gathered in both home and school settings and on both parent and child behaviour. The tape recordings ensured that full data on parents' programme implementation was available for analysis as well as for conveying specific information to the school about children's performance at home. However, no component analysis was attempted on the separate tutoring behaviours.

These two studies demonstrate that parents can successfully remedy their children's reading at home, without the direct involvement of the teacher. However, generalization of reading gains to school reading was more effective in the Birmingham study, where the teacher operated a reading programme that included oral reading from books of similar difficulty to those used in the home reading programme. Demonstration of generalization of home tutoring gains from an oral reading programme is difficult, if not impossible, in situations where older children receiving remedial reading are not given the opportunity to read with support from texts at school.

In retrospect, one disappointing feature of both the early studies has been that the home–school contact was provided by a third party – an outside professional – independent of home and school. It was this professional who provided the mechanism for the exchange of information between parent and teacher about the child's performance in the other setting. Despite the best efforts of this professional, both parent and teacher were thus deprived of a source of mutual reinforcement and mutual recognition of competence. The relationship stopped well short of a working partnership, and still did not capitalize fully on the advantages of the school setting. There is a need for research to address the problem of engineering direct parent–teacher contact and exchange of data, without dependence on a third party.

As previously mentioned, Glynn and McNaughton (1985) recently reviewed these two studies and nine further studies employing 'Pause, prompt and praise' remedial reading tutoring procedures. These studies replicate the findings of the original studies, with widely differing samples of readers and tutors, and so greatly expand confidence in the effectiveness of the 'Pause, prompt and praise' procedures. For example, Wheldall and Mettem (1985), working in the UK, report major gains for low progress 12 year-old readers who were tutored by means of these methods by 16 year-old pupils from the same school. Another study introduced the 'Pause, prompt and praise' procedures concurrently to teachers and parents of four 11–12 year-old readers, who had reading deficits of three to five years (Scott and Ballard, 1983). This procedure necessitated the participation of both teachers and parents from the outset. Scott and Ballard report reading gains of 32 to 36 months over a duration of 3.25 months. This is the study that reported the greatest gains among those reviewed by Glynn and McNaughton. These large gains result mainly from the concurrent intervention in two settings (home and school), but also from the sharing of responsibility for the tutoring task between parents and teachers.

The home-based remedial reading studies offer data to show that gains in behaviours made at home can generalize to school as long as the school provides a supportive context in which these behaviours can occur. Surprisingly, there is even less evidence to show that academic behaviours learned at school generalize to the home. This generalization seems simply to be taken for granted by schools. Yet, currently, very few parent training programmes would be accepted by the behavioural research community without data to show that behaviours acquired in the training setting generalize to other appropriate natural settings (Miller and Sloane, 1976; Forehand and Atkeson, 1977; Koegal, Glahn and Nieminen, 1978; Jewett and Clark, 1979; Sanders and Glynn, 1981).

One study that did examine school to home generalization was that of Jewett and Clark (1979), who implemented the correspondence training procedure devised by Risley and Hart (1968). Jewett and Clark showed that conversational skills during family meals at home could be modified through intervention in the pre-school setting. This involved delayed reinforcement of children's accurate verbal reports corresponding to their actual conversation at home. The correspondence training procedure is suggested as particularly applicable in programming generalization of skills from a training setting to a less accessible setting, where the new skills are expected to be used but with less support available. The procedure certainly holds promise as a means for teachers to programme changes in children's academic behaviour at home, for example, increasing the opportunities for children to practise oral reading or writing skills. However, the procedure depends on access to good-quality reliable data in the generalization setting. The setting may be less accessible in terms of introducing a training programme, but it must remain quite accessible as far as data gathering is concerned.

Data gathering in the home setting for incorporation in evaluation of school-based programmes, whether done by independent observers or by parents themselves, requires frequent and specific contact and a degree of co-operation between parent and teacher. If frequent contact and parent–teacher co-operation are needed merely to collect data on school to home generalization, why not programme generalization directly (Stokes and Baer, 1977) and involve parents not only in data gathering but also in sharing teaching of academic skills?

Spelling and writing at home

One study, in which a parent and teacher shared not only in data gathering but also in teaching academic skills, is that of Glynn and Glynn (1980). In this study, the teacher and parent together implemented both a spelling programme and a writing fluency programme, to improve the performance of an 11 year-old boy, Michael, who was grossly under-achieving in these areas.

The two programmes were introduced independently of each other, so that opportunities to practise fluency in writing could be provided under conditions where accuracy of spelling, grammar and letter formation was not required. Parent and teacher suspected that the very small amount of writing Michael displayed may have resulted from the extinction effects of writing under conditions designed to reinforce accuracy of form, spelling and grammar almost to the exclusion of content. This is a feature of many school writing programmes.

Accordingly, 10-minute 'speed writing' sessions were conducted daily for 57 days, either by the mother at home or by the teacher at school. These sessions could occur at any time of the day or evening, including weekends. Michael was required to write as much as he liked on the clear understanding that letter formation, spelling, punctuation and grammar did not matter.

Concurrently, a daily spelling programme was conducted in both settings. This programme required daily random testing and sentence writing, with words selected from the Alphabetical Spelling List of Arvidson (1977). At the outset, Michael performed below the criterion for Level One (the level usually achieved by children in infant classes).

Of particular interest to this discussion is that not only were there expected gains in spelling and fluency of written expression but the data also showed generalization effects of the spelling programme into the written expression (see Figure 4.4). Results of the spelling programme showed that Michael passed criterion tests for Spelling Levels 1, 2 and 3 at the point indicated by the dotted vertical lines in Figure 4.4. The accuracy scores (cumulative totals of words right minus words wrong) for each of Arvidson's first four levels are also shown in Figure 4.4. It can be seen that gains in accuracy of words at Levels 1, 2 and 3 occurred during phases

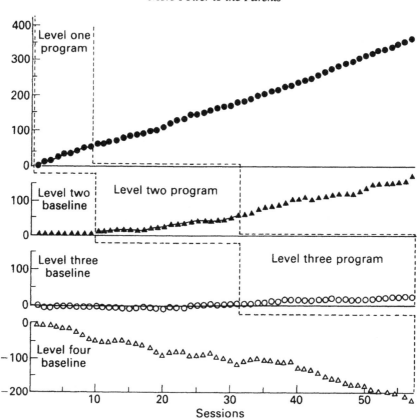

Figure 4.4 Cumulative accuracy scores for spelling words at levels 1, 2, 3 and 4 across 57 samples of speed writing.

when the spelling programme was introduced, successively, for each of these levels. In contrast, the accuracy of the Level 4 words not included in the spelling programme decreased across the 57 sessions. These gains in spelling accuracy were not made at the expense of fluency, since Michael was also found to use proportionately more words from Level 4 and above as the programme progressed. It is this proportionate increase in use of Level 4 words, not included in the spelling programme, that resulted in the apparent decrease in accuracy of those words shown in Figure 4.4.

The close sharing of teaching and data-gathering in this study enabled the parent to appreciate the rationale behind the spelling and writing programmes. She also learned how to sample her child's written work in order to monitor the occurrence of academic behaviours specified by the teacher. Parent and teacher regularly exchanged actual writing samples, produced in both settings under similar conditions, and discussed changes in data gathered from these samples. As with the parents in the reading tutoring studies, this parent later began tutoring a second child with the spelling programme.

Conclusions

The research reviewed suggests that the power of parents to remedy their own children's academic learning difficulties is great. Behavioural skills training procedures demonstrate that parents are capable of being just as effective as co-teachers as they are as co-therapists. Home-based remedial teaching programmes have produced gains in children's academic behaviour which generalize to school. When it comes to generalizing school gains in academic behaviour into the home setting, it seems that the power of parents is grossly under-used.

The challenge for applied behavioural research lies in devising a technology to make better use of the power of parents inherent in their availability in the home setting. To date, there has been an over-emphasis in research on the power of parents as agents of re-inforcement. The power of parents to provide opportunities for children to perform academic behaviours and to promote generalization of behaviours acquired at school has been underestimated in applied behavioural research. The challenge might be taken up by first providing a better technology of home and school contact. Existing behavioural research permits a tentative specification for such contact.

1 The frequency of parent–teacher contact on an individual basis should be increased, to something approaching one per week.
2 The type of contact should be modified, so that both parties give as well as receive information about children's performance of a skill.
3 The amount and type of information exchanged should be modified. Specifically, work samples and tape recordings (i.e. actual data) should replace judgements and opinions or even global notes about data.
4 To utilize the advantages of the home setting, home–school contact should provide parents with specific information about which behaviours are being introduced at school and with the rationale behind the curriculum that prescribes these.
5 Parent–teacher contact should lead to the formulating of a joint strategy for monitoring, for providing opportunities to practise and for shared teaching of particular academic behaviours in both settings.

6 Parent–teacher contact should provide teachers with specific information about the occurrence at home of academic behaviours acquired at school and about new behaviours being acquired at home.

Further research into the generalisation of academic behaviours from home to school and from school to home should be designed to call upon the competence and expertise of both parent and teacher. Such research should incorporate strategies which require behaviour change from both parties, in directions mutually agreed upon. Improvement of children in target behaviours mutually selected may provide reinforcement to both teacher and parent. Perhaps co-operative or partnership behaviours themselves will be reinforced. At least, in this way, successes can be credited equally to parent and teacher and failures may be seen as a challenge to further effort, rather than as cause to blame the inefficiency of the other. Research of this kind may help to build links between the settings in which people live out their lives, rather than contribute further to the isolation of the family from the rest of society, as feared by Bronfenbrenner (1979).

References

Allington, R. L. (1983), The reading instruction provided readers of differing reading abilities, *The Elementary School Journal*, vol. 83, no. 5, pp. 548–59.

Arvidson, G. L. (1977), *Learning to Spell: A Manual for Use with the Alphabetic Spelling List* (Oxford: Pergamon).

Atkeson, G. L. and Forehand, R. (1979), 'Home-based reinforcement programs designed to modify classroom behavior: a review and methodological evaluation', *Psychological Bulletin*, vol. 86, pp. 1298–1308.

Berkowitz, B. P. and Graziano, A. M. (1977), 'Training parents as behaviour therapists: a review, *Behaviour Research and Therapy*, vol. 10, pp. 297–318.

Blackstone, T. (1979), 'Parental involvement in education', *Education Policy Bulletin*, vol. 7, pp. 81–98.

Bronfenbrenner, U. (1974), *Is Early Intervention Effective? A Report on Longitudinal Evaluations of Pre-School Programs*, vol. 2 (Washington, DC: Department of Health, Education and Welfare).

Bronfenbrenner, U. (1979), 'Beyond the deficit model in child and family policy', *Teachers' College Record*, vol. 81, pp. 95–104.

Chilman, C. S. (1976), 'Programs for disadvantaged parents: some major trends and related research', in Leitenburg, H. (ed.) *Handbook of Behaviour Modification and Behavior Therapy.* (Englewood Cliffs, NJ: Prentice-Hall).

Clay, M. M. (1979), *Reading: The Patterning of Complex Behaviour* (Auckland: Heinemann Educational Books).

Deakin, M. (1973), *The Children on the Hill: The Story of an Extraordinary Family* (London: Quartet Books).

Donachy, W. (1979), 'Parental participation in pre-school education, in Clark, M. M. and Cheyne, W. M. (eds) *Studies in Pre-School Education* (London: Hodder and Stoughton).

Forehand, R. and Atkeson, B. F. (1977), 'Generality of treatment effects with parents as therapists: a review of assessment and implementation procedures', *Behaviour Therapy*, vol. 8, pp. 575–93.

Fry, L. (1977), 'Remedial reading using parents as behaviour technicians', *New Zealand Journal of Educational Studies*, vol. 12, pp. 29–36.

Gath, A. (1979), 'Parents as therapists of mentally handicapped children', *Journal of Child Psychology and Psychiatry*, vol. 20, pp. 161–5.

Glynn, T. (1980), 'Parent–child interaction in remedial reading at home', in Clark, M. M. and Glynn, T. (eds) *Reading and Writing for the Child with Difficulties* (Birmingham: Educational Review Occasional Publications).

Glynn, T. and Glynn, V. (1980), 'Generalization of spelling gains into written expression with parent–teacher remedial programme', unpublished manuscript, Department of Education, University of Auckland, New Zealand.

Glynn, E. L. and McNaughton, S. S. (1975), 'Trust your own observations: criterion referenced assessment of reading progress', *The Slow Learning Child*, vol. 22, pp. 91–108.

Glynn, T. and McNaughton, S. S. (1985), 'The Mangere Home and School Reading Procedures: continuing research on their effectiveness', *New Zealand Journal of Psychology*, vol. 15, 66–77.

Glynn, T., McNaughton, S. S., Robinson, V. and Quinn, M. (1979), *Remedial Reading at Home: Helping You to Help Your Child* (Wellington: New Zealand Council for Educational Research).

Graziano, A. M. (1977), 'Parents as behavior therapists', in Herson, M., Eisler, R. M. and Miller, P. M. (eds), *Progress in Behavior Modification*, vol. 4 (New York: Academic Press).

Jewett, J. and Clark, H. B. (1979), 'Teaching pre-schoolers to use appropriate dinnertime conversation: an analysis of generalization from school to home', *Behaviour Therapy*, vol. 10, pp. 589–605.

Johnston, C. A., and Katz, R. C. (1973), 'Using parents as change agents for their own children: a review', *Journal of Child Psychology and Psychiatry*, vol. 14, pp. 181–200.

Koegal, R. L., Glahn, T. J. and Nieminen, G. S. (1978), 'Generalization of parent training results', *Journal of Applied Behavior Analysis*, vol. 11, pp. 95–109.

Love, J. M. and Van Biervliet, A. (1984), 'Training parents to be home reading tutors: generalization of children's reading skills from home to school', *The Exceptional Child*, vol. 31, no. 2, pp. 114–27.

McNaughton, S. S. and Delquadri, J. (1978), 'Error attention tutoring in oral reading', in Glynn, T. and McNaughton, S. S. (eds) *Behaviour*

Analysis in New Zealand, 1978 (Auckland: Department of Education, University of Auckland).

McNaughton, S. S. and Glynn, T. (1981), 'Delayed versus immediate attention to oral reading errors: effects on accuracy and self correction', *Educational Psychology*, vol. 1, pp. 57–65.

McNaughton, S. S., Glynn, T. and Robinson, V. (1981), *Parents as Remedial Reading Tutors: Issues for Home and School* (Wellington: New Zealand Council for Educational Research).

Miller, S. J. and Sloane, H. N. (1976), 'The generalization effects of parent training across stimulus settings', *Journal of Applied Behavior Analysis*, vol. 9, pp. 355–70.

Morgan, R. and Lyon, R. (1979), 'Paired reading: a preliminary report on a technique for parent tuition of reading retarded children', *Journal of Child Psychology and Psychiatry*, vol. 20, pp. 151–60.

Neale, M. (1966), *The Neale Analysis of Reading Ability* (London: Macmillan).

Nicholson, T. (1979), 'What parents know about reading – and what we need to tell them', paper presented at A.N.Z.A.A.S. Congress, University of Auckland, New Zealand, February 1979.

O'Dell, S. (1974), 'Training parents in behaviour modification: a review', *Psychological Bulletin*, vol. 81, pp. 418–33.

Risley, T. R. and Hart, B. (1968), 'Developing correspondence between the non-verbal and verbal behavior of pre-school children', *Journal of Applied Behavior Analysis*, vol. 1, pp. 267–81.

Ritchie, J. C. (1984), 'Parents as teachers: home based reading instruction, unpublished MEd thesis, University of Waikato, Hamilton, New Zealand.

Ryback, D. and Staats, A. W., (1970), 'Parents as behavior therapy technicians in treating reading deficits (dyslexia)', *Journal of Behavior Therapy and Experimental Psychiatry*, vol. 1, pp. 109–11.

Sanders, M. R. and Glynn, T. (1981), 'Training parents in behavioral self management: an analysis of generalization and maintenance', *Journal of Applied Behavior Analysis*, vol. 14, pp. 223–37.

Scott, J. M. and Ballard, K. D. (1983), 'Training parents and teachers in remedial reading procedures for children with learning difficulties', *Educational Psychology*, vol. 3, no. 1 pp. 15–31.

Stokes, T. F. and Baer, D. M. (1977), 'An implicit technology of generalization', *Journal of Applied Behavior Analysis*, vol. 10, pp. 349–67.

Tizard, J. and Tizard, B. (1979), 'Parents as teachers and educators', in Doxiadis, S. (ed.) *The Child in the World of Tomorrow: A Window into the Future* (Oxford: Pergamon).

Wheldall, K. and Mettem, P. (1985), 'Behavioural peer tutoring: training 16-year-old tutors to employ the 'pause, prompt and praise' method with 12-year-old remedial readers', *Educational Psychology*, vol. 5, pp. 27–44.

Woodward, K. L. (1978), 'Saving the family', *Newsweek*, 15 May 1978.

Young, M. and McGeeney, P. (1968), *Learning Begins at Home* (London: Routledge & Kegan Paul).

Yule, W. (1975), 'Commentary after paper by C. C. Cunningham', in Kiernan, C. C. and Woodford, F. P. (eds) *Behaviour Modification with the Severely Retarded* (Amsterdam: Associated Scientific Publishers).

5

The Teacher–Child Interaction Project (TCIP): Implementing Behavioural Programmes with Troublesome Individual Children in the Primary School

MICHAEL BERGER, WILLIAM YULE and
VERONICA WIGLEY

Evaluations of the use of behavioural methods in educational settings are characterized by encouraging results, studies of individual and group applications and a high level of professional staffing. There is still, however, a dearth of control-group studies and studies of service applications. This chapter describes a control group study that was carried out by the Teacher–Child Interaction Project (TCIP), focusing on how teachers involved with the project and their children changed in the classroom.

The TCIP was a collaborative project between staff of the University of London Institutes of Education and Psychiatry and the Inner London Education Authority (ILEA), which ran for eight years from 1973. The major goal of the project was to foster positive teacher–child interaction as a means of reducing the mutual difficulties experienced by teachers and a proportion of children in their classes. It aimed to achieve this goal through the application of principles and techniques of behaviour modification adapted to the special needs and circumstances of teachers and children in local schools.

The project was developed following successful pilot work by Berger and Yule and by Barcroft (1971) in a London primary school. As a result of this work, in 1973, the ILEA seconded the third author (an experienced teacher) as the teacher-tutor to collaborate in developing and evaluating service models based upon behavioural techniques. The work was actively fostered and encouraged by the Divisional Inspector and by the local Heads Consultative Committee. The project also enjoyed the collaboration and co-operation of the Schools Psychological Service and its local staff.

The philosophical basis of the project's work was very much in line with the approach to be advocated by the Warnock Committee (Department of Education and Science, 1978). The project recognized that, for a proportion of children experiencing and presenting difficulties, specialist help through child guidance, special schools and classes would continue to be needed. The majority of children and their teachers encountering difficulties might be able to benefit, however, from help in their normal classrooms.

Coping with difficulties in the classroom is an integral part of the teacher's professional expertise but, every so often, some children present difficulties which do not respond to the teachers' attempts to deal with them. The relevance of behavioural techniques in extending teachers' classroom management skills is now widely recognized, but there is still a dearth of service provision directed at transferring such knowledge and skills to where they are needed most, namely, the teacher working in the classroom. There is still relatively little evaluation of such provision. TCIP was one of the first attempts in Britain to train teachers systematically in behaviour management, so that they would be able to utilize whatever skills they acquired in their own classroom and to pass on their experience to their colleagues.

The theoretical principles of the project were derived from the work of social learning theorists. In practice, this meant that the project was based on the premise that many of the problems experienced by teachers are a function of the interaction between them and children. To the extent that ways in which teachers and children interact are learned, they can be modified through the systematic use of approaches derived from the principles of relevant learning theories. Great emphasis, therefore, was placed on the active involvement of teachers, since it is believed that what they do, and do not do, in response to the behaviour of children influences to a great extent the behaviour of most of the children. Naturally, teachers are affected by the response of the children. A child who consistently fails to respond to teacher praise or positive attention is likely to induce in the teacher a tendency not to praise or positively attend. It is in this sense, that of mutual responsiveness, that we use the term 'interaction'.

There are several ways of helping teachers to learn about and use behaviour approaches in the classroom. Simply providing lecture courses and hoping that teachers will then be able to implement what has been learned has been shown to be inadequate by McKeown, Adams and Forehand (1975) and others. Training teachers must involve teaching *how* as well as teaching *about*, but problems may arise because it may be difficult, even for some psychologists, to translate behavioural principles into practical action tailored to the special needs and characteristics of individual children or classes, and their particular teachers. Further, it is essential to ensure that the teacher's behaviour in the classroom conforms to the requirements of the behavioural programme – in our experience, verbal reports about what was done did not always coincide with the reports of an independent observer. Finally, questions and problems always arise once a programme has begun and, unless someone with experience is readily accessible, the programme is likely to founder (Berger, 1982).

In view of these considerations and influenced by approaches adopted in the USA (Hall, 1971), it was decided to develop a service model built upon a basic lecture and discussion course complemented by practical project work in the classroom. A teacher–tutor, having completed a basic training, assisted in running further courses and in providing practical advice to colleagues. A major task of the teacher-tutor was to maintain regular and frequent contact with teachers participating in the courses, observe interactions in their classrooms, feed back to them information on their classroom performance and assist them with any problems that arose.

Several courses for teachers in primary schools were run in pilot form by the project team. During this period various observation schedules were devised to gather data on teacher–child interaction. The derived data were used as part of the monitoring process. A questionnaire to be completed by teachers at the end of each course was also developed. This enabled teachers to comment anonymously on the quality and usefulness of the various aspects of the approach. This information was also used to help modify the courses. Following several courses, a controlled study was carried out to obtain data for a systematic evaluation of our approach. The rest of this chapter is devoted to a description and discussion of the findings of this study, focusing on data obtained about changes in teacher and child behaviour in the classroom as recorded by an outside observer. In addition, questionnaires were completed anonymously to obtain data on teachers' perceptions of the course and how their own and their pupils' behaviour changed. Further data were also obtained by teachers during the course of their own work with a selected child.

Aims and design

Initial evaluation of TCIP work was based on case studies of changes in children's behaviour and on responses to question-naires given to all teachers who attended courses. These findings were encouraging, but it is likely that many forms of intervention will produce effects because of a number of factors such as the offers of help and the on-going monitoring and support which need not be specific to behaviourally based programmes. Children and teachers accommodate to each other over time, and other factors are likely to reduce the nature and severity of difficulties. For these and other reasons, evaluations are most appropriately conducted on the basis of systematic controlled studies involving a number of groups subjected to different forms of intervention, coupled with intensive and objective monitoring.

Several important constraints limited the evaluation of this project. Although the teacher–tutor was available on a full-time basis, most of her time was taken up in running courses and assisting participants. Because of this, it was difficult at any one period to secure data from more than twenty or so teachers. We also felt that teachers who had agreed to be observed (as a control group) should receive the help offered once this role had ended. Moreover, as the courses lasted a school term, and as we felt it inappropriate to evaluate interventions in the first term of the school year, it was not feasible to run more than one control group.

With these and other practical constraints operating, the following design was implemented (Design 4, Campbell and Stanley, 1966). Twenty teachers recruited at the end of the first term were randomly divided into two groups of ten. One group was then randomly chosen to participate in a course during the second term (Group 1), the other group acting as a control (Group 2). In the third term, the control group participated in the course, the experimental group continuing without further help. The control group teachers were told that they could not be given a place on the course during Term II, but would be guaranteed a place in the next term. They were asked, however, to identify difficult children, and all teachers and children were observed during both terms. Teachers were observed on eight occasions, twice at the beginning and twice at the end of each of the two terms covered by the study.

Each teacher identified at least one child who was regarded as 'difficult'. One teacher selected a child who was anxious and withdrawn as well as one other child. All other teachers selected a child who showed disruptive behaviour or who was passively inattentive. These children were observed at the same time as their teacher on the same number of occasions. We identify these children as the 'selected' group.

Twenty teachers initially agreed to participate. Although ten teachers were chosen for each group, the study groups were reduced to eight and nine teachers respectively, because of factors such as sickness. This degree of attrition is to be expected. However, the actual numbers involved for each group are not such as to lead to bias in one but not the other. Eighteen selected children (one teacher decided to work with two children) and a random sample of children in seventeen clases were monitored. As is common in this type of research, we were not always able to observe each teacher and child on all eight occasions. All the observations were carried out by one person and had to be carried out at fixed times. It was not possible to compensate for absences of teachers and children, so that observational data were sometimes incomplete. This was taken into account in the data analysis by statistical adjustments.

Course structure

The courses evaluated in the study followed a standard format. Each course presented material on systematic observation procedures, the behavioural orientation, basic principles and derived techniques. Time was always allocated for discussion of the nature of behaviour problems in childhood, ethical issues on behaviour modification and the importance of tailoring the curriculum to the child's abilities. Emphasis was placed on assessment of the nature of difficulties through observation. The importance of peer influence was also taken into account in this process. Courses were not focused solely on conduct problems. Attention was also paid to academic problems, anxiety problems and to classroom organization. Individual project work formed the central focus of the course. Each teacher clarified in behavioural terms the nature of the difficulty experienced with the selected child, carried out structured observations (while teaching) and, with the help of the project team (the present authors), devised and implemented an intervention programme. The teacher then evaluated the effectiveness of the intervention through continued structured observations and other less formal means. Courses were held after school hours at a local centre. During the school term, there were eight weekly sessions, which lasted two to three hours after school. About half of each session was devoted to formal teaching, the remainder to discussions about individual projects.

Data collection

(a) Instruments used

In addition to data gathered by the teachers as part of their project work, two special observation schedules were utilized to gather data on teacher behaviour and on child behaviour. One of these schedules focused on teacher behaviour (TCIP Schedule 1), which was recorded together with the behaviour of the child interacted with, if any. The other (TCIP Schedule 2) focused on child behaviour, which was recorded together with any interaction between the child and teacher and child and peer. This schedule was used to monitor the behaviour of selected children and the random sample of children. Both the teacher and child schedules were completed during direct observations by the teacher–tutor, and inter-observer agreement checks were undertaken for both schedules by a postgraduate psychology student. The teacher was observed for three seconds, and behaviour was then coded in terms of what the teacher was doing and what the child or class she was interacting with was doing. Three seconds were allowed for recording. Ten observations, therefore, were obtained in one minute and a ten-minute observation period yielded one hundred observations.

Where the teacher was called out of the class by another teacher or helper, recording stopped until her return. If the teacher left the class to fetch a child or for some other purpose, records of 'not interacting with the class' were made until her return, unless she could be heard outside the room, in which case any interactions were recorded appropriately.

Observations were carried out when the teacher was involved in normal teaching activity – supervising individual work and marking it or taking a class or a group lesson. Observations were not carried out during PE periods, or when the teacher was reading to the class as a whole or when the class was watching television.

As far as possible, a ten-minute teacher behaviour observation session followed a child behaviour observation session, but this was not always possible owing to the exigencies of timetabling for use of the hall, television, etc. Child behaviour was coded as appropriate or inappropriate, using previously agreed definitions.

Each child was observed for five seconds and his/her behaviour recorded in the next five seconds. After the behaviour of a selected child had been observed and recorded, the behaviour of a random child was observed and recorded. Observers selected the random child by mentally dividing the room into quadrants and taking each child in the area as a random choice before moving to the next area. No child was recorded twice until the behaviour of all the children in the class had been recorded. Five seconds were allowed for observation because of the difficulty of 'finding' specific children in a busy classroom.

Generally, the observer aimed to get 20 samples of behaviour for each observation session for each child selected and for random children. Where there were two selected children, observation sessions lasted approximately ten minutes, including the observation time devoted to random children. Before starting observations, the observer discussed with teachers which times they thought would be most likely to show up the kind of problems that concerned the teacher. Observation was then carried out during these times.

Teachers on the course also monitored the behaviour of the child they had selected by structured observation in the classroom. Most teachers used methods based on time-sampling or interval counts, depending on the nature of the problem with which they were concerned. Teachers were able to use these methods while continuing to teach normally. Examples of this sort of observation and consequent intervention carried out by teachers on TCIP courses have been published elsewhere (Berger, Yule and Wigley, 1977; Wigley, Yule and Berger, 1983; Yule, Berger and Wigley, 1984).

(b) Reliability

The reliabilities of the observational data were assessed as the percentage agreement between the teacher-tutor and a trained observer, a postgraduate psychology student. Reliabilities were computed for each separate item on the observation schedules, using the formula given by Maxwell (1970). The measure is a stringent one in the sense that it monitors agreement on each of the three second observation intervals. Parallel observations were undertaken throughout the two terms of the study, and an attempt was made to sample most of the teachers (14 out of the 17 teachers were observed at least once) and most of the children (16 out of 18 being observed at least once). This procedure avoids some of the problems characteristic of reliability studies, in which observer accuracy is assessed only at the start of the study.

For teacher categories, agreement ranged between 40 per cent and 89 per cent, the average being 75 per cent. This level of agreement is not high, but is adequate and similar to that reported in many other studies. Disagreement usually arose because observers were sometimes positioned in such a way that the view of one was restricted by the position of the teacher and children. Agreements on the less complex coding scheme for children averaged 93 per cent, with a range of 83–100 per cent.

Results

It was predicted that both experimental and control group teachers and their children would improve, but that the group participating in the course would show the greatest improvement. 'Improvement' was defined operationally in the sense of statistical significance and specifically in terms of the individual measures selected for monitoring. In terms of a behavioural approach and the thrust of the courses, it was predicted that there would be a greater increase in 'approval' behaviour and a greater diminution in 'reprimands' for teachers attending the course than for the control teachers.

This hypothesis does not preclude the possibility that teachers, during the course of the school year, would become more effective in classroom management or that children who were 'difficult' would become less so. It simply asserts that the differential improvement in TCIP teachers would be greater and that associated with this would be a relatively greater diminution in the difficulties presented by the children. It was also predicted that those selected children whose teachers had participated in the course would show a greater increase in appropriate behaviours than was shown by selected children in the classes of control teachers. It would be anticipated that the selected children eventually would not differ substantially from their randomly selected peers.

It is essential that evaluation of efficacy be assessed in terms of individual change as well. It is not sufficient that overall average change is significant; rather, the majority of individuals within the experimental group should change. There is little point in achieving statistical significance between groups if this is due only to large changes in 30 to 40 per cent of the group members.

I   *Changes in teacher behaviour*

At each point in the study, two sets of observations were made using the observation schedule. These observations – eight in all – were averaged so that data set one is the average of the two observations at the start of Term II, data set two from the two observations at the end of Term II, and so on. The observation categories were combined to produce four major variables: Instruction, Approval, Reprimands and No Interaction. Each is made up of the sets of discrete categories included within the schedules. By averaging over occasions, it was hoped to produce a more representative characterization of teacher behaviour than would be obtained from the single observations. In those instances where only one observation was possible, the observed frequency for that occasion was utilized in the analysis. Raw cell frequencies were transformed into proportions and multiplied by 100 to standardize for the differences in the raw numbers of observations. This was necessary because, in practice, it was not always possible to observe every teacher for the prescribed observation period.

For a number of reasons, the resulting data were analysed by means of t-tests. The data themselves do not satisfy all the assumptions necessary for more sophisticated analyses and t-tests are among the most robust of the statistical procedures. This leaves open the charge that with multiple comparisons a proportion of significant findings would arise through chance factors. While this is conceded, it is counterbalanced by the availability of very specific directional hypotheses, which were generated from a substantial pre-existing literature. Further, the major analyses were carried out by contrasting the experimental group with a control group, so that the interpretation of findings can be balanced by parallel observations within the control group. It is recommended by Campbell and Stanley (1966) that within-group change scores be computed initially and that the t-test be applied to the difference between the average gain scores for the experimental and control groups. In the final analysis, of course, any assessment of the study is based on factors additional to statistical tests. Statistical significance serves as a guide and not as the criterion. The means, standard deviations and ranges for all data are given in Table 5.1.

On inspection, it appears that the teachers in both groups increased the proportion of Approval and Instruction and decreased Reprimands and No Interaction. The important question is whether or not teachers participating in the course showed these changes to a greater extent than teachers not participating in a course directed at producing such changes. To answer these questions mean change scores were computed for each group and

Table 5.1 Means standard deviations and ranges for observations of teacher behaviour (combined categories – percentages)

Observation Point	Start Term II 1			End Term II 2			Start Term III 3			End Term III 4		
	MEAN	SD	RANGE	MEAN	SD	RANGE	MEAN	SD	RANGE	MEAN	SD	RANGE
APPROVAL												
Group 1	2.3	1.8	0.5 – 5.2	3.7	3.8	0.0 – 10.5	3.6	2.9	0.0 – 7.0	7.1	4.8	1.5 – 13.3
Group 2	2.3	2.3	0.0 – 5.5	2.1	2.2	0.0 – 6.0	3.3	3.6	0.0 – 10.5	4.6	4.4	0.0 – 12.6
REPRIMAND												
Group 1	14.7	7.0	3.0 – 24.7	8.8	5.9	1.0 – 16.0	8.8	7.8	2.5 – 27.0	7.2	6.0	2.0 – 19.2
Group 2	10.4	4.8	3.1 – 16.3	6.8	4.8	0.8 – 17.6	9.2	4.2	3.6 – 16.0	5.5	4.0	0.5 – 12.5
INSTRUCTION												
Group 1	73.7	6.1	67.2 – 83.7	80.9	7.7	67.1 – 91.8	79.9	10.2	59.0 – 90.0	81.7	3.6	75.3 – 86.0
Group 2	80.5	5.3	73.2 – 90.0	83.2	7.5	70.9 – 93.2	80.3	4.4	73.8 – 87.3	85.1	4.9	79.0 – 93.0
NO INTERACTION												
Group 1	9.4	6.7	2.6 – 23.5	6.5	3.6	1.0 – 11.9	7.7	4.1	3.0 – 14.6	3.7	1.9	1.0 – 7.0
Group 2	6.8	3.0	1.9 – 10.9	8.0	4.6	2.0 – 14.6	6.3	3.9	1.0 – 13.3	4.7	3.1	0.5 – 9.5

(a) *Approval* At the start of the study, there was no significant difference in the frequency of teacher approval between the two groups. At the end of Term II, however, there was a statistically significant improvement in the course group, when compared with the improvement in the no-course group ($t = 1.83$, one tailed, $p = 0.041$, d.f. $= 15$). Examining next the within-group changes, the course group (Group 1) showed an increase in average approval, whereas the no-course group showed, if anything, a marginal decrease. The increase within the course group is, on a one-tailed test, significant ($t = 1.94$, $p = 0.047$, d.f. $= 7$). (A one-tailed test is appropriate for these t-tests because of the prediction that course participation would lead to an increase in the frequency of contingent approval.)

Compared with their performance at the start of the course, Group 1 teachers showed a significant increase in approval by the end of the study ($t = 2.95$, $p = 0.01$, d.f. $= 7$). Although Group 2 also evidenced an increase, this was not significant, despite their participation in a course during the third term. It should also be noted that Group 2's participation in the course was not associated with a statistically significant improvement in approval, possibly because of the variability within this group. (It may seem unusual that increased teacher approval in Group 1 of 1.5 per cent over Term I is statistically significant, whereas an increase of 2.3 per cent for Group 2 between the beginning and end of the study is not. This is due to the greater variability of data in the latter case.)

Given that Group 2 did not show a significant increase immediately after the course, whereas Group 1 did, the significance of the latter finding must be qualified. That is, in so far as group performance is concerned, participation in the course does not unequivocally lead to significant improvement.

It is worth drawing attention to the increased approval level in Group 1 over the term following their completion of the course (Term III). Statistically this increase is significant ($t = 3.56$, two-tailed $p = 0.01$, d.f. $= 7$) and was not anticipated. This is probably a consequence of changes in two Group 1 teachers. Neither had completed their project work by the end of Term II and only began to implement what they had learned on the course during Term III. This suggests a possibly delayed or 'sleeper' effect. In the absence of data for Group 2 after a similar interval or data from a control group, this finding is only suggestive, and monitoring of 'sleeper' effects should be planned in future studies.

A proper evaluation of change must take into account the number of *individuals* who improved, balanced against those who were unchanged or made worse by the intervention. In small samples, one or two individuals evidencing large changes can distort the group means. In examining individual change data, a cut-off of 1.5 per cent or more increase or decrease in Approval following the course is used as an index of change.

Five teachers increased their Approval responses following the course, whereas none of the no-course teachers did so. By the end of the study, four of these five maintained their improvement. One who had improved initially reverted to the original level, and one who had not changed had improved by the end of the third term. In the no-course group, all but one of the teachers showed no change and one got worse. Following their participation in the course in Term III, four teachers in Group 2 improved. Again, in the absence of additional suitable control groups, we cannot draw strong conclusions from these data. However, from the data on changes over Term II, it would appear that the course did effect some positive changes in the use of Approval behaviour.

(b) *Reprimands* The two groups did not differ significantly in their frequency of use of reprimands at the start or at any other time during the study. Also, although both groups showed a significant decrease in reprimand frequency over Term II (Group 1 $t=3.01$, $p=0.01$, d.f. $=7$; Group 2 $t=1.91$, $p=0.46$, d.f. $=8$, one-tailed), their relative decrease did not differ significantly. Thus, the results show no impact of the course as such on the use of reprimands. Compared with their initial levels, by the end of the project both groups showed a significant decrease in their use of reprimands (Group 1 $t=2.64$, $p=0.03$, d.f. $=7$; Group 2 $t=2.69$, $p=0.03$, d.f. $=18$, two-tailed). This finding has to be qualified, because the second group also showed a significant change without course participation.

In the results for individual teachers, seven teachers reduced their frequency of reprimands over the period of the course and six of them maintained this change. Five of the Group 2 teachers who showed a reduction in reprimands maintained this to the end of the project. From this data, it can be seen that, in terms of individual change, course participation did not produce a 'striking' overall impact on the use of reprimands.

(c) *Instruction and no interaction*. Since these two categories are less directly related to the effectiveness of behavioural training, and since changes were minimal anyway, we shall not dwell on these results here. The relative changes in the use of instruction within each group did not differ significantly. There is thus no evidence that course participation had any significant differential impact. Both groups, however, do show a trend towards increased instruction.

The overall trend for no interaction means is in the direction of a reduced frequency for both groups. At no point, however, did the groups show any significant differences in no interaction or in their relative frequency on this observation category.

II Changes in children's behaviour

Children's behaviour was coded either as appropriate or as inappropriate. Any change in one category was therefore accompanied by an opposite direction change in the other. The mean percentage appropriate behaviour for selected children as well as means for randomly selected controls are shown in Table 5.2. Group 1 children are those whose class teacher attended the course during Term II; those in Group 2 had teachers who attended the course during Term III.

At the start of the project all selected children showed a lower frequency of appropriate behaviour than randomly selected children. Statistically, this difference just missed being significant, in the conventional sense, on a one-tailed test ($t = 1.64$, $p = 0.056$, d.f. $= 32$). Although a reliable difference was predicted, there is, on reflection, no reason for such a difference to emerge. Given that one or, at most, two children could be selected by each teacher, that no attempt was made to select controls randomly from among only non-disruptive children, and given also the high base rate of 'deviant' behaviour in the local population (Rutter, Cox, Tupling, Berger and Yule, 1975), the absence of a marked difference is understandable. Nevertheless, the magnitude and direction of the differences (10.5 per cent less appropriate behaviour in the selected children) suggests that there is some validity in the teachers' selection of children.

Although the means in Table 5.2 indicate an increase in the average frequency of appropriate behaviour in both groups of selected children over Term II, neither group showed a statistically significant increase. Further, there was no *differential* increase in appropriate behaviour, despite the fact that the teachers of Group 1 children had been on the course, whereas those in Group 2 had not. Indeed, with one exception, none of the important comparisons was statistically significant. To some extent, this is likely to be a consequence of the substantial variability between individuals.

The only significant increase in appropriate behaviour is that shown by Group 1 children over Term III. These children improved from their initial level at the start of the project ($t = 4.92$,

Table 5.2 Means, standard deviations and ranges of percentage appropriate behaviour in selected and random children.

Observation Point	Start Term II MEAN	1 SD	RANGE	End Term II MEAN	2 SD	RANGE	Start Term III MEAN	3 SD	RANGE	End Term III MEAN	4 SD	RANGE
SELECTED CHILDREN												
Group 1 Teachers	59	22.3	23 81.4	70.6	15.3	50- 93	71.2	19.2	50 -96.7	84.6	9.0	75 -97.1
Group 2 Teachers	59.5	18.7	30 -87.8	71.7	25.2	28-100	68.6	16.8	36.6-85.3	68.8	15.0	36.7-92.5
RANDOM CHILDREN												
Group 1 Teachers	66.7	25.0	15.8-95	81.9	11.5	64-100	79.1	16.1	45 -96.5	80.8	17.7	49.4-100
Group 2 Teachers	67.5	12.1	56.3-91.7	79.3	8.5	70- 92	80.4	10.4	58.8-94.1	78.6	9.1	62.5- 90

p=0.003, d.f.=6, two-tailed) and show a greater differential improvement over Term III when compared with Group 2 children over the same period (t=2.36, p=0.03, d.f.=15, two-tailed). This 'sleeper' effect is probably due in part to the factors noted earlier, namely, that two Group 1 teachers only began to apply what they had learned in the course the following term. This 'sleeper' effect in the behaviour of children was not anticipated, but its coincidence with the change in the positive behaviour of their teachers suggests that the course did have an impact, although delayed. If this interpretation is correct, then a similar change in Group 2 would not be detected because of the limitations in the design of this study.

All selected children increased their average frequency of appropriate behaviour to a significant degree when the initial level is contrasted with the level at the end of the project (t=3.35, p=0.004, d.f.=16, two-tailed). Randomly selected children, however, showed a similar change (t=3.46, p=0.004, d.f.=14, two-tailed). Randomly selected children within each group showed increases in appropriate behaviour over Term II, but only that for children in Group 1 was statistically significant (t=2.45, p=0.05, d.f.=6, two-tailed). The increase for the Group 2 children is not quite significant, but is in the same direction (t=2.30, p=0.055, d.f.=6, two-tailed). As is obvious from Table 5.2, the levels of appropriate behaviour in the randomly selected children do not alter over the subsequent term. As noted above, all randomly selected children on average increased their appropriate behaviour between the beginning and end of the project.

Apart from the tendency for selected children to show less average appropriate behaviour at the beginning of the project, no other differences between the combined groups (all selected versus all random) were statistically significant. Further, there was no significant difference in the measures of differential change. Had the initial difference been more striking, the fact that selected children were indistinguishable from the random children by the end of the project would provide some support for the effect of the courses attended by teachers.

As was the case with their teachers, the children showed varied changes in appropriate behaviour, defined here as an increase or decrease greater than or equal to 5 percent. The majority of children for whom data were available change over Term II towards increased appropriate behaviour, irrespective of their status (Selected/Random) or their teacher's participation in the course. Taking changes over the two terms of the study, twelve out of eighteen selected children improved (67%) whereas ten out of seventeen randomly selected children improved (59%). Despite the absence of a striking overall change, the data indicate the operation of a 'sleeper' effect. That is, by the end of the course, six of the eight selected children in Group 1 increased their appropriate behaviour and none were worse whereas six out of ten selected children in Group 2 showed similar improvement and two were worse than at the start of the study. At this stage it is not possible to co-relate these changes with the changes specific teachers made in their own behaviour.

Discussion

There is little doubt that the trends in the data on teacher behaviour are in the direction consistent with the aims of the TCIP. That few of the comparisons reached statistical significance is perhaps not surprising, given the small numbers and the striking within-group variability.

The courses organized as part of the TCIP, focused on increasing the frequency of positive behaviours and on decreasing negative actions by teachers, indicated by the variables approval and reprimand. Our data suggest that the increases in approval behaviour and instruction were made through a decrease in reprimands and no interaction, which are desirable changes consistent with the aims of the project. The data, despite their limitations, indicate that the courses had a positive effect on the behaviour of teachers, even though some of the teachers failed to respond immediately, and others not at all. The longer-term impact of the courses, for reasons discussed earlier, could not be assessed, but, from the available data, it would appear that 'sleeper' effects may have been operating and thus the longer-term impact may have been greater and more pervasive than is apparent in our data.

The initial level of approval in both groups was low, but data from other studies suggests that these levels are not abnormal (White, 1975). By the end of the study the average percentage level of approval had risen and the average level of reprimands had decreased, so that they were now similar.

However, verbal approval only accounted for an average of about 7 per cent of all interactions at this point. This raises important questions about the balance of approval and reprimand behaviour. We do not know whether it is the absolute level of approval that is most critical and, if it is, to what extent this needs to be increased above existing levels in order to secure improved classroom behaviour. This study suggests that very small increases in approval and small decreases in reprimands can be effective. It may be that it is the magnitude of the relative differences between approval and reprimands that is most effective. These issues warrant further investigation.

Within the framework and assumptions of a behavioural approach, the difficulties that children present to their teachers are seen as being partly a function of the ways in which their teachers respond to them. This, without any doubt, is an incomplete analysis, in that other influences, such as the way in which the classroom is organized, are contributory. So, too, are the characteristics and experiences of the child, to the extent that some children will not change substantially, irrespective of the actions of teachers. The role of the teacher appears to be crucial in helping to reduce the extent and severity of difficulties if only as a first step in amelioration. Changes in the actions of teachers may involve the development and use of new patterns of interacting with children or may require an extension and redirection of already present patterns. However, the difficulty individuals experience in modifying their habitual patterns should not be underestimated; several teachers involved in the project commented on the conscious effort that had to be exerted in applying the systematic approach emphasized on the courses.

The second major task of the TCIP, that is, to increase appropriate behaviour in the selected children, produced less clear-cut results; although they increased their frequency of appropriate behaviour, the changes were not significantly greater than those in the various control groups. Further, not all individuals changed. In one case, that of the anxious child, there was a high level of appropriate classroom behaviour to start with. Unfortunately, at this stage, it is not possible to re-analyse the data, excluding this child. The overall trend in the data is encouraging. The observation of a 'sleeper' effect and the finding that on average by the end of the project the selected and random children were indistinguishable gives some basis for optimism.

These findings have some implications for future evaluative studies. In particular, they highlight the need for further control groups made up of selected children who are not the focus of a behavioural programme, a form of 'yoked' control. In addition, it became apparent that a somewhat more differentiated system was needed, as was the incorporation of procedures to detect 'sleeper' effects. Following this study, an observation schedule of children's behaviour was developed in consultation with classroom teachers. This was used in later TCIP work.

The absence of clear-cut effects on children's behaviour is attributable to some extent to the within-group variability and the absence of an adequate long-term follow-up when 'sleeper' effects might have become manifest in Group 2 children. The design limitations affecting the analysis of teacher behaviour apply as well to the assessment of changes in the children. In addition, a further design refinement is necessary, resources permitting. It would be more appropriate to set up several control groups of children. In particular, teachers should identify two 'difficult' children, only one of whom would be worked with, the other serving as a control child. This would be a more appropriate control group than simply selecting a random control. Although a 'difficult' control group was present in this study (Group 2 selected children over Term 1), insufficient time was available during which to monitor behaviour changes. As was the case with the assessment of teacher effects, the data on the children reinforce yet again the need for control groups in this, as well as in other studies attempting to produce changes in performance.

All teachers who attended TCIP courses were subsequently asked to complete a questionnaire anonymously. The questionnaire focused on how teachers felt about the course and the way it was organized, how various aspects of the course had affected their behaviour in the classroom, how they felt about the role of the teacher-tutor, whether they had perceived any changes in the behaviour of their selected child, or the class as a whole, which they attributed to the course, and whether they felt that behaviour modification should be taught to teachers. Questionnaires were received from five of the Group 1 teachers and eleven of the Group 2 teachers. Their answers to the questionnaire were generally positive and their overwhelming approval of teaching behaviour modification to teachers was encouraging.

The initial service model of a central course with a practical in-school component, however, proved to be unsatisfactory for a number of reasons. It had been hoped that involving two teachers from each of a number of schools would lead to a diffusion within schools of the knowledge and skills acquired by participating teachers. For practical reasons, this diffusion could not be monitored. The amount of travelling time between schools diminished the time available for observation and consultation with teachers, and time was wasted when the teacher-tutor arrived at a school to find the teacher and/or pupil was absent or that an unscheduled event (for example, practice for a concert) was taking place, making observation impossible. Several school-based courses, in which the team worked in one school during one term, were carried out following the completion of this study. No formal evaluations of these courses were undertaken, however.

This control group study shows that, even where teachers attended a course *and* carried out supervised practical work in the classroom, the extent to which skills were integrated into their normal teaching was limited. This, and other work, strongly suggests that a lecture-based course alone would have been even less effective and underlines the need to utilize staff with sufficient experience and time to be able to cope with the varied needs of teachers. Time must be available for observation, discussion and elaboration of procedures aimed to help teachers and children. In addition to the service at the 'shop-floor' level, there must be provision, at least initially, of back-up consultation provided by psychologists familiar with behavioural methods, schools and educational and psychological difficulties. These issues involved in training teachers are discussed more fully in Berger (1979).

The role of the teacher-tutor poses professional and administrative problems which, while apparent in a service research context, become crucial in planning a wider service. It is possible that the role could be integrated into the existing structure of advisory teachers.

A common feature of published behavioural studies is the ready availability of one or more independent observers who monitor teacher and child behaviour during the project. The provision of such observers on a service basis would greatly increase the cost of such a service and make it unworkable in practice. This difficulty was tackled in the TCIP by training the participating teachers to gather data on child behaviour at the same time as running the class. That this is feasible within limits and reliable was established early in pilot investigations.

The study described in this chapter was a pioneering one in attempting to assess the effectiveness of training teachers by going into classrooms to identify changes in teachers' behaviour and children's behaviour in the normal situation. The use of a waiting list control group provided a feasible method of evaluating changes. However, the study has a number of shortcomings, which could, we hope, be avoided in a replication. The most important of these methodologically is the absence of 'blind' observers (O'Leary, Kent, and Kanowitz, 1975). The teacher involved in training the teachers on the courses also carried out classroom observation and was not 'blind' with regard to the purpose of the study or the group membership of teachers and children. Although the project team were aware of the problems this raised, funds were not available at that time to avoid this difficulty. Other problems centre on the analysis of data – it is probable that approval levels and changes are slightly underestimated since non-verbal warmth, e.g. smiling, was not included in the analysis. The data available suggests, however, that this was at a low level before intervention and appeared to rise in line with verbal praise after intervention.

Although direct observation yielded results that were inconclusive, the teachers involved in the study produced their own case studies, which demonstrated changes in children's behaviour. In some cases such changes were quite dramatic (Berger, Yule and Wigley, 1977; Yule, Berger and Wigley, 1984). The majority of the intervention studies carried out by teachers focused on increasing appropriate conduct in the classroom. Only one teacher focused on achievement. This is a common problem in studies such as this and is partly due to the relative ease of measuring and ensuring changes in conduct levels compared with changes in trends in academic achievement. Recent work in precision teaching has much to offer in this area (Neal, 1981).

A number of spin-offs were reported by teachers, such as increased liking for the children they focused on, a change in their perception associated with measuring the behaviour of selected children, and greater feelings of competence. One headteacher reported that discussion in the staffroom was at a much higher level following the school's participation in a TCIP course. These sorts of effects are difficult to quantify, but nevertheless need to be monitored.

The favourable response to these courses by teachers, headteachers, educational psychologists and the divisional inspectorate suggests that the courses were meeting an important need and that teachers obtained information and skills from them. However, observation carried out in the classroom suggests that, although the changes in teachers' behaviour had dramatic consequences for some children, these changes were quantitatively very small. It appears either that very small changes may be very important or that the observation schedules were not picking up important changes in teachers' behaviour. Our experience suggests that the former is the case.

Conclusions

Work carried out by TCIP suggests a number of areas in which further research is needed. For example, an evaluation of the relative efficacy of clinic-based versus school-based help for individual referrals would yield important data on current services. Further, there is not much information on the 'natural history' of difficult children in the classroom or on the development of teachers' coping skills over an extended period of time. Our data suggest that important changes take place in both groups, yet we know little about who is most likely to change, what changes occur and what conditions facilitate or hinder changes. These questions have important theoretical and practical implications and are well worth investigating.

There is also a need for further work that evaluates the relative efficacy of interventions and service delivery models, including the major area of the relative efficacy of modes of teacher training. The project team found that the problem of helping teachers to change their behaviour was not as simple as some early American work suggests. Following this study, the team experimented with a number of ways of supporting teachers who wished to change the nature of their interaction with a child. Such methods as role play, in vivo modelling, self-monitoring and learning to cue another teacher were tried. There is a need for further systematic work in this area.

Although some of the results of this study are gratifying, they suggest that courses of this nature need to focus on implementation. It is clearly not enough to teach teachers about behaviour modification or even to ensure that they can use the skills. Emphasis must also be placed on optimizing conditions in such a way that teachers do use the skills. Such work would need to recognize the importance of the school as an organization and the influence this has on the change potential of individual teachers. These points are further considered in Chapter 7.

References

Barcroft, J. (1970), 'Behaviour modification in the school', unpublished MPhil thesis, University of London.

Berger, M. (1979), 'Behaviour modification in education and professional practice: the dangers of a mindless technology', Bulletin of the British Psychological Society, vol. 32, pp. 418–19.

Berger, M. (1982), 'Applied behaviour analysis in education: a critical assessment and some implications for training teachers', Educational Psychology, vol. 2, pp. 289–300.

Berger, M., Yule, W., and Wigley, V. (1977), 'The Teacher–Child Interaction Project', Bulletin of the British Association for Behavioural Psychotherapy, vol. 5, pp. 42–7.

Campbell, D. T. and Stanley, J. C. (1966), Experimental and Quasi-

Experimental Designs for Research (Chicago: Rand McNally).

Department of Education and Science (1978), *Special Educational Needs,* Warnock Report (London: HMSO).

Hall, R. (1971), 'Training teachers in the classroom use of contingency management', *Educational Technology,* vol. 11, pp. 33-8.

McKeown, D., Adams, H. and Forehand, R. (1975), 'Generalisation to the classroom of principles of behaviour modification taught to teachers', *Behaviour Therapy,* vol. 13, pp. 85-92.

Maxwell, A. E. (1970), *Basic Statistics in Behavioural Research* (Harmondsworth: Penguin).

Neal, D. (1981), 'The data-based instructional procedures of precision teaching', *Educational Psychology,* vol. 1, pp. 289-304.

O'Leary, K. D., Kent, R. N. and Kanowitz, J. (1975), 'Shaping data collection congruent with experimental hypotheses', *Journal of Applied Behavior Analysis,* vol. 8, pp. 43-51.

Rutter, M., Cox, A., Tupling, J., Berger, M. and Yule, W. (1975), 'Attainment and adjustment in two geographical areas: the prevalence of psychiatric disorder', *British Journal of Psychiatry,* vol. 126, pp. 493-509.

White, M. (1975), 'Natural rates of teacher approval and disapproval in the classroom', *Journal of Applied Behavior Analysis,* vol. 8, pp. 367-72.

Wigley, V., Yule, B. and Berger, M. (1983), 'A primary solution to soiling', *Special Education - Forward Trends,* vol. 9, pp. 27-30.

Yule, B., Berger, M. and Wigley, V. (1984), 'Behaviour modification and classroom management, in Frude, N. and Gault, H. (eds) *Children's Aggression at School* (Chichester: Wiley).

6

The Behavioural Approach at Chelfham Mill School for Emotionally Disturbed Boys

ROGER BURLAND

Chelfham Mill School is an independent, residential school approved by the Department of Education and Science. It was established in 1966 to develop and effect methods of behaviour change with emotionally disturbed children. The school is situated some four miles from the market town of Barnstaple in picturesque North Devon, England. It is a small country house set in 57 acres of woods and pasture with its own trout stream. Many of the outbuildings have been converted to classrooms or accommodation, but the whole atmosphere has been kept homely rather than institutional.

The professional staff consists of the director, who is an educational psychologist, head teacher, social worker, assistant teachers and residential behaviour therapists concerned with all aspects of the care of the children outside school hours. The staff work very much as a team, but have individual responsibilities, which may vary from time to time, e.g. co-ordinating social skills training, curriculum development, leavers' programme, and so on.

The school environment has been structured to provide an exciting and interesting set of surroundings. The traditional hard playground is bordered by a formal garden, which merges into the informal, leading to fields and woods. The trout stream running through the grounds provides for water play, fishing and boating in an area that has been developed with an island and stockade. The more level fields serve as playing fields as well as providing grazing for the school farm animals. The farm includes a dairy in which milk is processed and cheese made. The children are very involved in helping with the six milking cows, the beef herd and their followers, the flock of breeding ewes, and pigs (Burland and Chichester, 1978).

The classrooms are all outside the main house, and have individual characteristics as most are converted from agricultural buildings. They all open directly outdoors. Other school facilities include a small attractive theatre, a library and a studio, which contains the school printing equipment, the T.V. video set-up and computers. The boys sleep in the main house, in bedrooms that vary in size and character but all have fitted carpets, are colourfully decorated and most have wash-basins. The dining room is carpeted and warm, and cosy recreation rooms adjoining have been specially designed to be the children's leisure rooms.

Many of the children attending the school need remedial help and a well-developed reading scheme, including Distar (Thorne, 1979), with a remedial resources centre, is of great assistance. Each child has his own individual programme, which is constantly monitored, with target areas clearly described for him. The Distar mathematics scheme is used as the central pivot of number education. In the teaching of religious knowledge and environmental studies (which includes history, geography and science) work is programmed so that basic information is learned but presented in project form. In addition to this, the importance of developing a sense of awareness of life around each individual is always stressed. The development of appropriate attitudes to learning and good study habits are encouraged and programmed where necessary. A scheme has been established for developing fine and gross co-ordination of physical movement, which has remedial and sporting elements. The music and movement programme is linked to this last scheme, but has speciality divisions so that the children can enjoy tuition in percussion, brass, keyboard and stringed instruments (see also the description of leisure skills training on p. 125).

The main concept underlying much of the work with the children is that many behavioural disorders of the most divergent types are essentially learned responses and that applied learning theory provides the most effective means for permanent behaviour change. The term, applied learning theory, refers particularly to the techniques evolved from the work of B. F. Skinner (1953), variously described as behaviour modification, behaviour therapy or applied behaviour analysis. Staff at this school have been trained in these behavioural techniques and are able to formulate and implement behaviour change programmes. The training is mostly in-service, with attendance at workshops and conferences wherever possible.

No problem behaviour is looked at in isolation. Reference is always made to the child's history, his family situation and cultural background. It is important to attempt to assess the personality of an individual, to put the problem behaviour in perspective. Lack of educational, self-help or social skills can promote behaviour problems and these aspects must be considered before any behaviour change programme is envisaged. A question always to be asked is, 'Has the child an alternative behaviour in his repertoire?' It is no use encouraging the use of an alternative behaviour if the child simply does not know what to do or how to do it.

Instruction is often required. In fact, most behaviour modification programmes require an element of teaching, and hence should fit in well with the traditional role of the teacher. The instruction can be a simple explanation of what is required, or the teacher or other children may need to model the required behaviour. Sometimes, behaviour rehearsal is needed, in which the child practises the behaviour for several sessions before being asked to use it in actual situations (e.g. Burland and Mather, 1978).

Before inappropriate behaviour can be modified, eliminated or replaced, it is vital to ensure that we know all about that particular behaviour. Accurate observation must be undertaken so that analysis of the situation is meaningful. Baseline information is always required, and this is usually obtained by the observer/ manager, i.e. the teacher or residential therapist. Of course, it is ideal in many ways to have an independent observer, but this is not always possible. It is, however, usually possible for another member of staff to take observations for a short while at the same time as the observer/manager so that the reliability of the observer/manager is checked. Naturally it is not easy to observe and teach a class of disruptive children at the same time. Thus, some traditional observation techniques are impossible, but adaptations can be made in order to obtain accurate results (Burland and Burland, 1979). For example, one teacher in a class of eight disruptive children looked around at five-minute intervals at each child in turn, marking (+) or (−) on a prepared sheet according to whether they were on-task (in their work area, attending to their work, or to the teacher) or off-task (further categorized into O/L − out of location, V − verbal disruption, M − motor disruption or N − non-active). Thus, she obtained in an hour 96 samples of behaviour accurately recorded. This was continued for five days, giving 2,000 samples. The observations gave the 'temperature' of the class and an assessment of problem areas for each individual. It is important to note that each category was operationally defined before observation began. For example, verbal disruption would be defined as using sounds, words or phrases to upset or disturb others or even to cause them to react in retaliation.

The timing of observations can be difficult for the observer/ manager as she or he is usually very busy. One way this problem can be overcome is to have the observer wear an earpiece linked to an electronic pre-timed pulsor. There are difficulties when lights flash or sounds are heard by the whole group, as the children can interpret what is going on and immediately go on-task. Observations sometimes have to be taken in difficult situations, on walks or on the beach, for example, and here a clip-board would be incongruous – but it is amazing what can be written on the back of one's hand! In such situations, to allow for unbiased recording, a therapist or teacher may decide he or she wishes to observe a child five times in half an hour. She is allowed to choose these five times when she likes, but must wait until the second hand reaches 12 before she observes for five seconds. This avoids the possible temptation of choosing a time when he or she sees a behaviour occurring and thus allows for true sampling.

When the data have been collected on an individual or group of individuals, analysis can be undertaken to formulate various behaviour goals and the best way to reach them. The progress of a behaviour change programme should be monitored continually. This on-going process and the final evaluation when we feel a goal has been reached render it unnecessary to resort to such comments as 'I think he is beginning to settle in class' or 'He appears to be concentrating more on his work.' We can say instead that 'whereas six weeks ago he was only 27 per cent on-task he is now 79 per cent on-task and verbal provocation has fallen from 40 per cent to 8 per cent'. This sort of information is very reinforcing, of course, to the observer/manager in giving accurate feedback on her/his methods, and so is helpful for informing colleagues, parents and others of a child's progress and for resetting goals.

The token economy

One of our main concerns early in our development was to establish a workable reward system and, as such, a token economy was instituted. The token economy works because it basically controls most rewarding situations in a contingent manner. If a child can obtain sweets, unlimited television viewing, visits to town, etc., he will not be particularly motivated to work for these if they are classed as rewards. If he can obtain them only by certain appropriate behaviours, his motivation will be higher. A token system is introduced because it is inconvenient for the teacher to carry a lot of rewards around and it also allows behaviour to be evaluated in small units and consequently reinforced. In addition, it allows a saving system to operate, so that there can be a greater variety of rewards. Moreover, it has the advantage of providing a way of keeping records and monitoring the activities of an individual class, house group or the whole community. Basically, when an appropriate behaviour occurs, a unit of recognition – a token – is given immediately. This unit can be a plastic disc, a piece of paper, a star stuck on a card or even a 'verbal' token that is recorded centrally. We have used three different types of tokens at different times with different children. There is some evidence that children prefer some types of tokens to others, but earning is not significantly different (Burland and Burland, 1978).

Since the introduction of the first token economy, which covered both in-school and out-of-school activities, there have been many modifications to suit specific needs at different times (Burland, 1978). At the present time (1985), there is a token economy that operates during the school day only and covers the learning of classroom skills, individual difficulties (e.g. accepting correction appropriately), peer interaction, etc. Tokens can be earned in certain areas: (1) class routines such as lining up appropriately; (2) work completion and standard; (3) involvement; (4) classroom skills; (5) individual areas. The system is known as the Levelled Token Economy (Mendham and Thorne, 1984) as children can proceed from level 1, which expects only basic skills and achievements, to level 4, which gives very high prestige status and where tokens can purchase special rewards and privileges. The system involves elements of management, skill training and behaviour change. By level 4, children will have overcome behavioural difficulties, be achieving academically at the appropriate level and be showing social skills suited to more independent living. Other token economies in operation include a management system for ensuring that morning and evening routines are conducted efficiently and speedily. Small boys are not greatly interested in washing, bedmaking and clothes care so the token system BOOSTS (Behaviour Out Of School Token System) operates. Boys earn tokens for their routines and they spend these on dormitory-based rewards, e.g. bubble baths, breakfast in bed, spending time in other bedrooms, late nights, etc. Another system operates during leisure skill training, where the rewards are spares from the day, given out at supper time, and other edibles such as 'Coke', crisps, fruit and sweets (see later). Having several economies can be useful. A child who happens to be talented academically cannot earn well in this area alone and then be tempted to neglect his bedtime routines or leisure skill training. It also helps to have exchange of rewards at different times of the day and provides novelty from the main and important exchange centre – the token shop.

A token shop should contain as many different rewards as possible (i.e. the reinforcement menu should be wide and varied) and at Chelfham there are sweets and cakes, small cheap plastic toys, transfers and higher value items such as Dinky cars, models, fishing tackle, etc. Tickets may be purchased for certain privileges, such as coffee at break times, extra TV, cookery sessions, private dining, etc. A token value is put on all these and adjusted, as in any economy, in terms of supply and demand (the value placed on them by the consumer). We have found that novelty items increase earning rate, and it is also necessary to publicize and 'sell' the wares. Tokens can be spent on various special items such as raffles and competitions. Also, *Chelfham Token News* is distributed to inform its readers of good performances. We have an actual shop with attractive displays, so that the children can see at any time what is available and how much each item costs. Sometimes, younger or duller children cannot understand the token system and require rewards such as small sweets immediately after appropriate behaviour. Short delays are built in after a while, so that the child may gradually be weaned to the more convenient token systems. Various numeracy aids have been invented to enable boys to cope with the amounts involved. At present, the children fill in a token-earning record card, which is also checked by their teacher, and they are able to see immediately how many tokens they have earned.

One of the main advantages of the system is that, when formulating a programme, the staff do not have to enquire specifically about the child's personal reinforcement choices as there are certain to be several things to his liking at the shop. Also, he is allowed the pleasure of buying a variety of small rewards or the option of being able to save for some larger item. Monitoring of the whole system is very necessary so that overall general earning is seen to be high enough and the community well motivated, that the staff are actually giving tokens and that individual children are earning and spending. A standard earning potential has been used as a guide to ensure that each child has the chance to earn as many tokens as his peers.

Research and experience have indicated that loss of tokens is also effective in producing behaviour change. At this school at various times it has been possible to lose tokens and this provides an effective measure for enforcing community rules in a fairly easy way. Token loss is rarely built into a behaviour change programme but has been reserved for such misdemeanours as wearing boots in the lounge, playing in the car park, using the secretary's office as a short cut and so on. (It is interesting to note that one can regard an infringement of the above, and the consequential loss of tokens, as a child in fact opting to *spend* two tokens on this activity, e.g. in taking a short cut!) All such set token losses have been agreed with the children, the whole community taking part in the discussion and the staff and children coming to a decision about what is a fair token loss for each misdemeanour. At the present time there are no loss contingencies on any of the token systems.

Visitors to the school often ask how we wean children from the token economy. This is no problem. Often older children will tell staff that they no longer need tokens. In individual programmes, praise is always paired with the giving of tokens, so that at the end of the programme the tokens are gradually faded out but the praise stays at a high level and self-reinforcement is encouraged and programmed: for example, in BOOSTS, older children monitor their own performance and award their own programmes and rewards.

Sanctions

Apart from the minor sanction of token loss, other sanctions are occasionally used. It is as necessary to ensure that inappropriate behaviour is not reinforced as it is to ensure the opposite. Therefore, one must be able to control consequential reinforcement following an inappropriate behaviour. The concept of 'time-out' is useful for this function and has been shown to be effective in many studies. Time-out is short for 'time-out from a reinforcing situation'. Thus, if a child knocks over some desks in a classroom he will gain attention from all the other children and probably the teacher as well, which could be very reinforcing and rewarding for him. We would, of course, prefer him to gain attention in an appropriate way, but in this first instance we must take immediate action, minimize the rewarding effect and remove him from the scene. At Chelfham, some classrooms have a time-out area, and there is a time-out bench as well near the dining room. The area should be in a situation that has minimal reinforcement, e.g. a cloakroom (but don't forget to remove the wet-day comics!) or behind a cupboard in the classroom. It can be an advantage to have a chair in the time-out area to minimize movement and to designate the area precisely. One class used a two-foot square outside the classroom door as time-out, but, to let the teacher know that the child stayed there, a board was placed in the square which, on pressure of body weight, lit a bulb in the classroom. This 'presence indicator' proved most useful. It is impossible to cut out all reinforcement for inappropriate behaviour, but the reinforcement can be minimal.

It is not easy to put a disturbed child on time-out. Some children will openly defy the teacher and will need to be carried to the area and firmly placed there. Some will then stay and others will run away. One cannot get round the fact that the teacher must have some 'natural' control to use this method. On the other hand, it is possible to reward a child by praise when he has performed even the slightest approximation to time-out, e.g. 'Well Johnny, you did sit on the time-out bench for a short time and that was good' or 'Jimmy, it was good to see that you were not so noisy on time-out today'. This technique is known as shaping and is much used in behaviour modification, usually in other contexts. Generally, one reinforces the nearest approximation to the desired behaviour, e.g. slight control of temper would be reinforced as a stage in reaching complete control. Returning to the time-out discussion, it is important that time-out lasts only three to ten minutes and that the teacher is in control of the situation all the time. For instance, a child saying 'I'm sorry' should not curtail the time-out period. A child who can avoid an unpleasant sanction by apologising is being reinforced for uttering this phrase, so that all we are likely to do is increase the frequency of saying 'I'm sorry' without reducing the frequency of the inappropriate behaviour for which the child was put on time-out. If the period is longer than three to ten minutes a young child can forget why he is there. Also, if a child is sitting quietly, he is behaving appropriately, i.e. following instructions, and can, in effect, be punished for this apppropriate behaviour if time-out is too long. Finally, the time-out period should begin immediately after the inappropriate behaviour. There is some interesting research on the duration of time-out by Kendall, Nay and Jeffers (1975), indicating that the time-out period must be consistent and never shorter than previous periods.

Over-correction is another technique that is applied in certain situations. This was originated by Azrin and Foxx (see, for example, Foxx and Azrin, 1973). For instance, a child who has just knocked over some chairs in the dining room, dropped cutlery on the floor and spilled water would be immediately required to mop all the floor (not just the area where the water was spilled), replace all chairs, re-align the tables, re-lay all the tables (not just the disturbed ones) and check that all was clean and tidy. These measures might have to be repeated if unsatisfactory. This procedure is time-consuming, requires good manager control of the child, an emotional neutrality and patience. The over-correction should be continued until the child has obviously had enough – he can enjoy mopping a floor for quite a while! If the above actions occurred during a meal, it would obviously be inappropriate to use the technique immediately, as the child would be reinforced by making capital out of the situation in front of his peers. In this case he can be put on time-out, which would possibly last longer than the time normally advised, until it was convenient for the over-correction to take place. Other examples of the use of over-correction would be requiring a child to lie very still for some 45 minutes after a temper tantrum, or to practise being quiet sitting in a chair downstairs in a non-reinforcing situation, if he could not settle at bedtime. This is not an easy technique, but can be effective on occasions. It should not be viewed as punishment but as a restitutional procedure containing an element of learning the alternative appropriate behaviours.

It is possible to eliminate inappropriate behaviour by applying sanctions every time it occurs. For example, every time a child has a temper tantrum he is given time-out. It is well known, however, that the immediate effect is for an increase in frequency of temper tantrums before a quite dramatic fall. This increase in frequency is very difficult to live with, especially for parents and less experienced staff. It is always more pleasant to operate a programme of change, which has some positive element to it. Thus, in our example, we might use time-out as suggested but reward periods of temper control in an appropriate manner.

Contracts

Very often, children themselves are very unhappy about their own behaviour, but are suffering from an old learned response to which they are shackled. These children react well to a suggestion of practical help and can become well motivated if allowed to participate in the formulation of the programme and to choose their own reinforcer. The more practical the help is, the more motivated the child becomes. If he is just asked to try harder 'to be good', how can he succeed? For example, Ernie was concerned about the temper tantrums he was having in class. His teacher had obtained a measure of the frequency and duration of these and had made notes about possible triggers. This baseline information gave clues to a possible programme of change. Ernie was consulted and said he would like to work each evening on the school farm as a reward and would like a chart over his work area in class to show his progress. Because of the intensity of the temper tantrums, it was decided that a stage programme would be necesary.

In Stage 1, if Ernie felt that he was going to lose his temper in class, he would put up his hand and call out his teacher's name. Immediately, his teacher would go across to him and Ernie would put his head on the desk and they would talk quietly about an alternative behaviour. For example, if the trigger had been a boy calling him a name he could ignore it, call him a name in return, inform his teacher, or tell the boy he did not mind how many names he was called. Then Ernie would put into practice the behaviour decided upon. If he could do this he earned a point towards evening farming. Stage 2 was put into practice after sufficient rehearsal at Stage 1 level and required Ernie to put his head on his desk immediately he felt the cue for a temper tantrum and to put his hand up without calling out (which was quite disruptive in Stage 1), when he had selected the behaviour. His teacher would then go over immediately to reinforce his choice and the alternative behaviour would be put into operation. The same reinforcer was used as in Stage 1. Stage 3 required Ernie to put into operation the alternative behaviour straight away and to inform his teacher afterwards of the complete circumstances. Stage 4 was a generalization stage to situations such as the playground, dining room, etc. At all times, if in difficulty, Ernie could regress to one of the previous stages. This was an extremely successful programme.

The preceding example was not formulated as a written contract, but this can often be extremely helpful. This is shown in the example given overpage (p. 122), in which is described a contract worked out after a lot of discussion. Most of the ideas came from Freddie himself. A chart was made on which the score could be kept and Freddie hung it over his bed. The important elements in this contract are that it is specific in its requirements, giving examples of what to do and what not to do. Also, provision is made for temporary failure on the programme or complete failure. One of the main advantages of contract formulation, with heavy emphasis on the child's personal involvement, is that if it does not work out it is a technical problem rather than a personal one, and it is 'back to the drawing board' to effect a more efficient contract. No party need feel let down or that they are letting someone else down. The relationship can, in fact, be strengthened. A fuller discussion of the elements of contracting is given by De

Risi and Butz (1975) and by Homme, Csanyi, Gonzales and Rechs (1970).

> I, Freddie, agree to be helpful with others in my housegroup (e.g. helping to make beds, sharing my comics and toys, being nice to other boys, being a good example by following instructions) and will not disturb other boys by teasing them, taking their belongings, calling them names, or getting in their way. I will be able to earn two points in the morning and two points in the afternoon if I am helpful, but if I do any unhelpful things I agree that I should be put on time-out. When I reach a total of 36 points earned, whether I have spent them or not, I can be allowed 70 pence worth of fishing tackle from the Rod Room, Barnstaple. If this contract does not work in some way I agree to it being changed.
>
> Signed ....
> Freddie

.... Susan

Date...........   .... Roger

Other strategies

At Chelfham Mill School, there can be some 200 individual, group and class programmes proceeding at the same time. Data collection, record-keeping and communication, then, are of the utmost importance and need efficient organization. The writer has the function in this school of acting as a 'therapeutic clearing house.' Programmes are formulated usually for specific situations (e.g. by a teacher for her classroom setting), but often there are links, for instance, across a therapy group or to playground behaviour. Sometimes, programmes are worked out from the beginning by several members of staff, or possibly by one who will have it approved only when it reaches implementation stage.

In addition to individual programmes, there are group and class programmes for management and sometimes whole community programmes. Group programmes, with titles such as 'living together', have been instituted to help children get along together in what is rather an artificial situation and, in addition, programmes affecting one individual and the group are often needed. For example, Daniel obtained most of his rewarding experiences from disturbing other boys or getting them to laugh at his antics. To control this, his peers were rewarded for ignoring Daniel's inappropriate behaviour. They were successful at doing this, but realizing that Daniel could reduce their earnings by being well-behaved and that this situation could actually encourage Daniel's peers to incite him, it was arranged that the group also earned if Daniel behaved well. This system effectively controlled the inappropriate behaviour and Daniel's reinforcer.

Happiness House is a game where a doll's house has rewards in each room and a plywood cut-out operates like an advent calendar. A card is placed behind the cut-out and windows and doors are opened in a Happiness House session. The card contains legends, which are changed for each session and are concerned with community or individual behaviours which are not controlled by other programmes. For example: (1) If the senior therapist visits the bootroom and finds no more than three boots out of cubicles, all boys receive a sweet (apart from those whose boots were out). (2) Can the therapist nominate two boys who are always polite or who greet them with a nice smile? During the session, a buzzer sounds at random intervals and the name of a boy or of a member of staff is drawn out of a bag. If they can demonstrate a social skill nominated, for example, apologizing appropriately, or perhaps demonstrate that they have earned full tokens on BOOSTS that day, they may choose a reward from the house. Staff also pick cards, and they might have to show that their files are up to date or that their shoes are clean (modelling appropriate behaviour) etc., and then they can earn a reward. Novelty games and staff bonuses (a bottle of wine or a free hair style etc.) add excitement for all of us. The formulation, implementation and evaluation of behaviour change programmes is an exciting process. Each problem is individual and unique. The teacher or residential therapist needs to be creative and to have professional sensitivity to be really successful.

When a programme has reached a successful conclusion or a stage is reached which sees a goal attained, we must be sure that the behaviour pattern established is maintained. Although possibly the rate of reinforcement was high during the programme, this can be reduced for maintenance and we should aim for maintenance reinforcement, as far as possible, to be from the natural conse-quences of the new behaviour. Maintenance reinforcement must be built in as an integral part of the programme. Another important consideration is that behaviour learned in one situation does not necessarily generalize to another situation, and again this has to be built into the programme. The need for generalization to

other situations should always be borne in mind when a programme is being constructed.

Children copy the behaviour of children or adults they live with
and the principles of modelling, well described in the literature
(e.g. Bandura, 1969; Cullinan, Kaufman and Lafleur, 1975)
should always be remembered when attempting to implement
behaviour change programmes. Children can easily model either
appropriate or inappropriate behaviour and the latter, unfortunately, often seems the choice. Programmes can be based on the
following principles of choosing a model for certain behaviours
that one would like to be learned by another individual:

1   The model must have status (this can be discovered by using
    sociometric tests).
2   The model must have the power to reward (i.e. he must be in
    a position to praise or give out tangible rewards).
3   The model must be shown to be reinforced (i.e. he must be
    shown to be praised or otherwise rewarded by others).
4   The observer must have the chance to practise immediately.
5   The observer must have the components of the modelled
    behaviour in his repertoire.
6   The observer himself must be reinforced.

Thus, one can affect a whole class or group by establishing a new
behaviour pattern in an individual member with high prestige.
Programmes in table manners, routine completion and social
approach have been instigated, using an effective model.

Skills training

Although it is important to eliminate inappropriate behaviour, it
has become apparent at this school that for a child to function
happily and effectively when he returns to his home environment
(or indeed in life) he will need a full repertoire of self-help and
social skills. To achieve this a scheme has been developed to check
whether these skills are in each child's repertoire or whether they
need to be taught by using the principles of learning on which the
behaviour change programme is based. The checklist comprises
nearly 400 skills and the manual that accompanies it gives detailed
instructions on how to test for these skills and, subsequently, to
teach them (Burland, Brown and Mendham, 1977). The skills
range from the basic everyday self-help skills of washing, dressing,
etc., to the use of leisure. The social skills, which are taught where

necessary, include assertion skills, conversation skills, denial acceptance, social approach and interaction, social prediction, questioning instructions, self-reinforcement, etc. These last-mentioned are sophisticated skills, but are usually broken down into their components, e.g. social approach, eye-to-eye contact, appropriate hand movement, facial expression, speech clarity and emphasis, verbal content and body attitude. When a child masters such skills he is more confident to deal with situations in which he finds himself, and every successful outcome of a problem when such skills are used reinforces their use and his feeling of confidence.

Children commence learning social skills at an early age and, although perhaps somewhat artificial initially, they become more spontaneous and natural with practice. These social skills are incorporated into a special scheme 'Survival in the Comprehensive School' for older boys due to leave. They are combined into social strategies, which will enable these boys to relate well to their teachers and peers and to cope overall with adapting to a very much larger school. They are taught, and practise, how to organise their time, how to study and to present their work on time and tidily. They learn how to approach teachers, apologizing if necessary, and also how to compliment them. With peers, they learn how to be accepted, how to deal with teasing and bullying and how to avoid being drawn into trouble. These older boys also learn how to organize homework and to study effectively. They are aided in their learning by visits from 'old boys' who discuss and demonstrate all the above skills.

The team of residential therapists, with part-time specialist coaches, is responsible for the leisure skills training programme. This programme is separate from the leisure activities engaged in by the children, although there can be some overlap. The training is seen as a way of preparing young children for the more structured and organized forms of leisure in their future, replacing their more general and freer imaginative play as they get older. It is considered that participation in hobbies and sport is normally incompatible with inappropriate, delinquent behaviours. It also provides a young person with the means of using his time constructively if he is in the position of having a surfeit of leisure time as, for example, during the school holidays or periods of unemployment. Leisure skills training for junior boys is provided to give experience and understanding of as many leisure and sporting pursuits as possible. This allows a boy to select a hobby or sport from some direct experience. It also calls for understanding of others' hobbies and sports and improves spectator skills.

Training takes place after tea each weekday and at weekends. Each course lasts from 4–6 sessions and teaching is based on a carefully compiled syllabus which includes pre- and post-evaluation tests. The boys earn tokens for level of concentration, motivation, co-operation and instruction-following. These are called SMARTS and may be earned for social skills also. They are part of the scheme, BE SMART, which stands for 'Behavioural Enhancement through Social Mastery And Recreational Training'.

Working with parents

Generalization of acquired appropriate behaviour from one situation to another has already been mentioned. At this school, a lot of time and effort is put into working with parents to help achieve this end. Parents can be very effective behaviour modifiers, and this is well illustrated by Becker (1971) and Patterson (1971). Those parents who live fairly close by are invited to attend parent meetings regularly where training is given in management. For example, one group of parents attended a course of ten evening training sessions and received a printed certificate to signify their participation and interest. Other parents visit the school for days or week-ends and, in the course of their stay, are able to talk to staff and observe management techniques in operation.

The idea of self-help in the family commences at the initial interview. At this point, usually, but not always, parents are concerned that their child will be accepted and can be helped. It is then that a verbal contract can be formulated to ensure their co-operation in working with the school staff on behavioural programmes. The ways in which we require them to co-operate are outlined and illustrated by charts, diaries, observation forms and so on, already completed by other parents. One has to assess how far to go so that parents are not confused; it is sufficient to describe techniques in a very simple manner. Other parents can become involved at a more sophisticated level and can, if they live near enough, be given training in theory and practice. We have used certain books to good effect in this area, including *Children and Parents* by Peine and Howarth (1975).

When there is co-operation with good understanding, progress can be quite dramatic. It is most important that any co-operation is reinforced and, in fact, some parents can be 'shaped' gradually to observe behaviour and implement programmes, sometimes when they were originally unconvinced (even hostile) about the techniques. Often it is of the utmost importance to involve other members of the family, as it can seem most unfair to brothers and sisters that the member of the family who has caused them so much unhappiness is the one to have an attractive chart on the wall and who is able to earn rewards that they cannot. Therefore, other children in the family have programmes devised for them as well, perhaps to deal with some area of difficulty or just to maintain some behaviour that is already in their repertoire. Older children often like the role of programme manager. We have used with some success a page-a-day diary for parents, with a large section for reporting 'good' things done, another for jobs and helping, and a smaller section for 'not good' things. The diary gives a good record of each holiday and encourages a positive attitude. Some older children enjoy filling this in and ensuring that their parents have signed it. The SPOT scheme, 'Special Programme Of Training', is a token system (Burland and Burland, 1981) that has proved very effective in the home. Parents find it easy to operate and it is designed so that it can be evaluated at a sophisticated level. The children like it because they can earn a SPOT dog mascot, SPOT T-shirts and so on.

The school social worker visits families and keeps a liaison between school, home and referring clinic. He can also help parents, when necessary, with their relationships, marital and sexual problems, and can advise, in consultation with other staff, on management. Sometimes a member of staff will live with a family, sleeping and taking all other meals there, so that he or she can observe and be of practical help. For example, George obsessionally repeated questions and refused to follow instructions. His parents were very co-operative and wanted to try a home token economy. Here, most of George's leisure activities, such as TV, swimming, cinema visits, as well as sweets, crisps, lemonade, etc., were made contingent upon non-repetition of questions and upon instruction-following. The parents were afraid that George would be angry with them if they were strict about it, and so one of the female residential staff lived with the family to help them institute the programme and reinforce their efforts. She was able to encourage them to ignore George when he was angry and to praise him when he was not. The parents were able to complete this programme successfully and then to take part in further holiday follow-up programmes. Repetition of questions decreased and instruction-following improved. Work in the home is essential to achieve a child's happy and successful return there.

Concluding comments

The use of behavioural techniques should be a creative and sensitive process. There should always be the aim of getting the children to use behaviours because they are self-reinforcing or because the reinforcement comes from the natural consequences of their behaviour (for example, the intrinsic worth of the task or other people's pleasure). There will, of course, always be behaviour that humans do not find reinforcing, and systems are needed to find a way to ensure that the appropriate behaviour takes place. The aim is to help the children to become positive, caring individuals who accept the principles of reinforcement as part of their everyday life. To teach all the skills necessary to enable a child to feel confident is time-consuming. We have to adopt a way of looking at problem children which is different from that shared by some advocates of 'behaviour modification', who see the techniques mainly as a particularly quick, effective and economic way of dealing with particular behaviour problems. At Chelfham Mill School we are committed and convinced that if we do not spend time and effort in improving self-help, social, and academic skills, the individual child could revert and resort to inappropriate manipulative behaviour to cope with his environment, even if his main presenting problem at referral has been quickly modified.

References

Bandura, A. (1969), *Principles of Behavior Modification* (New York: Holt, Rinehart & Winston).

Becker, W. C. (1971), *Parents are Teachers* (Champaign, Ill.: Research Press).

Blackham, G. J., and Silberman, A. (1971), *Modification of Child Behavior* (Belmont, Calif.: Wadsworth).

Burland, J. R. (1978), 'The evolution of a token economy in a residential school for junior maladjusted boys', *Behavioural Psychotherapy*, vol. 6, no. 4, pp. 97–104.

Burland, J. R., Brown, T. W., and Mendham, R. P. (1977), *Steps to Self-Sufficiency*. (Barnstaple: Chelfham Publishing and Distribution Co.).

Burland, J. R. and Burland, P. M. (1978), 'The nature of tokens – a preliminary study', *Newsletter of the Association for Behaviour Modification with Children*, vol. 2, no. 1, pp. 12–15.

Burland, P. M. and Burland, J. R. (1979), '... and teacher came too!', *Behavioural Psychotherapy*, vol. 7, no. 1, pp. 11–18.

Burland, J. R. and Burland, P. M. (1981), 'SPOT – Special Programme Of Training for parents and children: The development of evaluation of a behavioural programme for maladjusted children operated by parents in the home environment', *International Journal of Behavioural Social Work and Abstracts*, vol. 1, no. 2, pp. 87–107.

Burland, J. R., and Chichester, A. G. M. (1978), 'Educational and therapeutic aspects of a school farm', *Journal of the Association of Workers with Maladjusted Children*, vol. 6, pp. 49–57.

Burland, J. R. and Mather, M. R. (1978), 'Teaching alternative behaviours', *Therapeutic Education*, vol. 6, no. 2, pp. 21–5.

Cullinan, D., Kaufman, J. M. and Lafleur, N. K. (1975), 'Modelling: research with implications for special education', *Journal of Special Education*, vol. 9, pp. 209–21.

De Risi, W. J., and Butz, G. (1975), *Writing Behavioral Contracts* (Champaign, Ill.: Research Press).

Foxx, R. M., and Azrin, N. H. (1973), 'The elimination of autistic self-stimulatory behaviour by over-correction', *Journal of Applied Behavior Analysis*, vol. 6, pp. 1–14.

Homme, L., Csanyi, A., Gonzales, M. A. and Rechs, J. (1970), *How to Use Contingency Contracting in the Classroom* (Champaign, Ill.: Research Press).

Kendall, P. C., Nay, W. R., and Jeffers, J. (1975), 'Time-out duration and contrast effects: a systematic evaluation of a successive treatment design', *Behaviour Therapy*, vol. 6, pp. 609–16.

Mendham, R. P. and Thorne, M. T. (1984), 'A description and evaluation of a Levelled Token Economy operating within the school day in a residential school for junior maladjusted boys', *Behavioural Psychotherapy*, vol. 12, pp. 151–62.

Patterson, G. R. (1971), *Families* (Champaign, Ill.: Research Press).

Peine, H. A. and Howarth, R. (1975), *Children and Parents* (Harmondsworth: Penguin).

Skinner, B. F. (1953), *Science and Human Behavior* (New York: Macmillan).

Thorne, M. T. (1979), 'Direct instruction in the classroom', *Visual Education*, June, pp. 27–9.

7

Training Teachers to use the Behavioural Approach to Classroom Management: the Development of BATPACK

KEVIN WHELDALL and FRANK MERRETT

Student teachers (and indeed many experienced teachers, with hindsight) frequently complain about the content of their initial teacher education courses. Although strong on theory, such courses are often weak in terms of passing on relevant classroom teaching skills. For example, James Cross, a student teacher in the late 1970s, cited his experiences (which we believe to be not untypical) in an article published in *The Observer* in March 1983.

Discipline was an ugly word at college, although our everyday teaching is affected and possibly shaped by it. Not once in three years was it discussed. How should one react if a child refuses to do as he is told? What if a child swears at you? How do you establish silence? What forms of punishment should be used?

Moreover, academic critics have questioned, in particular, the relevance of much of what is taught as the 'psychology of education'. For example, Riding and Wheldall (1981) commented:

Teachers frequently complain that educational psychology has little to offer them that is of real value in the classroom. We think that it is important to admit that, to some extent, they are right. (Riding and Wheldall, 1981, p. 5)

Recent attempts to remedy this situation, however, have been disappointing in terms of their inability to identify coherent areas of psychological research in education that have manifest, practical applications in the classroom. For example, Merrett's article, 'What has psychology to offer the teacher?' (Merrett, 1986) provides an extended critique of a recent collection of chapters on this theme (Francis, 1985) written by psychologists 'actively involved in teacher education'. He writes,

If there is a consensus of opinion in this collection it might well be that what has gone on so far in teacher education is not up to much, but I can see few suggestions for improvement. The one or two that are put forward remind one of practices common in the training colleges of the fifties and earlier ... I find it strange, that none of the contributors to this volume (except perhaps Desforges and Evans, and they only in passing) find a word of commendation for the only branch of psychology whose adherents would be prepared to stand up and affirm their interest in a technology of behaviour change and of skills learning, namely behavioural psychology.

In our view, and as we hope the contents of this book demonstrate, the behavioural approach to classroom management offers precisely the sort of practical help and advice in the area of classroom discipline that Cross and others were seeking. Moreover, as Fontana (1982), already quoted in Chapter 1, affirms, behavioural studies provide proof 'that psychological research does, after all, have something very definite to say about the practicalities of teacher–child interaction'. There is now no doubt about the effectiveness of behavioural methods of classroom management, as countless studies have demonstrated, (see, for example, Chapters 2 and 3 and Wheldall, Merrett and Glynn, 1986). A remaining problem is how best to pass on the benefits of behavioural methods to teachers. In this chapter, we shall describe the development of a behavioural training course for teachers.

Previous attempts to train teachers to use behavioural methods

Attempts to train teachers to use behavioural techniques have been many and varied and have met with varying degrees of success (reviewed by Merrett and Wheldall, 1984). The most successful have tended to be those in which a behaviourally oriented educational psychologist has worked with one teacher, or a very small group of teachers, on a specific intervention strategy with a particular class or classes. The less successful, but more desirable on both cost effective and pedagogic grounds, have involved attempts to teach larger groups of teachers to implement and maintain their own intervention strategies following a lecture course in behavioural techniques. In Merrett and Wheldall (1984), we reviewed the literature which reports and criticizes attempts to run training courses for teachers in the behavioural approach to teaching. In this section, we shall describe how the lessons we drew from these attempts influenced our Behavioural Approach to Teaching Package (BATPACK). We shall subsequently report on its development and review evaluations of its effectiveness.

The writing of an extensive review of American and British attempts to 'give away' behavioural psychology to groups of teachers led us to certain conclusions. Our review showed clearly that teachers can be taught to use behavioural methods and to understand the accompanying theory. As a result, the behaviour of their classes may also change in a more positive direction. However, there is some disagreement among researchers about how easy it is to bring about such changes. Hall, Panyan, Rabon and Broden (1968) and Andrews (1970), for example, suggest that it is a relatively simple process, while others warn that it is quite difficult (e.g. Altman and Linton, 1971; Thomas and Adams, 1971; Rosenfield, 1979; Kazdin, 1981; Berger, 1980).

Some of the earlier studies involved the training of teachers for specific intervention experiments. These are useful in relation to specific aspects of technique, but we are chiefly concerned here with those studies that aim to train groups of teachers in order to improve their general knowledge about and their use of behavioural techniques in classroom management. Berger (1980) was among the first to articulate the difference between courses which teach *about* behavioural methods (i.e. the theory) and those that seek to teach *how* (i.e. skills training). He makes a strong plea for the inclusion of courses in initial teacher training: 'Teaching about behavioural approaches can be presented at any time in the career of a teacher but should become an essential part of initial training.' (p. 47) It is not clear exactly what sort of courses Berger has in mind, but it is extremely doubtful if, in the present climate of teacher education, anything more than a rudimentary theoretical course could be offered. Skills-based training, therefore, can be provided only by in-service courses. Berger shares our fear that delaying such courses brings extra difficulties, which are embodied in the aphorism about teaching old dogs new tricks.

MacKrell (1983), like Berger, points out that, although teaching specific management skills may be relatively easy, to teach the skills of applied behaviour analysis is another matter altogether. He refers to the fact that it is all too easy for the student with a little theoretical knowledge to confuse a *strategy* (shutting a child in a room for a short period) with a *principle* ('time-out') and to fail to understand that the point of the short period of isolation in a situation giving minimum stimulation is, in fact, *time-out from positive reinforcement*. 'Therefore, it is important to provide nurse, teacher and parents with the skills necessary to analyse behaviour rather than to teach techniques with little or no reference to functional analysis.' (p. 11)

In addition to the points raised above, we feel that the following distinctions are also necessary. Courses may be designed:

(a) for teachers in special *or* in 'ordinary' schools;
(b) for teachers in secondary *or* in primary schools;
(c) to help teachers to deal with individual problem children *or* to teach the basic skills of classroom management;
(d) for individuals from several schools coming to a course *or* for the whole staff of a school.

We shall consider each of these points in turn.

(a) Behavioural methods are already in general use in many special schools. Because their problems are more obvious and more serious, teachers in this area have been forced to examine their methods and to adopt a more systematic and powerful model of instruction. Since the level and pace of learning are different and because some special schoolteachers will already have had practical experience, the type of course suitable for teachers in special education must be different from that for teachers in ordinary schools. The needs of teachers in special schools for the mentally handicapped have been largely satisfied already by such courses as the Education of the Developmentally Young (EDY) project materials, for example (Foxen and McBrien, 1981; McBrien and Foxen, 1981). There are very few well-designed and effective courses for teachers in main-stream schools, however.

(b) One of the crucial issues in the use of behavioural methods in schools is that of consistency. Where children are taught in the same room by the same teacher for long periods every day, it is possible to establish a rule structure within a particular milieu and for the teacher to apply this structure consistently. This is the pattern in most primary schools, but it is not so in secondary schools, except for the small number of pupils who may find themselves in a remedial department. Generally, secondary schools are organized to allow for teacher specialization, so that classes move from one subject specialist to another throughout the day. In schools where single periods are favoured, a child could meet up to seven or eight teachers in a day, each with different standards and methods for attempting to enforce them. Moreover, older children may be less responsive to teacher approval and more influenced by peer group reinforcement. This does not mean to say that the behavioural approach has nothing to offer teachers of older children, but simply that courses for teachers in secondary and primary schools will have to concentrate upon different strategies for behaviour management. Since much of our original experimental work had been carried out in primary and middle school classrooms, we decided to devise a training programme for teachers at this level, initially.

(c)   Some of the courses we reviewed attempted to teach behavioural methods to teachers and, at the same time, recommended teachers to carry out interventions with individual children with social or academic problems. This appears to be a sound idea, because it is encouraging the teacher to apply the theory and to learn through carefully monitored practice (e.g. Hall and Copeland, 1972; Greenwood *et al.*, 1979; Yule, Berger and Wigley, 1977; see also Chapter 5). However, this calls for a lot of theoretical knowledge before the process can begin, which means a rather lengthy course and involves the student in the complex business of applied behaviour analysis at an early stage. For this, expert guidance is needed, which means that the number of students on the course has to be limited. Some courses that adopt this model arrange for course members to be visited in their schools so that their programmes can be overseen (e.g. Firman and Hastings, 1980; Raymond, 1980). This is an excellent practice, but is very expensive in tutor time. There is another type of course, however, which focuses upon class teaching as a series of techniques and seeks to impart a package of teaching skills to be applied to the class as a unit rather than to individual members. The Program of Academic Survival Skills (PASS) (Greenwood *et al.*, 1974). Classroom Management Teaching Project (CMTP) (Jones and Eimers, 1975) and our own BATPACK are all examples of such packages. Packages such as these give teachers the opportunity to learn a number of well-tried management techniques, which they can then implement with a background of theory that may be relatively simple and rudimentary.

Zimmerman *et al.*, (1971), Hall and Copeland (1972) and Sanders (1978) suggest that it is very important for teachers to be able to monitor the results of the strategies they employ. If this is satisfactorily achieved then it should not only provide positive reinforcement and thus lead to programme maintenance but, in addition, provide a good basis for further courses, in which the more complex skills of analysis and individual intervention programmes could be tackled. Greenwood *et al.* (1979) and Jones,

Fremouw and Carples (1977) showed that such courses can be taught on a pyramid model, making for cost-effectiveness. The EDY programme for teachers of severely mentally handicapped children is a British example of a pyramid model course. (McBrien and Foxen, 1981). Our own interest was in providing a general introduction to behaviour management techniques as a means of promoting good classroom discipline.

(d)   Most of the courses we reviewed brought together groups of teachers, usually from schools at a similar level, who volunteered for a course in behavioural methods applied to the classroom. Such a course may well appeal to individuals, perhaps because they feel a special need for help, but when they go back into school the climate of opinion and custom may well be against them. Georgiades and Phillimore (1975) have spelled out in some detail how difficult it is for the individual 'hero-innovator' to make headway against the 'system'. (We will return to this point in the following section.) Some course organizers (e.g. Firman and Hastings, 1980; Merrett, 1981, 1982 and 1984) have tried to arrange for two or more teachers from the same school to attend courses in order to provide mutual support against the 'system', and have found this to be useful, especially if one of the pair holds a position of responsibility as head or deputy. School-based courses would appear to enjoy many advantages. When all the staff, including the head and other management staff, agree to take a course and to apply behavioural management strategies, then many of the difficulties detailed by Georgiades and Phillimore can be overcome.

Taking account of all these issues, we decided that the Behavioural Approach to Teaching Package should be designed to meet the needs of teachers of children of up to about twelve years of age in ordinary (mainstream) schools, that it should concentrate upon classroom management skills and be taught on-site to the whole of the school staff, including classroom assistants and the head teacher. Having decided what the nature of the course was to be, it was then necessary to decide the content and the best way of teaching it.

The consensus of experiments in this field seems to suggest that it is necessary to teach theory as well as technology (c.f. especially Berger, 1979; MacKrell, 1983). The questions are: how much and when? Most researchers have come to the conclusion that enough theory to allow teachers to know what they are doing is essential and that it should, as far as possible, accompany the practical work. This is usually done by using a class textbook or specially prepared handouts. For example, Firman and Hastings (1980) used Leach and Raybould (1977), Wolff and Rennie (1977) used Poteet (1973), Moss and Childs (1981) used Vargas (1977). A further constraint upon an in-service course is how much extra effort can reasonably be expected from teachers who are already fully engaged by their regular employment. By using a skills package in which the techniques are introduced in sequence, it is possible to underpin these with the minimum necessary theory, both in the session notes and in take-home notes written specially for the purpose.

When a package of skills is being introduced, it is necessary to ensure that the teachers involved do, in fact, make an effort to apply them. This is a point made by many experimenters, as is the need for the teachers to be observed in this. Even when all the teachers are in the same school, it is difficult to observe them all. To teach teachers to monitor their own behaviour is one way out of this predicament. This can be accomplished by arranging for the carrying out of some of the suggested strategies and the self-monitoring of teacher behaviour to be part of a contractual agreement between tutor and student. The contractual basis has the added advantage of showing, in the structure of the course itself, an element from the behavioural approach. Moss (Moss and Childs, 1981) claims to do this and McKeown, Adams and Forehand (1975) use shaping as a behavioural example in a similar way.

Two other devices that have been found to be useful in training courses are cueing and modelling. Saudargas (1972) found cueing a valuable help. To some extent the monitoring of the teachers' own response rates contains an element of cueing. The use of a tally counter or some other device for self-recording tends to become a conditioned stimulus or cue for the behaviour. Modelling has also been found to be effective (Ringer, 1973; Jones and Eimers, 1975; McKeown et al., 1975). The use of course members as surrogate pupils is one possibility, but role play is not always popular with teachers. However, an alternative is to include short video sequences in which good practice is modelled for comment, discussion and for subsequent copying.

Hall and Copeland (1972), Harris et al. (1975) and Greenwood et al. (1979) suggest that, apart from success in the course itself, the members do best if they are provided with some bonus or back-up reinforcement. Hall and Copeland arranged for this in the form of academic credits. Cossairt, Hall and Hopkins (1973) and McKeown et al. (1975) found that teachers learned more effectively when their efforts were rewarded with social praise. This is manifestly in line with the precepts of the behavioural approach to teaching and, as Cossairt *et al.* (1973) found, contingent social praise was even more effective when delivered on an intermittent schedule. The inclusion of the management staff on a course might allow a special role for the headteacher and others, who may be in a position to oversee their colleagues as they attempt to apply behavioural strategies. The fact that authority figures are aware of all that the teachers have learned and what they are attempting to do will make them very effective in guiding and reinforcing their colleagues. They would probably be more effective than outsiders (such as course tutors), offering an occasional visit. They would also have an important role to play in programme maintenance.

We now turn to a vital issue in the development of any training programme, that of evaluation. Some of the later American studies attempted to pay proper attention to evaluation. However, few of the courses devised and run in Britain have included attempts to evaluate outcomes systematically and those that have done so have used non-behavioural devices, such as questionnaires. Some tutors who have run behavioural courses for teachers have evaluated outcomes in terms of knowledge gained, e.g. Moss and Childs (1981). But, for a course which aims at changing children's behaviour through bringing about change in teacher behaviour, and which is behavioural to boot, nothing short of the demonstration of behaviour change, using some objective method of observation, can be considered sufficient. Milne (1984) notes that: 'Dissemination of the behavioural approach to a variety of client groups and problem areas has proceeded rapidly in recent years' but comments that there 'has not been any comparable growth in the evaluation of the training of such groups'. He continues, 'somewhat paradoxically, evaluations of *behaviour* in behaviour therapy are outnumbered by assessments of knowledge and attitudes, with very few controlled examinations of the most relevant parameter of all, skill'. He then describes five measures of behavioural skill, presenting reliability and validity data for each, but none of these, however, is based on systematic observation of trainees' behaviour *in vivo*. Topping and Brindle, writing generally about in-service training courses, put it this way:

Few studies have demonstrated relevant post-course behaviour changes by a substantial proportion of the course members, and even when these did occur, they proved mostly short-lived at longer term follow up. (Topping and Brindle, 1979, pp. 49–50)

Thus, there are two problems. First, we have to demonstrate

behaviour change in teachers and their pupils as a result of the training course. Secondly, we have to be able to demonstrate generalization across types of problems and situations and, above all, over time. The latter is basically a problem of programme maintenance. Most of the British reports have contented themselves with reporting case studies of successful interventions by some of the students attending courses (e.g. Merrett 1981, 1982 and 1984). Some have obtained data from the completion of anonymous questionnaires (e.g. Clayton, 1983), but none has attempted to measure behaviour change *per se* (except our own studies reported later in this chapter). Even where tutors have been able to go into the classrooms of course members (e.g. Firman and Hastings, 1980; Raymond, 1980), it has been for the purpose of monitoring the progress of interventions and not to gain objective observational data on behaviour change of teachers or children. Farrell and Sugden (1984), who report an evaluation of some of the outcomes of the EDY programme, have made an attempt to show behaviour change, by observing video-tapes made during the course.

Generalization of behavioural teacher training was examined by Robinson and Swanton (1980). They identified six reports of behavioural teacher training courses, all of which were published in the *Journal of Applied Behavior Analysis*. In their summary and conclusions section they state:

> There are very few studies available that have attempted to establish that behavioural training of teachers results in generalized change. Of those that have attempted this demonstration (approximately six studies) only half provides convincing evidence of generalization. On this criterion, the efficacy of behavioral training has not yet been established ... The design and methodology of teacher training studies suggest that researchers do not consider a clear demonstration of generalization to be a necessity. Only a small proportion of the resources invested in any one study is devoted to collecting data in a nontraining condition, and to establishing the reliability of that data. (Robinson and Swanton, 1980, p. 496)

If hard-nosed American behaviourists have generally failed to demonstrate generalization, we should hardly expect to find it in British contexts. Woods and Cullen (1983) have been concerned with this problem in the context of long-term hospitalized mentally handicapped patients. They suggest that the rate of client behaviour change and its permanence are of prime importance. Measures of how much the students enjoy a course or how much they think they have gained from it, or even measures of their improved knowledge, have little bearing upon their behaviour in the wards. Woods and Cullen suggest that the business of programme maintenance is a highly complex one and difficult to demonstrate, which probably accounts for the fact that not many researchers have attempted to do so.

In this section we have discussed some of the relevant literature concerning the topic of how best to train teachers in the behavioural approach. We have also tried to provide an analysis of this research, yielding a series of critical features which a successful model of training for teachers should embody. Some progress has been made towards designing an appropriate model but, equally, many of Kazdin and Moyer's points made in 1976 are still true.

effective teacher training techniques exist ... unfortunately, effective techniques have not been implemented on a large scale to train teachers to utilize the available technology ... dissemination of information is often a substitute for actually training teachers to implement the procedures effectively. Even when specific procedures are used to train teachers, they are rarely evaluated in terms of their effect on teacher or student classroom behavior.

Their concluding paragraph is worth quoting in its entirety, because it still sums up admirably the current state of the art. It also reflects the views of the present authors on the need for continued attention to be devoted to the problems of generalization and programme maintenance and for change in the educational system *per se.*

Preliminary evidence suggests that various approaches alter teacher behavior in the classroom. Certainly additional work needs to be conducted to determine the most effective and efficient training 'package'. Hopefully, such a package can be incorporated into the curriculum of student teachers when their actual classroom behavior is supervised. Whatever training procedures are implemented, schools need to foster continued use of skills after training has been terminated. Presently, there is no empirical justification for the notion that desirable teacher behaviors will be reinforced (by change in the students) while undesirable or ineffective teacher behaviors will extinguish. Specific procedures need to be implemented to sustain teacher performance. Perhaps, one means to ensure the long-term maintenance of teacher behavior is to restructure the contingencies of reinforcement in which teachers operate. Teachers represent only one position or level in the educational structure. It is unrealistic to expect performance of certain teacher behaviors unless those behaviors are actively supported by the environment. Perhaps, changes in educational systems will be required to ensure effective and accountable teacher classroom practices. (Kazdin and Moyer, 1976).

Distinguishing characteristics of BATPACK

From our review (Merrett and Wheldall, 1984), discussed in some detail above, we arrived at ten general observations relating to the ideal content and structure of an effective training course for teachers in behavioural methods of classroom management. These are as follows:

1 Teachers can be taught, in groups, to use behavioural methods.
2 Different courses are needed for different types of schools.
3 Successful courses are skills-based.
4 Courses should have specific, limited objectives.
5 Ideally, courses should be school-based and for the whole staff.
6 Observation skills are a key component of such courses.
7 Contracts encourage commitment and skills practice.
8 Cueing and modelling are important aids to skill acquisition.
9 Teachers need positive reinforcement too.
10 Courses should programme for generalization and mainte-nance of skills.

We also learned from our own research. In Chapter 2, we reviewed the continuing programme of experimental research into the behavioural approach to teaching carried out by the 'Birmingham Group' (Wheldall, Merrett and associated students) based in the Centre for Child Study at the University of Birmingham. This research has been concerned with the practical applications of behavioural psychology in British schools and has, during the last ten years, involved the active participation of many local teachers. The influence of our programme of research can be clearly seen in the development of BATBACK (see, especially, the fifth distin-guishing characteristic of BATPACK later in this section). We have also benefited from the evaluative comments made by consumers, both teachers who have taken BATPACK courses and tutors who have taught the courses, as detailed later.

Our experience in actually teaching the behavioural approach to teachers during the past ten years has been another influence on course content. For example, we learned the hard way that animal studies put teachers off. The elegance of rat or pigeon studies and the paradigmatic clarity they present is bought at the expense of relevance and credibility, and so we have ceased to use them. Similarly, American studies are avoided, because British teachers tend to be suspicious of foreign products and practices. Moreover, the educational system and climate in the United States are radically different from those of the UK and, hence, important points can get lost in translation. We now cite our own (British) demonstration studies throughout.

Our debt to some of the ideas underpinning Direct Instruction (Becker and Carnine, 1980) and the EDY materials for training mental handicap practitioners (McBrien and Foxen, 1981) will be obvious to many. However, we believe that the pulling together of these various influences into one package constitutes an original approach to the problem.

The Behavioural Approach to Teaching Package (BATPACK) was developed by a project team, based in the Centre for Child Study, in the University of Birmingham, made up of Kevin Wheldall (Project Director), Frank Merrett (Research Fellow) and, in the initial stages, Alan Russell (an LEA Educational Psychologist). Our aim was to develop a package that would train practising primary and middle school teachers in a number of key behavioural skills. The development of BATPACK was assisted in its early stages by a research grant awarded by the Schools Council.

BATPACK is distinguished by the following features:

1   BATPACK *is skills-based*

As we have already mentioned, Berger (1980) has made the distinction between teaching *about* and teaching *how*. This distinction is supported by the experience of many researchers, including ourselves (Merrett and Wheldall, 1982). It is relatively easy to run a course on the behavioural approach that will effectively teach knowledge of the theory and methods. Following such courses, teachers will readily be able to spot explanatory fictions, define negative reinforcement and use operant jargon in a most convincing way. Moreover, as we have shown (Wheldall and Congreve, 1980; Merrett and Wheldall, 1982), such courses can be very effective agents for attitude change. Once teachers know what the behavioural approach really entails (and equally importantly, what it does *not* entail) then they become much more positively disposed and receptive to the idea of implementing it. What such courses fail to do, however, is to change teacher behaviour in the classroom; to improve their teaching skills at the chalk face. This is not surprising, for no behaviour analyst would expect that radical behaviour change, including the learning of new skills and the extinction of ineffective but deeply ingrained teaching habits, could be brought about merely by talk.

We believe that good, positive teaching is dependent upon the learning of a set of specific classroom management skills and techniques. Many good teachers use such techniques intuitively, but, as our research showed (Merrett and Wheldall, 1986a), this is not true of most British teachers nor, according to the research reviewed in Chapter 2, is it true of teachers generally. Few teachers typically use positive behavioural methods involving overt approval for desired social behaviour. Many teachers think they do, but the data show that approval of social behaviour is very infrequent while disapproval occurs at a high rate. Most teachers have learned negative methods of attempting to achieve classroom discipline, which is probably maintained by negative reinforcement, i.e. by the occasional, immediate (albeit very temporary) cessation of undesired classroom behaviour. Unfortunately, this is exhausting and the result is temporary.

Behavioural teaching seems simple until you attempt to do it without adequate training in the necessary skills and techniques. A teacher using behavioural methods without proper training may, at best, gain only a small improvement at great cost. For example, a full-scale token economy requiring a very time-consuming observation schedule may severely reduce the actual teaching time. Such an attempt at the learning of new skills is unlikely to be maintained by the consequences. What is needed is specific training in basic classroom skills, which can be implemented directly in the teacher's own classroom. By such skills we are referring, for example, to pin-pointing behaviours, positive rule-setting, effective praising, etc. These skills and techniques and many others are taught overtly as part of the BATPACK course.

In BATPACK we are not primarily interested in improving knowledge of and attitudes towards the behavioural approach, although we expect, and have evidence to show, that these follow our course. Our primary aim is to change teacher behaviour by teaching new skills and techniques. Consequently, by way of contrast with other courses, we believe that BATPACK can only be assessed by, and its success measured by, changes in observed teacher behaviour. As we will show later, BATPACK does bring about changes in teachers' actual behaviour in the classroom.

We have referred continually in this section to another important aspect, which is closely related to learning skills and changing teacher behaviour, and that is the importance of reinforcing events in the learning and maintenance of teacher behaviour. A teacher's colleagues are an important factor here, and this brings us to the fact that BATPACK is school-based.

2   BATPACK *is school-based*

Georgiades and Phillimore's (1975) influential paper did much to promote the concept of systems theory in both clinical and educational psychology. The basic message was that, however good the product, the hero-innovator is doomed to failure if he enters the system alone, without allies: 'The fact of the matter is that organisations such as schools and hospitals will, like dragons, eat hero-innovators for breakfast' (p. 315). While the hero has a vested interest in success, many others in the system have a vested interest in his failure. Successful programmes, they argue, need to involve key management figures, who are in a position to encourage group cohesion.

Returning to the school situation, it has often been observed that a teacher can be enthused by the behavioural approach, only to be firmly squashed by staff resentment or even by ridicule of his/her efforts, which will sometimes take the form of mild teasing but is insidiously effective. After a while, many teachers cave in under group pressure and return to the security of being part of the system. Consequently, BATPACK is not 'sold' to individuals but to whole schools or sections of very large schools. Training is typically carried out in groups of about eight or ten, which would usually include the entire staff of an infant, junior or middle school. It is essential for the head and deputy head to attend and for the staff to accept BATPACK as something for all of them, which will become basic to *their* system. (We shall return to the important role of the headteacher later.)

We do not encourage the lukewarm to take part. If individuals are not keen initially they may well drop out later, wasting time and effort. We advocate leaving such individuals out of the course, provided that a large majority within the school is committed to BATPACK training. Similarly, there is no point in running a course if the staff as a whole are not keen to take part, even if the headteacher is. A school-based training system provides support by instilling a team spirit whereby all members of the staff are working together. The message is conveyed that it is possible to change children's behaviour by changing your own behaviour. In addition, the BATPACK course gives a common language for talking about children's behaviour problems within the school context and with visiting educational psychologists. Remembering Georgiades and Phillimore's simile, the role of the BATPACK tutor is best summed up in a phrase from the Book of Job, 'I am a brother to dragons, And a companion to owls.' (Job xxx, 29, RV). In other words, the tutor works within the system from a secure knowledge-base in behavioural psychology.

3 BATPACK *is contract-based*

There is no shortage of in-service courses for teachers, all of widely differing type, level and duration. Most teachers will have had experience of attending a number of such courses. A common feature, and frequently a cause for complaint, is that courses do not specify in advance what will be provided and what will be expected. This is important to a busy teacher. In BATPACK we specify precisely, in advance, and in practical terms, what is expected and what the course tutor will provide: this is stated in the 'Preview'. These points are then embodied in a contract, which is agreed and signed by each course student and the tutor.

As we say in the Preview, 'We think it is important to make explicit what responsibilities each party will accept in the successful running of the course.' The student is informed that the course is rather different from other courses, since it is presented on-site and is 'concerned less with theoretical knowledge and more with practical skills'. It is emphasized that active participation by course members both in the weekly sessions and in mid-week assignments is essential. By signing a contract, teachers commit themselves to trying out the new skills and methods they have learned, in their own classrooms. Precise details of the times and dates of course sessions are written into the contract.

The Preview and contract are discussed thoroughly in a preliminary pre-course session with the staff, and only if sufficient course members contract to attend is the course run. The contract, which is signed by the tutor and each course member, states that:

The tutor agrees to:

1 Start all sessions on time.
2 Finish all sessions on time but to be available afterwards for further discussions if requested.
3 Provide all necessary materials.

Course members agree to:

1 Attend all six sessions and to be in good time.
2 Complete work assignments between sessions. This includes using the hand-tally each week for self-recording and completing the summary sheet.
3 Try out suggested techniques in class.
4 Complete the evaluation sheets at the end of the course.

It is made clear that the BATPACK course completion certificate will be awarded to, and *only* awarded to, those teachers who score at least 11 points out of 12 by attending sessions and completing the assignments (one point for each attendance and one for each completed assignment). The Preview also makes clear the limited remit of the course and this brings us to the fourth distinguishing characteristic.

4 BATPACK is limitation-based

The limitations of BATPACK are deliberate and are made explicit. We are not attempting to provide training in behaviour therapy. We aim only to train teachers in a limited series of key behavioural teaching skills and techniques. As we say in the Preview, 'We shall be concerned with the improvement of classroom management generally, not the remediation of individual problems, except incidentally.' Other courses have attempted to teach operant learning theory in unnecessary depth and to provide an overview of highly specialized techniques, including fading, shaping, over-correction, etc. We believe this to be unnecessary and counter-productive. BATPACK has no pretensions to anything other than basic training in the behavioural approach to the management of classroom (social) behaviour. Moreover, the present version of BATPACK is meant to be used only in 'ordinary' schools dealing with children between the ages of five and twelve.

We also accept the fact that teachers' time is limited, hence the course sessions last only sixty minutes. In addition, we realize that busy teachers cannot be expected to read large amounts of theoretical material. The amount of theory taught is, therefore, limited to that needed to back up the skills learned in the sessions and is provided in the form of 'take-homes' which never exceed two sides of A4-size paper. Another limitation that we accept is the inability to train successfully all teachers on a course. As we say in the Manual (Wheldall and Merrett, 1985): 'We do not expect 100 per cent success with BATPACK, nor should you ... Not all teachers will be sympathetic to the method and some will not be able to stay the course.'

5 BATPACK is research-based

It is a proud feature of BATPACK that it is soundly based on knowledge and principles derived from rigorous behavioural research in classrooms, as described in Chapter 2. Since this research is referred to overtly in the course, tutors need to be familiar with it.

From our demonstration studies (see Chapter 2) we have fed in specific behavioural techniques. For example, our 'Playing the game' study is featured as a demonstration study (with accompanying video) in the final unit of the package. The importance of setting events and classroom ecological variables (for example, our research on seating arrangements) is also very heavily stressed in comparison with other behavioural courses for teachers. Explicit reference is made to our surveys of troublesome behaviour and our findings concerning natural rates of approval and disapproval of British teachers. This also influenced our decision to include specific skills-training designed to increase use of praise and to decrease use of disapproval. The work on teacher attitudes and the findings from the study on the classroom performance of student teachers, following a course about behavioural methods, led us to make important decisions about the nature of the course content we would include in BATPACK, with its heavy emphasis on skills and its relative neglect of the history of behaviourism. This means that all of the material presented is backed by research evidence rather than mere assertion or opinion. Moreover, the content and techniques employed are also the result of continuing experimental evaluation (see below).

6   BATPACK *is evaluation-based*

From the outset, teachers who have attended BATPACK courses have been required, as part of the contract, to contribute to the evaluation of the package. As a result of constructive criticism from teachers and BATPACK tutors, many changes have been made to the content and structure of the course. BATPACK has now passed through several metamorphoses and at each stage an attempt was made to evaluate what had been achieved. This was done through:

(a)   evaluative comment from students by means of post-course questionnaires;
(b)   evaluation of student knowledge before and after courses;
(c)   objective observation of teacher behaviour in the classroom;
(d)   objective observation of children's behaviour in the classroom;
(e)   evaluation of children's work completed, i.e. product measures;
(f)   evaluation of the above measures again after a lapse of time.

Outcomes of some of these evaluations completed to date will be reported in a later section, in which the gradual evolution of BATPACK will be described. It will be seen that BATPACK was successively modified in the light of the findings from these evaluations in order to achieve its main objective of changing teacher and pupil behaviour. Typically, teachers on the course increase their use of approval and decrease their rates of disapproval, and these changes, in turn, lead to the children in their classes spending far more of their time actually getting on with their work.

BATPACK described

The description of BATPACK that follows illustrates the ways in which the authors have responded to the requirements for a practical, skills-based course in classroom management.

A BATPACK course is designed typically:

(a) to be run on-site in a classroom, staff-room or other spare room;

(b) to start ten or fifteen minutes after school finishes for the afternoon;

(c) for the whole of the staff, including classroom assistants and the head teacher (an ideal number would be between eight and twelve; a larger staff would need to be subdivided);

(d) to begin after all members have had the chance to read an outline of what is to be attempted and have signed a contract to attend all sessions and to give their full co-operation;

(e) to result in all successful course members receiving a copy of the BATPACK course completion certificate at the end. (They keep their own records of attendance and completion of the weekly assignments as they go along, in order to qualify for the certificate.)

The course is designed to be taught by a tutor who has attended a BATPACK tutors' training course. Prospective tutors must have a good working knowledge of behavioural psychology and its applications in schools. Many will be educational psychologists, but we are also beginning to train senior teachers who have followed advanced courses in the Behavioural Approach to Teaching. At the training course, which lasts about six hours, tutors receive a copy of the BATPACK manual. This manual contains all the detailed instructions necessary for a *trained* tutor to run a BATPACK course. Full step-by-step tutor's notes are given for every element of each unit, including scripted details of what to say at critical points. It also includes advice on how to set up and run an effective course, how to involve the head teacher, how to maintain behaviour change, in addition to background reference material and so on. A copy of the BATPACK VHS training cassette, OHP transparencies and a supply of tally counters, in addition to unit notes and 'take-homes', are also needed to run the course.

The BATPACK video comprises two programmes. The first is an introduction to the package and the behavioural approach in general and includes interviews with classroom teachers who have taken the course. The second programme consists of classroom behaviour sequences, which are used in the package to train the teachers in various skills. For example, teachers use tally counters to record the frequency of praise and disapproval in some of the sequences. OHP transparencies, specially prepared for the course, are employed to illustrate various points and to summarize group discussion.

The original version of BATPACK was a package meant for teachers in ordinary (mainstream) *primary and middle* schools only, i.e. for those who teach children aged from about five to twelve. It has been planned as a complete, integrated package and it is essential that tutors follow the framework provided closely. The BATPACK course consists of six one-hour sessions called units, taught at weekly intervals. A session length of one hour was judged to be the most teachers could cope with at the end of a teaching day. Six sessions fit neatly into a half term. We decided to operate within these practical constraints and limited our course accordingly. Each unit has its own set of unit notes, which teachers complete during the session. For each unit there are five objectives. Every unit is divided into five elements, so that each corresponds to an objective. The first objective is always a review item, giving the opportunity for students to ask questions and for the tutor to review aspects of the earlier units. The last objective of each unit is concerned with the practical assignments for the following week. These always include some reading and time for the student to observe and record his/her own behaviour in responding to the class. The three other elements are used to explore practical problems (identifying problem behaviours), develop skills (pinpointing, observing) and explain techniques (setting rules, defining work demands). The latest version of BATPACK consists of the following:

Preview and Contract

Unit 1:   Identifying troublesome behaviour
Take-home 1: The five principles of the behavioural approach to teaching

Unit 2:   Focusing on desirable behaviour
Take-home 2: The behavioural teacher's A B C

Unit 3:   Eliminating (or, at least, reducing) the negative
Take-home 3: Negative consequences

Unit 4:   Accentuating the positive
Take-home 4: Using positive reinforcement effectively

Unit 5:   Getting the classroom setting right
Take-home 5: Antecedents – settings for behaviour

Unit 6:   Where do we go from here?
Take-home 6: The behavioural charter

Every unit has an accompanying weekly reading assignment or take-home. The take-homes attempt to supply some of the theoretical material that underpins the practical skills learned in the unit. In the last unit, an attempt is made to review all the skills and techniques that have been covered and to present some successful classroom strategies tried out by other teachers in a school of the same educational level. At all stages, the tutor tries to be accepting and encouraging when course members attempt to express a point of view or to respond during a skills-learning session.

BATPACK concentrates upon improving the teacher's ability to manage the classroom situation as a whole rather than the behavioural/learning problems of particular children. It attempts to do this by helping teachers to define clearly the commonest classroom behaviour problems and to observe them carefully, while concentrating upon positive measures to bring about change. BATPACK attempts to change teachers' responses to their classes principally by skilful attention to antecedents and by being more positive towards specifically defined child behaviours that they wish to encourage. In addition to specific skills, techniques and procedures, we also teach the general principles of the behavioural approach to teaching. This enables teachers to use behavioural methods creatively as well as being able to follow our proven procedures in appropriate situations. More specifically, the contingent and effective use of praise is emphasized. Teachers are also taught related skills, such as 'rule setting', and video-tapes of classes are used to train teachers in how to 'catch children "being good"' (i.e. appropriate times for praise). Various techniques are practised by which teacher praise can be increased, and more elaborate strategies and techniques derived from research in behavioural ecology are suggested.

The development and evaluation of BATPACK

Since the beginning of the project in 1981, BATPACK has been subject to continual change and modification; each succeeding version incorporating changes in structure, content, layout and organization (see distinguishing characteristic 6, p. 146). We could not hope to detail here the minutiae of the changes wrought in each of these succeeding versions, nor would it be particularly instructive or profitable to do so. It is helpful, however, to conceptualize the development of BATPACK in a series of phases, each phase being loosely associated with a version of the package (Mark I, Mark II, etc.) that was substantially similar. In this way, we can chart progress and show how the major changes eventually led to the current version.

As we have already said, all teachers who have taken part in BATPACK courses have helped in its evaluation and hence its development. BATPACK tutors have also contributed to this rolling programme of development and evaluation. Because our aim has been to change teacher behaviour, the main focus of our other attempts at evaluation has been to see, quite simply, whether BATPACK does bring about such change. To this end, we developed classroom observation schedules as briefly mentioned in Chapter 2. Our first schedule was the Class Teacher/Pupil Observation schedule (CTP 1), which allowed the observer to look systematically at and sample three main aspects of classroom behaviour: teacher responses, children's disruptiveness and on-task behaviour. This was developed over a number of years and eventually became Observing Pupils and Teachers In Classrooms (OPTIC) (Merrett and Wheldall, 1986b).

Phase I

The prototype package (Mark I) was designed and written early in 1981 with Alan Russell, who taught the course in a large middle school. (We would like to acknowledge here Alan Russell's valuable contributions to the prototype package.) Teachers were randomly allocated to a BATPACK experimental group and to a control group, with eight teachers in each. All staff were observed on three separate occasions, both before and after the BATPACK course, and estimates of teacher and class behaviour were thereby obtained. Other, more subjective, pre- and post-measures were obtained which basically assessed (a) commitment to the general behavioural approach and (b) whether the teacher would opt for a behavioural solution to classroom problems.

The prototype version taught was admittedly primitive. Rough unit notes (and take-homes) were provided for the teachers for six one-hour sessions, but the sound quality of the (black-and-white) video sequences employed was very poor and no clear notes for the guidance of the tutor were available at this stage. The teachers were merely encouraged to try out the suggestions made and to attempt to self-record their responses by using tally counters.

The findings from our evaluations were mixed. The teachers were asked to complete two questionnaires: one asked for feedback on what they thought of the content and organization of the course and the other attempted to assess how far the package succeeded in teaching its objectives in terms of how much of the material presented was retained and understood. Analyses of these proved very favourable, a view supplemented by informal feedback. The teachers reported that they had enjoyed the course, that they had generally found it one of the most useful they had attended and that it was particularly pertinent in their school where there were severe problems with disruptive behaviour. Administration of tests before and after BATPACK showed clearly that teachers' theoretical knowledge of the behavioural approach had improved significantly in the experimental group compared with the control group. The results thus showed that the pilot BATPACK was fulfilling at least one of its aims of making teachers aware of the behavioural approach to teaching. Perhaps the most striking behavioural evidence for the success of the course was in the traditional 'voting with your feet' evaluation – attendance by the eight teachers over the six sessions was more than 95 per cent.

Analyses of the observational data, however, were not so encouraging. Although observation of teachers' behaviour in the classroom showed changes in the predicted direction (i.e. positive responses increased and negative responses decreased slightly), the differences in mean changes between the experimental and control groups were not statistically significant. Of even more concern was the fact that the behaviour of the children had barely changed: rates of disruption remained at the same level and on-task behaviour improved by only a few percentage points. Full details of the extensive evaluations completed with this prototype package are reported in two unpublished dissertations (Childs, 1982, and Cooper, 1983).

Consequently, we were forced to conclude that, although the basic content and structure of the package were acceptable to and indeed appreciated by teachers, for whom it was designed, it would need revision in order to achieve its primary objective of bringing about major changes in teachers' and children's behaviour.

Phase II

During the second phase, which lasted from autumn 1981 for about a year, numerous small changes and refinements were made and small-scale evaluation studies conducted. During this period, minor amendments and additions to content and structure were incorporated into a more consistent, word-processed prototype manual for tutors. Unit notes were reduced to a record of activities carried out during the session, specific content being transferred to take-homes and/or the tutor notes. Possibly the major innovation of BATPACK Mark II was the decision, taken towards the end of this phase, to introduce the formal contract between course tutor and teachers. This contractual commitment required teachers to monitor their own behaviour weekly and to try out the strategies presented in the units. Moreover, the course completion certificate was made contingent upon fulfilment of this contractual agreement. By the end of this phase, BATPACK was beginning to resemble its current format.

Courses based on versions of BATPACK Mark II were taught to a variety of groups of teachers by the authors, but they were not always objectively evaluated. These included groups of students attending courses in the Faculty of Education at Birmingham University and school-based courses. Evidence accumulated supporting the fact that BATPACK significantly improved both teachers' knowledge of and attitudes towards behavioural teaching methods.

In addition, one school-based course taught in a middle school by the second author was objectively evaluated. All eight teachers took part, four of whom it was possible to observe working in their classrooms before and after the course (children's behaviour was not observed in this study). The observational data showed little change brought about by BATPACK in teachers' responses (positive or negative) to academic behaviour. However, teachers' positive responses to children's social behaviours were shown to increase substantially and negative responses to social behaviour decreased in all cases, overall by about 50 per cent. It is also worth mentioning that the teachers were sufficiently impressed by the behavioural rule-setting aspect of the course to attempt to devise general rules that would apply throughout the school as a whole.

These positive results encouraged us to begin the production of a version of BATPACK that could be made more widely available. However, teacher criticism had identified the video sequences as being in urgent need of improvement. To this end, we began to produce new video material in an experimental classroom in the Centre for Child Study at Birmingham University, during the summer term of 1982.

Phase III

The main aim of this phase was to produce a version of BATPACK that could be taught by tutors other than members of the development team; for this, a proper manual was necessary. The manual included some general guidance for BATPACK tutors and transcripts of the video sequences were listed in an appendix to the manual, with photocopied master sheets for producing the necessary OHP transparencies. The opportunity was also taken to revise completely the content and structure of the package, based around the new (colour) VHS material. Structurally, BATPACK Mark III was now made internally consistent, so that each unit comprised five elements relating to five quasi-behavioural objectives, which were clearly identified for the tutor at the beginning of the unit. Tutors were also given a checklist of materials needed for each unit. During this phase, which lasted for about two years, the behavioural charter was introduced and, towards the end, the BATbooster or follow-up checksheet (mentioned later) was included.

The Mark III package was initially taught to fifteen teachers and nursery nurses in two infant schools. All the staff and both head teachers attended. Eight of the teachers were observed before and after the course using a version of OPTIC which concentrates solely upon teacher behaviour, since it is that which BATPACK sets out to alter. In addition to completing an evaluation sheet, course members answered questions in a structured interview. A much more detailed analysis was now possible. The data showed that total positive responses increased overall by 25 per cent, with positive responses to social behaviour increasing by 87 per cent; total negative responses decreased by 36 per cent with negative responses to social behaviour decreasing by 38 per cent. All these results were statistically significant at the 1 per cent level, using the non-parametric Wilcoxon test. In addition, positive responses to academic outcomes increased and negative responses to academic outcomes decreased, but neither of these changes was large enough to be statistically significant.

Only one teacher failed to increase the number of positive responses given to social behaviour, and only one failed to decrease the number of negative responses given to social behaviour. All but one of the teachers had developed and were displaying a set of simple rules, and all but two had rearranged their rooms to ameliorate management problems. Results from a structured interview suggested that the teachers were all more aware of their responses to children, and all but one said that they would recommend the course to colleagues. Half of the course members thought that they had increased their positive responses; twelve out of fifteen thought that they had reduced their negatives.

As a result of these positive outcomes, we now felt confident enough to begin to train others to use the package and to release a version of the manual for their use. However, we felt that future BATPACK tutors needed more guidance than could be contained in a manual, and we have always insisted that tutors should attend a training course. Informal courses were given in Liverpool and Grimsby prior to the first 'official' training course for BATPACK tutors, held at the Centre for Child Study in Birmingham in Spring 1983. The content of BATPACK tutor training courses has itself evolved over the years in the light of feedback from tutors. BATPACK courses have subsequently been held at regular intervals in Birmingham, for individual school psychological services and for other groups in various parts of the UK.

The most thorough, truly experimental evaluation of the Mark III package was carried out early in 1983. This study used an independent observer (with some measurement of inter-observer agreement) and involved the comparison of a group of teachers who had experienced a full BATPACK course with a control group in another school who had not. All teachers were observed on three separate occasions, both before and after a seven to eight week interval during which the experimental group received BATPACK training. The control group received one seminar on the behavioural approach during this period, and were given two papers to read that set out the guidelines for the application of behavioural methods in the classroom. One of these was given to the teachers before the seminar in order to provide a basis for discussion. The other, given afterwards, set out in clear and simple terms the steps involved in carrying out a behavioural intervention.

The results of this study, summarized only briefly here, have now been reported fully (Wheldall, Merrett and Borg, 1985). It was shown that mean inter-observer agreement for both teacher and class behaviour was high (94 per cent and 91 per cent respectively, on average) which supports the reliability of the measures employed. The data obtained from the schedules showed that prior to BATPACK training the two groups of teachers did not differ significantly and, in fact, were very similar in terms of their use of approval and disapproval. Rates of disapproval to both academic and social behaviour were very low in both groups, as was approval of social behaviour. Approval for academic behaviour, however, was (relatively) very high. Average on-task behaviour of the classes was around 75 per cent in both groups, again quite high.

At the end of the experiment the control group had barely changed, except to increase their rates of negative responding to both academic and social behaviour, and this was accompanied by a 6 per cent drop in the average on-task behaviour of their classes. Positive responding to both academic and social behaviour was almost identical to the rates found on the initial testing, despite the fact that these teachers had read about and discussed the importance of using positive reinforcement. The experimental group, however, who had now completed the BATPACK course, showed marked increases in approval rates and maintained their low levels of negative responding. Positive responses to academic behaviour more than doubled, and those to social behaviour increased by a factor of one hundred! Whereas only 10 per cent of the positive responses given before the BATPACK course were accompanied by an explanation, more than 35 per cent of positive responses after the course were rule-related, accompanied by a reason or used as example to encourage others. (We refer to these sorts of more effective positive responses as REX responses; see Merrett and Wheldall, 1986b.) On-task behaviour in the classes in the experimental group increased by 9 per cent to 84 per cent (compared with a decline to 68 per cent in the control classes). In short, after the BATPACK courses was completed, there were significant differences on all the measures favouring the experimental group, showing them to be more positive, less negative and with higher on-task behaviour levels among their pupils.

Turning now to the results for individuals, it was shown that all teachers in the experimental group doubled their previous rates for use of positives, with the exception of two teachers whose responses to academic behaviour (only) did not quite meet this criterion. Moreover, five out of the six teachers showed increasing use of positives over the three post-test observation sessions. In the control group, only a few minor increases in positive behaviour were in evidence. These were limited to marginal increases in positive responding to academic behaviour only, and were seen to be decreasing over the post-test observation sessions. On-task behaviour was seen to increase in five out of six experimental classes, with the sixth class maintaining its already high on-task level (81 per cent). In the control group, on-task behaviour fell in all classes except one, which increased by 5 per cent.

All the teachers who took the course completed (anonymously) the BATPACK questionnaire, which replaced the structured interview. All of them regarded BATPACK more favourably at the end than at the beginning and all were prepared to recommend the course to colleagues. All believed that their own responses to children had improved and that they had increased their rates of positive responding. They were less sure about the levels of their negative responses. Some of the teachers reported that they had attempted to manipulate antecedents: for example, four of them had set up rules in their classrooms. Comments about the structure of the course were very favourable and attendance at the course was excellent; one teacher only was absent for one session. (Typically attendance rates for BATPACK have been in the upper 90 per cents, infrequent absences invariably resulting from sickness or family crisis.)

Two subsequent evaluations of BATCPACK Mark III were undertaken without the direct involvement of any members of the development team. The first of these was carried out by Walker, Allsop and Ross (1986) before and after a BATPACK course taught to all twelve teachers in a school in Scotland run by the first two authors. Reports from the teachers after the course were almost entirely favourable, and the tutors reported: 'We feel that it (BATPACK) has long-term positive effects for all concerned'. Eight of the teachers were prepared to be observed, and this observation was carried out for each teacher three times both before and after the course. The results showed that for academic behaviour positive responses hardly changed, but there was a significant decrease in negative responding. For social behaviour, the results were highly significant, positive responses rising by more than four times and negative responses falling to less than half of the pre-course levels. Moreover, pupils' time on-task rose significantly from 68 per cent to 84 per cent.

The second evaluation was designed and organized by the present authors, but was carried out by Worsley, Colmar and Parry (Wheldall, Merrett, Worsley, Colmar and Parry, 1986). The course was taught by Colmar and evaluated informally by Parry, the head teacher, and objectively by Worsley. Nine class teachers took part in the course and six of them were observed by the independent observer. All inter-observer agreement percentages exceeded 90 per cent and averaged around 95 per cent. Teachers' positive responses to children's academic behaviour increased substantially and significantly, and the positive responses to social behaviour also increased, though not significantly. The use of more effective positive (REX) responses, especially those addressed to academic behaviour, increased dramatically by a factor of eight. Similarly, teachers' negative responding dropped sharply, especially in relation to children's social behaviour. Mean on-task behaviour for the six classes increased significantly from 67 per cent to 73 per cent.

Both of these studies were marked by clear demonstrations of improvement in children's on-task behaviour as measured by independent observations. However, the validity of on-task behaviour *per se* is sometimes questioned as a measure of whether children are working as the teacher has planned and whether they are producing satisfactory results. Evidence supporting the importance of time on task (sometimes referred to as academic engaged time) has been provided both by behaviour analysts and non-behavioural educational researchers. For example, Merrett and Wheldall (1978) (as reported in Chapter 2) showed that increased on-task behaviour in a junior school class, following a behavioural intervention based on a 'game' strategy, was accompanied by substantial increases in the quantity and quality of work produced. Similarly, it has been shown that the large increases in on-task behaviour associated with changes in seating arrangements (from table groups to rows) were associated with improved quantity and quality of work produced (Wheldall, 1981; Bennett and Blundell, 1983; Wheldall and Croft, in preparation). The results from these behavioural experimental studies (most of which employed OPTIC to measure on-task behaviour) are congruent with the findings of educational researchers such as Rosenshine, Berliner and Anderson, who have demonstrated that academic engaged time is a critical variable in academic progress in all subjects (Rosenshine and Berliner, 1978; Anderson, 1981; Fisher and Berliner, 1985). It would appear, therefore, that on-task behaviour is a good index of performance in the classroom. In as yet unpublished research, we have demonstrated that BATPACK training with groups of teachers appears to yield similar improvements in work produced, in addition to the expected gains in pupil on-task behaviour.

The main aim of our early work was to demonstrate measurable gains in teacher and class behaviours following BATPACK training. This we achieved with Mark III, as the studies reported above clearly demonstrate. However, an obvious question, frequently asked by behaviourally aware practitioners is, 'What evidence do you have for the long-term effects of BATPACK?' In other words, will the effects of BATPACK 'wear off' after a while with teachers returning to their pre- training modes of responding. Our expectation has always been that it is likely that it will and that they might, unless definite positive steps are taken to maintain changes in teacher behaviour. This appears to be a behavioural fact of life; behaviour changes will neither be maintained nor will they generalize unless contingencies have been structured to facilitate this. We will return to this point following a brief presentation of some relevant data.

Following the collection of the post-training data in our main experimental study (described above, Wheldall, Merrett and Borg, 1985), the teachers comprising the control group were subsequently given BATPACK training, as they had been promised. For a number of reasons, not least the fact that they were trained towards the end of the school year, it was not possible to observe this group of teachers and their classes for a third time (i.e. following training). It did prove possible, however, to observe both groups of teachers in the following academic year with their new classes. It must be emphasized that they were not teaching the same classes and had only been teaching their new classes for half a term (about eight weeks). Given the mutuality of behaviour between a teacher and a specific class, therefore, even the results for teacher behaviour are not directly comparable.

Members of the original experimental group of six teachers were again observed in November, some nine months after BATPACK training. Different (trained) observers were employed, who were deliberately kept in ignorance of the results of the original study. Inter-observer agreement figures were again high, around 90 per cent. The mean on-task behaviour of the six new classes 63 per cent (range 45 per cent–80 per cent) was appreciably lower than the pre-intervention mean of the original six classes, which had already been high at 75 per cent. The reason why their on-task rates were so low probably lies in part with the teacher's behaviour, which had reverted to pre-training levels or even worse. Approval for academic behaviour was still appreciably higher than at pre-test level, and this was also (marginally) the case for approval to social behaviour, but both had fallen back considerably from post-test levels. Moreover, very few REX responses were evident. In addition, use of negatives had increased appreciably, way above even pre-test levels, especially for social behaviour. (It must be noted, however, that pre-test levels of negative responding had been atypically low, as discussed in Wheldall, Merrett and Borg, 1985.)

Before attempting to suggest reasons for these disappointing outcomes, we shall examine the results for the control group of five teachers who were subsequently given BATPACK training in the summer term and were also observed again in November, some six months later. Observations of this group were made by the same observers as above, and once again inter-observer agreement was very high, around 95 per cent. Again, it must be stressed that the teachers were teaching different classes, but there is no reason to suspect the children taught to be radically different from those taught the previous year. Yet, for this group, mean on-task behaviour had risen to 86 per cent (compared with 72 per cent and 69 per cent respectively on the previous two 'testings'). This is consistent, from a behavioural perspective, with the marked changes apparent in teacher behaviour. Positive responses to academic behaviour had nearly doubled, whereas positives to social behaviour, which had previously been non-existent, were now very much more common. Negative responding to academic behaviour had also decreased since the second 'testing', but not to social behaviour, which had increased.

The results above show, as we expected, evidence of some fall-off in teachers' improved classroom management behaviour. In other words, behaviour change was not totally maintained. Our evidence, from these two studies, suggests that behaviour change appears to be maintained reasonably well for a period (perhaps six months) and then declines. We had anticipated this, since it is true not only of explicit behaviour change studies but of most, if not all, innovations. Without explicit attempts at programme maintenance, performance almost inevitably drops off. Our view is that you cannot expect behaviour change to be maintained: you must actively engineer it. To this end, towards the end of phase III we began to make it clear to tutors that they must assume a large part of the responsibility for programme maintenance, in partnership with the head teacher of the school and we provided two new means to help them to achieve this, which were subsequently incorporated into the published Mark IV package.

The first of these was a far more detailed definition of the role of the head teacher, with explicit instructions about what he/she is expected to do week by week throughout the course and during the weeks following it. Head teachers are, for example, explicitly instructed to look for opportunities to praise their staff for carrying out assignments and for trying out interventions and to be understanding of failure. Many other suggestions are made to head teachers for supporting colleagues in their attempts to adopt new strategies. These are the activities that the tutor would want to engage in if she or he could spare the time to be in the school. If we are to work with the system, we can probably do it best through the senior management.

The second innovation is the BATbooster, an analogous reference to the need for a second injection (a booster), several months after the first, in some inoculation programmes. Although not wishing to be thought adherents of the medical model(!), we argue that a booster shot of BATPACK is needed some months after the final session and subsequently at regular intervals (say, every six months). The booster takes the form of a follow-up check sheet, which reminds course members what the course included. The BATPACK tutor, in collaboration with senior management staff (i.e. the head and deputy), uses the check sheet in a follow-up seminar six months or so after the completion of the course, as a basis for recollection and discussion of strategies advocated in BATPACK. The tutor would suggest, for example, that teachers attempt to monitor their own behaviour once again. By such means, course members will be encouraged to try once more some of the strategies and techniques that had been employed initially but that may now have fallen into disuse (overt classroom rules, for example).

In view of the progress made with BATPACK Mark III, we now felt that the package was almost ready for more general release. To this end a final, thorough revision was undertaken.

Phase IV

In Summer 1984, we held a one-day workshop at the Centre for Child Study to which four experienced BATPACK tutors were invited. Our object was to pool ideas and suggestions for modifications in the light of our various experiences in teaching Mark III (including consideration of comments and criticisms provided by others). The invited tutors (Susan Colmar, Cedric Cramer, Pat Hay and Rick Story) made many helpful contributions and provided valuable feedback on the new video materials and other innovations we presented to them. We would like to take this opportunity to give public recognition of the contributions they have made to BATPACK. (A report of 'Initial experiences with BATPACK' was subsequently published by Cramer and Hay, 1985).

The 'final' version of BATPACK (Mark IV) was published in January 1985, following a thorough revision and the incorporation of new materials and methods. Briefly, in addition to the specification of the role of the head teacher and the elaboration of the BATbooster (as described above) completely new, higher quality video programmes were produced. The classroom sequences involve a wider age-range and transcripts of the relevant interactions are appended to the revised manual. (A new, introductory video programme about the package is also provided for showing to groups of teachers.) Other additions and changes to the manual include the colour coding of tutor notes, unit notes and take-homes, sections on how to set up and run BATPACK courses, advice on presentation and use of the materials, a tutor's course record, references to all the quoted research, recommended reading, a 'problem page' and copies of all the materials given to and kept by BATPACK course members. The content and order of the actual units has undergone major reorganization and the units now overtly refer to our research evidence supporting the points made and the strategies suggested (see distinguishing characteristic 5, p. 145). We believe that these changes have resulted in a more powerful version of the package.

As a result of the continuing industrial action by teacher unions throughout 1985, further evaluation studies by ourselves and others have been limited. However, in one small-scale study using the Mark IV version, pre- and post-course observational data were collected on five of some ten teachers attending a course, again taught by Susan Colmar. Although no control group data were available and the number of subjects was small, the gains made by this group of primary school teachers and their classes were impressive. On-task behaviour rose, on average, from 66 per cent to 84 per cent, that is, a mean gain of 18 per cent (range 5–30 per cent). The overall ratio of positive to negative teacher responses increased from about 1:1 to 3:1. All teachers sharply reduced their use of negative responses, especially to social behaviour. Positive responding was seen to improve, with markedly increased use of positives to social behaviour and/or increased use of positive REX responses to academic behaviour.

At the time of writing (January 1986) there are now nearly three hundred trained and registered tutors qualified to teach BATPACK Mark IV (not to mention those trained to use earlier versions). In addition, we have trained nearly one half of the educational psychologists in New Zealand and training courses in Australia are in prospect.

Concluding comments

Given our commitment to a rolling programme of research and

development, it is unlikely that BATPACK Mark IV will remain the final version for long. There is always room for further improvement. Having said this, however, we do believe BAT-PACK to be one of the most rigorously developed training packages (regardless of topic) yet produced in the UK. This is, perhaps, not saying much, since there is little tradition in British education for rigorous experimental evaluation of the effectiveness of educational methods and materials. (This is why we do not see real progress in education, only changes of fashion.) We are anxious to encourage more rigorous and more objective evaluations of the effectiveness of behavioural training programmes. We are particularly dismayed to see packages on 'general release' without adequate experimental evaluations of effectiveness having been carried out. It would be invidious to single out specific packages for criticism, since so few are supported by any hard evidence that they actually achieve their aims.

Murphy (1985) has recently provided a critique of BATPACK, describing the development and evaluation of BATPACK as 'a model for those involved in training human-service workers' (p.33) and endorsing the package as 'an exceptionally good program for training teachers in a number of key behavioural skills' (p.35). However, he rightly queries the steps taken so far to achieve maintenance and generalization of behaviour change in BATPACK-trained teachers, arguing that even more research is necessary to determine ways in which the school environment and organizational structure can be made to support the gains made. This will be especially important in the context of developing a version of BATPACK for use in secondary schools. Problems of scale and complexity will make more acute the sort of problems that can be overcome relatively easily in smaller, more intimate primary schools.

The need for a package like BATPACK is probably even greater in secondary schools than lower down in the system. But it appears that some of the techniques we have been advocating for infant, middle and junior schools will not work completely satisfactorily, without modification, for adolescents. The preliminary pilot studies we have conducted so far in secondary schools, using the Mark III (Primary) version, have confirmed this. Teachers were generally enthusiastic about the course and the methods advocated, but there was little, if any, evidence for appropriate behaviour change. This was certainly true of a BATPACK course taught by the second author in a secondary school in the West Midlands. In another unpublished study by Stokes (1985), carried out under our supervision in an ESN (M) school, changes similar to those we would expect in ordinary schools were evident in the primary but not in the secondary classes. We are encouraging secondary teachers to help us work out some appropriate modifications for this age-range. The prototype secondary version (BATSAC) currently undergoing trials involves the active participation of the children themselves in contracting and self-recording. The emphasis also tends to be more on academic and study skills than upon social behaviour *per se*. Preliminary results from studies employing the prototype secondary package are encouraging, showing evidence of appropriate behaviour change in both teachers and pupils.

As we have always maintained, BATPACK is deliberately limited to training in the general skills of everyday classroom management in mainstream schools, and teachers on our courses accept this. But we have been made aware of the need for a follow-up package. It is clear that an 'add-on module' concerned with more troublesome *individual* children would be greatly appreciated. This calls for a package that will teach an increased repertoire of more sophisticated behavioural skills. It is hoped to develop this in the future.

We have been able to achieve another of our aims more readily. This was to devise a course in behavioural methods for use on initial courses of training for teaching in colleges and universities (and for experienced teachers attending in-service courses for higher qualifications). The Positive Teaching Package has been developed for this purpose, based around our introductory text *Positive Teaching* (Wheldall and Merrett, 1984) and borrowing heavily from the methodology and content of BATPACK. Of course, immediate application of the skills is not usually possible (as is the case with BATPACK), but the course affords a more thorough theoretical grounding in the behavioural approach and includes training in behavioural observation, using our OPTIC schedule.

Although not being able to claim the achievement of all our aims, we can confidently report that it is possible to change teacher behaviour by means of an in-service school-based course. BATPACK has shown that skills-based *training*, carried out on-site, can yield major beneficial changes in teacher and class behaviour. Throughout this chapter, we have, unashamedly, referred to the need to 'train' teachers in behavioural methods. But, as Raths and Katz (1982) comment,

There appears to be a strong penchant among teacher educators to resist the notion that teachers are 'trained'. Training connotes to many an almost immoral, manipulative or unethical approach to students. Those who hold this view seem to believe that training a student to behave in a given way somehow transforms the content of the lesson and the student him/herself in a distorted or unnatural way.

This may well be the view of some teacher educators, but it is not, in our experience, shared by the teachers themselves who have to cope in the classroom. The feedback we have received has encouraged us in our belief that most teachers are caring, committed professionals who recognise their limitations and who are, in the main, only too keen to learn new, more relevant skills. Behavioural psychology has shown that it has something of practical value to offer to teachers.

References

Altman, K. I. and Linton, T. E. (1971), 'Operant conditioning in the classroom setting – a review of research', *Journal of Educational Research*, vol. 64, pp. 277–86.

Anderson. L. W. (1981), 'Instruction and time on task: a review with implications', *Journal of Curriculum Studies*, vol. 13, pp. 289–303.

Andrews, J. K. (1970), 'The results of a pilot program to train teachers in the classroom application of behavior modification techniques', *Journal of School Psychology*, vol. 8, pp. 37–42.

Becker, W. C. and Carnine, D. W. (1980), 'Direct instruction: an effective approach to educational intervention with the disadvantaged and low performers', in Lahey, B. and Kazdin, A. (eds) *Advances in Clinical Psychology*, Vol. 3 (New York: Plenum).

Bennett, N. and Blundell, D. (1983), 'Quantity and quality of work in rows and classroom groups', *Educational Psychology*, vol. 3, pp. 93–105.

Berger, M. (1979), 'Behaviour modification in education and professional practice: the dangers of a mindless technology', *Bulletin of the British Psychological Society*, vol. 32, pp. 418–19.

Berger, M. (1980), 'Behaviour modification and teacher education, *Psychology Teaching*, vol. 8, pp. 43–8.

Childs, J. (1982), 'In-Service training in the behavioural approach to teaching, unpublished MEd dissertation, University of Birmingham.

Clayton, T. (1983), 'The behaviour modification workshop: an antidote to mindless technology', *Behaviour Analysis*, vol. 4, no. 1, pp. 18–21.

Cooper, C. (1983), 'An evaluation of a school-based in-service training course in behavioural classroom management', unpublished MEd dissertation, University of Birmingham.

Cossairt, A., Hall, R. V. and Hopkins, B. L. (1973), 'The effects of experimenters' instructions, feedback, and praise on teacher praise and student attending behavior', *Journal of Applied Behavior Analysis*, vol. 6, pp. 89–100.

Cramer, C. and Hay, P. (1985), 'Initial experiences with BATPACK', *Behavioral Approaches with Children*, vol. 9, pp. 45–51.

Farrell, P. and Sugden, M. (1984), 'An evaluation of an EDY course in behavioural techniques for classroom assistants in a school for children with severe learning difficulties', *Educational Psychology*, vol. 4, pp. 185-98.

Firman, N. and Hastings, N. (1980), 'A teaching approach to managing classroom behaviour', unpublished manuscript, Bulmershe College of Higher Education, Reading.

Fisher, C. W. and Berliner, D. C. (eds) (1985) *Perspectives on Instructional Time* (New York: Longman).

Fontana, D. (1982), 'Review of *The Behaviourist in the Classroom: Aspects of Applied Behavioural Analysis in British Educational Contexts*', *British Psychological Society: Education Section Review*, vol. 6, no. 1, pp. 55-6.

Foxen, T. and McBrien, J. (1981), *Training Staff in Behavioural Methods: the EDY In-Service Course for Mental Handicap Practitioners (Trainee Workbook)* (Manchester: Manchester University Press).

Francis, H. (ed.) (1985), *Learning to Teach: Psychology in Teacher Training* (Basingstoke: Falmer Press).

Georgiades N. J. and Phillimore L. (1975), 'The myth of the hero-innovator and alternative strategies for organisational change', in Kiernan, C. C. and Woodford, F. P. (eds) *Behavioural Modification with the Severely Retarded.* (Amsterdam: Associated Scientific Publishers).

Greenwood, C. R., Hops, H., Delquadri, J. and Guild, J. (1974), 'Group contingencies for group consequences in class management: a further analysis', *Journal of Applied Behavior Analysis*, vol. 7, pp. 413-25.

Greenwood, C. R., Hops, H., Walker, H. M., Guild, J. J., Stokes, J., Young, R., Keleman, K. S. and Willardson, M. (1979), 'Standardised Classroom Management Program: social validation and replication studies in Utah and Oregon', *Journal of Applied Behavior Analysis*, vol. 12, pp. 235-53.

Hall, R. V. and Copeland, R. E. (1972), 'The responsive teaching model: a first step in shaping school personnel as behavior modification specialists', in Clark, F. W., Evans, D. R. and Hamerlynck, L. A. (eds) *Implementing Behavior Programs for Schools and Clinics* (Champaign, Ill.: Research Press).

Hall, R. V., Panyan, M., Rabon, D. and Broden, M. (1968), 'Instructing beginning teachers in reinforcement procedures which improve classroom control', *Journal of Applied Behavior Analysis*, vol. 1, pp. 315-22.

Harris, V. W., Bushell, D., Sherman, J. A. and Kane, J. F. (1975), 'Instructions, feedback, praise, bonus payments and teacher behavior', *Journal of Applied Behavior Analysis*, vol. 8, p. 462.

Jones, F. H. and Eimers, R. C. (1975), 'Role playing to train elementary teachers to use a classroom management skill package', *Journal of Applied Behavior Analysis*, vol. 8, pp. 421-33.

Jones, F. H., Fremouw, W. and Carples, S. (1977), 'Pyramid training of elementary school teachers to use a classroom management skill package', *Journal of Appied Behavior Analysis*, vol.10, pp. 239-53.

Kazdin, A. E. (1981), 'Behavior modification in education: contributions and limitations', *Developmental Review*, vol. 1, pp. 34-57.

Kazdin, A. E. and Moyer, W. (1976), 'Training teachers to use behaviour modification, in Yen, S. and McIntyre, R. W. (eds) *Teaching Behavior Modification* (Kalamazoo, Mich.: Behaviordelia).

Leach, D. J. and Raybould, E. C. (1977), *Learning and Behaviour Difficulties in School* (London: Open Books).

McBrien, J. and Foxen, T. (1981), *Training Staff in Behavioural Methods: the EDY In-Service Course for Mental Handicap Practitioners (Instructor's Handbook)* (Manchester: Manchester University Press).

McKeown, D., Adams, H. E. and Forehand, R. (1975), 'Generalisation to the classroom of the principles of behavior modification taught to teachers', *Behavior Research and Therapy*, vol. 13, pp. 85-92.

MacKrell, K. (1983), 'Teaching behaviour modification and behaviour analysis skills', *Behaviour Analysis*, vol. 4, no. 1, pp. 2-17.

Merrett F. (1981), 'Encouragement works better than punishment', *Behavioural Approaches with Children*, vol. 5, no. 3, pp. 1-34, and no. 4, pp. 17-26.

Merrett F. (1982), 'Encouragement works better than punishment', *Behavioural Approaches with Children*, vol. 6, no. 2, pp. 27-33.

Merrett F. (1984), 'Encouragement works better than punishment: a progress report of further studies', *Behavioural Approaches with Children*, vol. 8, pp. 66-75.

Merrett, F. (1986), 'What has psychology to offer the teacher?' *British Psychological Society Education Section Review*, vol. 10, pp. 20-23.

Merrett F. and Wheldall K. (1978), 'Playing the game: a behavioural approach to classroom management in the junior school', *Educational Review*, vol. 30, pp. 41-50.

Merrett F. and Wheldall K. (1982), 'Does teaching teachers about behaviour modification techniques improve their teaching performance in the classroom?', *Journal of Education for Teaching*, vol. 8, pp. 67-75.

Merrett F. and Wheldall K. (1984), 'Training teachers to use the behavioural approach to classroom management: a review, *Educational Psychology*, vol. 4, pp. 213-31.

Merrett F. and Wheldall K. (1986a), 'Natural rates of teacher approval and disapproval in British primary and middle school classrooms'. *British Journal of Educational Psychology*, (in press).

Merrett, F. and Wheldall, K. (1986b), 'Observing Pupils and Teachers In Classrooms (OPTIC): a behavioural observation schedule for use in schools', *Educational Psychology*, vol. 6, pp 57-70.

Milne, D. (1984), 'Skill evaluations of nurse training in behaviour therapy', *Behavioural Psychotherapy*, vol. 12, pp. 142-50.

Moss, G. and Childs, J. (1981), 'In-service training for teachers in behavioural psychology: problems of implementation', in Wheldall, K. (ed.) *The Behaviourist in the Classroom: Aspects of Applied Behavioural Analysis in British Educational Contexts* (Birmingham: Educational Review Publications).

Murphy, G. C. (1985), 'Designing an organisational environment supportive of in-service training programs: a comment on Wheldall and Merrett', *Behaviour Change*, vol. 2, pp. 33-5.

Poteet, J. A. (1973), *Behaviour Modification - A Practical Guide for Teachers* (London: Unibooks).

Raths, J. D. and Katz, L. (1982), 'The best of intentions for the education of teachers', *Journal of Education for Teaching*, vol. 8, pp. 275-83.

Raymond, J. (1980), 'Workshop on behaviour modification', *Links*, vol. 6, no. 1, pp. 13-17.

Riding, R. J. and Wheldall, K. (1981), 'Effective educational research', *Educational Psychology*, vol. 1, pp. 5-11.

Ringer, V. M. J. (1973), 'The use of a 'token helper' in the management of classroom behaviour problems and in teacher training', *Journal of Applied Behavior Analysis*, vol. 6, pp. 671-77.

Robinson, V. and Swanton, C. (1980), 'The generalization of behavioural teacher training', *Review of Educational Research*, vol. 50, pp. 486-98.

Rosenfield, S. (1979), 'Introducing behaviour modification techniques to teachers', *Exceptional Children*, vol. 45, pp. 334-9.

Rosenshine, B. B. and Berliner, D. C. (1978), 'Academic engaged time', *British Journal of Teacher Education*, vol. 4, pp. 3-17.

Sanders, M. R. (1978), 'Behavioural self-control with children and adolescents: a review and critical analysis of educational applications', *The Exceptional Child*, vol. 25, pp. 83-103.

Saudargas, R. A. (1972), 'Setting criterion rates of teacher praise: the effects of video-tape feedback, in Semb, G. (ed.) *Behavior Analysis and Education* (Lawrence, Kansas: University of Kansas Press).

Stokes, D. (1985), 'Behavioural observations of a single teacher teaching mathematics to three different classes in a secondary school', *Behavioural Approaches with Children*, vol. 9, pp. 52-7.

Thomas, J. D. and Adams, M. A. (1971), 'Problems in teacher use of selected behaviour modification techniques in the classroom', *New Zealand Journal of Educational Studies*, vol. 6, pp. 151-65.

Topping, K. and Brindle, P. (1979), 'Evaluation of in-service courses', *British Journal of In-service Education*, vol. 5, pp. 49-51.

Vargas, J. S. (1977), *Behavioral Psychology for Teachers* (New York: Harper & Row).

Walker, C., Allsop, N. and Ross, R. (1986), 'BATPACK - an evaluative study', *Behavioural Approaches with Children*, vol. 10, pp. 13-21.

Wheldall, K. (1981), 'A before C or the use of behavioural ecology in classroom management', in Gurney, P. (ed.), *Behaviour Modification in Education*, Perspectives No. 5 (Exeter: School of Education, University of Exeter).

Wheldall, K. and Congreve, S. (1980), 'Attitudes of British teachers towards behaviour modification', Educational Review, vol. 32, pp. 53 - 65.

Wheldall, K. and Merrett, F. (1984), *Positive Teaching: The Behavioural Approach* (London: Allen & Unwin).

Wheldall, K. and Merrett, F. (1985), *The Behavioural Approach to Teaching Package* (BATPACK) (Birmingham: Positive Products).

Wheldall K., Merrett F. and Borg, M. (1985), 'The Behavioural Approach to Teaching Package (BATPACK); an experimental evaluation', *British Journal of Educational Psychology*, vol. 55, pp. 65–75.

Wheldall, K., Merrett, F. and Glynn, T. (1986), *Behaviour Analysis in Educational Psychology* (London: Croom Helm in association with Positive Products).

Wheldall, K., Merrett, F., Worsley, M., Colmar, S. and Parry, R. (1986), 'Evaluating effectiveness: a case study evaluation of the Behavioural Approach to Teaching Package (BATPACK)', *Educational and Child Psychology*, vol. 3, pp. 33–44.

Wolff, D. and Rennie, E. (1977), 'Children with special needs: a workshop on teacher–child interaction', course report and evaluation to the Directorate of Educational Services, Kirklees Metropolitan Council.

Woods, P. A. and Cullen, C. (1983), 'Determinants of staff behaviour in long-term care', *Behavioural Psychotherapy*, vol. 11, pp. 4–17.

Yule, W., Berger, M. and Wigley, V. (1977), 'The teacher–child interaction programme', *British Association for Behavioural Psychotherapy Bulletin*, vol. 5, no. 3, pp. 42–7.

Zimmerman, J., Zimmerman, E., Rider, S. L., Smith, A. L. and Dinn, R. (1971), 'Doing your own thing with precision: the essence of behavior management in the classroom', *Educational Technology*, vol. 11, no. 4, pp. 26–32.

8

Behaviour Modification: Towards an Ethical Appraisal

ROBERT DEARDEN

It may be that the term 'behaviour modification' should be dropped and some more neutral-sounding term such as a 'behavioural approach' should be adopted. That would also be to shed some of the theoretical baggage that came from the Skinnerian origins of the movement. But, by the same token, it would become difficult to see how anything more was being discussed than the intelligent use of ordinary encouragement and discouragement. Certainly, from the point of view of philosophy of education, what is of most interest in the behavioural movement, however it is styled, is its concept of 'behaviour' itself. And preoccupation with behaviour, as opposed, say, to intention, desire or belief, can be understood only in terms of the origins of the approach and its pretensions to being a new science. In any event, a close scrutiny of the concept of behaviour is an indispensable preliminary to an ethical appraisal of the movement.

The concept of behaviour

According to B. F. Skinner, from whom behaviour modifiers generally acknowledge taking their inspiration, 'mental life and the world in which it is lived are inventions' (Skinner, 1974, p. 104). It is just this kind of detachment of physical behaviour from a mental world of belief, desire, trying, imagination, experience, attention and, in general, of understanding, that makes so necessary a preliminary inquiry into the concept of behaviour that is being taken for granted. Of course, it may immediately be said that the existence of such 'mentalistic' features is not denied. What is denied is that they have any important explanatory significance, or that they make much difference to behaviour. Yet, from an ethical point of view, the presence or absence of certain beliefs, desires or intentions makes a very great difference indeed. Legally, it could make the difference between whether you went to prison or not.

In the first place, it is clear that the same 'behavioural topography' can carry important different and even incompatible mentalistic descriptions. For example, suppose that someone's observable movements are to drive along a stretch of road at fifty miles an hour. What is he doing? He may be carefully observing or deliberately breaking a speed limit. He may be escaping from a crime or going to help someone. He may be thoughtfully conserving petrol or callously disregarding the victim of an accident. These fuller stories are of great ethical and also of legal significance. The different versions do not all come to the same thing.

It may be said that these differences can be accommodated by the behaviourist simply by looking at the driver's subsequent behaviour, when different topographies will emerge. But which of the descriptions is true is already an objective matter of fact, regardless of what the driver does subsequently. If in the next moment a meteorite fell on him and thus precluded any subsequent observations, the alternative mentalistic descriptions would nevertheless still each carry an objective truth-value (true or false). How we can find out whether something is true is a different question from what it is for it to be true.

My point is that there is more to behaviour than its topographical configuration. No doubt Skinner would try to meet this point by saying that the same 'topography' (his term) can be controlled by different contingencies of reinforcement. Thus a rat may press a lever on two occasions (same topography), though in the one case to obtain food when hungry and in the other case to obtain water when thirsty (Skinner, 1974, p. 90). Differences of 'meaning' can therefore be accommodated without reference to anything so mysterious and elusive as mind.

Although some critics would take Skinner to task here for supposing there to be a close analogy between rats and people, ethologists might very well wish to question whether justice has been done even to rats. What is the force of the phrase 'to obtain' food or water, for example? Attempting to cope with the important differences that there can be in behaviour that is topographically the same by referring to different contingencies of reinforcement shifts the problem elsewhere, but it does not solve it. Mentalistic explanations will reappear if we ask how environmental features can mean anything to us, how they can be selectively attended to and can be intelligently connected with what they are supposed to reinforce.

To approach the same difficulty from the opposite direction, consider what it means for two people to do the same thing. Initial plausibility may be given to a behaviourist account of this sameness, if we pick some example such as a child copying a teacher writing the letter 'a', for here there is an obvious topographical likeness. But take another case. Headteachers are often currently worried by the falling number of children on their school rolls. Two head teachers might 'do the same thing' in that they both actively set about making their schools more secure in this respect. Yet one of them does this by issuing to parents what he hopes is an attractive prospectus, while the other opens a nursery class. Where two pieces of behaviour are as topographically different as these are, reference must be made to the guiding intentions to bring out the important respects in which the behaviour is the same. Thus, whether we consider how topographically very different behaviour can yet be the same (the head teachers), or whether we consider how behaviour that is topographically the same can yet be very different (the drivers), in either case reference needs to be made to 'mentalistic' features if the behaviour is to be at all adequately characterized.

An absurd consequence of ignoring the understanding that accompanies and indeed essentially constitutes human behaviour is evident in Poteet's purportedly 'clever and useful' definition of 'out-of-seat behaviour'. Backed by references to suitable authorities, he defines this posterior irregularity as follows: 'the seat portion of the child's body is not in contact with any portion of the seat of the child's chair' (Poteet, 1973, p.7). The educational context, of course, is that of children improperly leaving their work to wander round the classroom. But, in that context, the behavioural definition is absurd. The spatial location of the child's bottom is not the point. If the child gets up to sharpen a pencil, or to pick up something that has fallen, or to show respect to a visitor, or to leave the room with permission, then all is well. It is only out-of-seat behaviour that the child knows to be in breach of a classroom rule that needs to be 'modified'. Only absurdity results from trying to dispense with the child's own recognition of what is appropriate behaviour. (This is elaborated in Wilson, 1971.)

Similar absurdities follow from misconceived attempts to specify regular laws of behaviour modification. For example, if a child becomes a nuisance by putting up his hand to answer a question when he does not in fact know the answer, it may sometimes be good advice simply to ignore his hand. But this cannot be some sort of law, since on a particular occasion it may be far more effective to hear the ridiculous answer, safe. in the knowledge that its reception by the rest of the class will be a strong discouragement to that child for the future. Again, it may be useful to praise a child in such a way that he may serve as a model, but on a particular occasion this may be so counter-productive that it merely embarrasses the praised child and produces detestation rather than modelling in the others. How behaviour is understood makes a very great difference indeed.

Consider next the nature of the connection between the occurrence of some reinforcing environmental contingency and the behaviour that it is to reinforce. How is that connection to be explained without reference to mind? A child enters a classroom, walks to his place, takes out various materials and starts working, and then the teacher looks at him and says 'very good'. What is being reinforced? Is it his punctuality, his appearance, his lack of clumsiness this time, his promptness in settling down, his choice of place, his silence ... and so on indefinitely? Whatever the problems may be with pigeons, with human beings the solution here is to convey to the child an understanding of just what it is for which he is being commended. Human interaction occurs within a web of shared understandings.

And how is the choice of the reinforcer to be made? If a child gets a sum right, might just anything be reinforcing, so that you have no alternative but to try many things, for example dusting the ceiling of the storeroom, blowing your nose, closing a window ... until something effective is eventually hit upon? Once again, we are driven to such mentalistic terms as a knowledge of people's desires and satisfactions. What those are and the range of possibilities that will occur to us will very much reflect a particular culture. Unconscious of this relativity, many behaviour modifiers take for granted as universally valid the model of a commercial transaction to guide their perception here. Other possibilities, such as an appeal to age-status, the enjoyment of skill mastery and respect for a proper instruction are often conspicuously absent. To the inadequacy of a topographical conception of behaviour is thus added poverty of imagination regarding what might be reinforcing and inexplicability of connection between reinforcer and reinforced.

One final perplexity regarding the behaviour modifier's concept of behaviour deserves mention. Teachers commonly draw an important distinction between a child's behaviour and his cognitive learning and, though we might quarrel with this distinction, there is point in it. The point can be brought out if we consider the problem that Skinner raises but does not solve under the heading 'the problem of the first instance', (Skinner, 1968, p. 206). Talk of reinforcing, of affecting the probability of recurrence or of shaping an emitted behaviour all assume that we do already have some continuing behaviour of the relevant kind to encourage or discourage. Often this assumption is entirely justified, especially with the troublesome behaviour that looms so exclusively large in the literature, such as aggression, temper, calling out, swearing and so on. But a large part of ordinary schooling is concerned to develop, by such means as explanation and instruction, an understanding of quite new topics and subject matters, such as chemical reactions, the fall of Rome, co-ordinate geometry, the teachings of some religion, economic terms of trade, delta formation and the nutritional values of food. In relation to topics and subject matters such as these, it is grossly inadequate to say that 'teaching is simply the arrangement of contingencies of reinforcement' (ibid., p. 5), as if in each case spontaneously emitted behaviour atoms needed only to be assembled into a repertoire of appropriate behavioural molecular topographies.

On the contrary, the learner must understand the context to be one of learning, with appropriately focused attention and attempts being made to get things right. A theory of cognitive learning is needed. And this will have as one of its very important determinants of sequence the nature of the subject matter being taught. A true understanding of the methods of inquiry, truth-criteria, working capital and standards of excellence of the subject will need to be developed. There will, of course, be a motivational side to this, but neither behavioural modelling nor behaviour shaping amount to giving such an understanding and we should wait forever for appropriate first instances even on the behavioural view. Grasping the reason why no even number except two can be prime is not an aspect of learning to behave yourself. There is point in the ordinary distinction between behaviour and cognitive learning.

In general, what I wish to suggest is this. Human behaviour does indeed present a certain 'topography' and it is indeed connected with environmental contingencies of reinforcement. But its nature and these connections are unintelligible without reference to the accompanying understanding. What someone is doing and why he is doing it are unintelligible without reference to certain of his beliefs, desires, intentions, experiences, imaginings, attitudes, sentiments or, in general, his understanding. To see what someone is doing and why he is doing it is therefore a work of constructive interpretation. Within a shared cultural stock of knowledge, rules, institutions, practices, self-images and styles, such interpretation becomes even easy and the behaviour of others may acquire such transparency of meaning that the presence of interpretation is hidden from us by familiarity.

An acquaintance with anthropology can restore a recognition of the place of such constructive interpretation here. For example, what is one to make of a man seated by a path with a chick held between his toes, who rocks backward and forward all the while muttering? Being unfamiliar with Azande culture, the behaviour modifier, like anyone else, will be mystified about what he confronts and about what reinforcers are operating. And, even within our own society, the variety of cultures and sub-cultures, not to mention insincerity, deception and self-deception, regularly make the behaviour of others opaque to us in ways that differ only in degree from that of the Azande witchdoctor.

Human interaction occurs within a web of shared understandings. We more or less readily interpret one another's behaviour in the light of these shared understandings. The physical topography presented by our behaviour has its place in this interpretation. But we do not first assemble hard behavioural data and then proceed by shaky inference to mentalistic speculations of no consequence. On the contrary, our tentative interpretations may guide us to those topographical bits to notice and to those patterns we shall be disposed to recognize.

It is an unfortunate historical contingency that the concerns of behaviour modifiers have arisen from Skinnerian behaviourism, since this theory in turn arose from others shaped by reaction to introspectionist psychology. This has made it seem to behaviour modifiers that, if they depart from talk of behavioural topographies such as 'out-of-seat behaviour', then they will be lost in a hidden and subjective world of private sensations or be groping in the darkness for the hidden machinery of psychoanalytic explanation. Given that restricted choice, it is not surprising that they go for topographies.

But I have been arguing that within a culture there exists such a degree of shared understanding that the meaning of behaviour is frequently public enough without its having to be misconceived as something merely topographical. Indeed, shrewd judges of other people may understand them better than those people understand themselves. I do not wish to deny that the meaning of behaviour is often public. It is the way in which it is public and the kind of understanding presupposed by this publicity that I have been trying to elucidate.

Ethical considerations

There are those who like to think that behaviour modification is an ethically neutral technology. In this connection, Skinner himself says that 'no theory changes what it is a theory about' (Skinner, 1972, p. 215). But where we are dealing with a theory of human nature this is just not true. People are significantly changed by the pictures that they form of themselves and that others form of them. The pictures embodied in educational practices, in different religions and in political and economic theories are themselves at least partially explanatory of why people regard themselves in the ways that they do, for example as autonomous, as immortal souls seeking salvation, as part of a socialist brotherhood working for the common good, as engaged in individualistic economic competition and so on. The same is true of psychological theories of human nature, for example 'Freudian analysis creates a Freudian patient' (Ingleby, 1972, p. 79). What people do and what they find reinforcing will be conceptually connected with these differing theories. With people, belief is apt to beget reality, though no doubt there are limits to such social malleability.

If we start with some picture such as that of shaping a pigeon's walk by reinforcing its chance movements, and we then move from that to people, a likely effect on human behaviour modification programmes will be for them to exhibit a certain manipulative remoteness and for them to deny the significance or even the existence of anything other than movement topographies. The ripples from dropping this particular stone into the educational pond have by now spread throughout the system, with some grossly distorting results. For example, objectives may have to be specified in behavioural terms, with a catastrophic narrowing as the result and with teachers 'teaching for the test'. (This is discussed more fully in Dearden (1976) and Dearden (1979).)

The very term 'technology' invites a pseudo-scientific fantasy of power and a pretentiousness of language. Suppose that a dairy hits on a scheme to boost milk sales to housewives in a new way. A behaviour modifier might report this as follows: 'A sector of female Ss with an average baseline consumption of 2.3 boviunits regarded delivery operatives as significant others sufficiently to select them as change agents having the Ss as targets. It has been shown that edible rewards are positively reinforcing (Smith, 1969; Brown, 1970; Robinson *et al.*, 1971) ...' The housewives have become remote things at whom some powerful manipulative offensive is to be launched. The element of fantasy, on the other hand, relates not only to overestimates of effectiveness (which are sometimes admitted) but also to ignoring the fact that there must already be a considerable measure of social control in operation before the behaviour modification game can be played.

And yet it is not entirely fair to make these criticisms of behaviour modification without qualification. Much justified criticism would be directed more appropriately at particular behaviour modifiers for the slant that their own personal attitudes, values and humanity (or the lack of it) give to these techniques. Examples could be cited from special education, where behaviour modification has ousted mystification and pretentious lab-coated authority and replaced it by co-operation with parents and policies based on shared understanding. Just as people drive their cars, for good or ill, in much the same way as they live generally (aggressively, considerately, competitively, impulsively, cautiously, etc.) so too will the perspective from which behaviour modification is viewed reflect the modifier himself. He may be a person of broad humanitarian sympathies or perhaps, at the other extreme, a human cripple who would quite naturally think of personal relationships in terms of mechanical engineering or animal training. And the ambiguity in the notion of 'behaviour', which runs right through behaviour modification, can mislead people of very different perspectives here into supposing that they are all really part of one and the same movement. The case is quite parallel to the apparent, but only apparent, sameness of principle as between the political left and right regarding 'equality of educational opportunity'.

Suppose that a more 'mentalistic' concept of behaviour is adopted and reference to beliefs, desires, intentions, experience and understanding is allowed to be in order, how might an ethical appraisal of behaviour modification proceed then? One obvious form that it might take is to look at the ends that the various techniques are used to serve. Skinner, for example, is openly hostile to the central liberal value of autonomy, although he grossly misunderstands it. In place of autonomy we are offered survival. But then it would be the manner of the surviving that mattered and, if we turned to *Walden Two* (Skinner, 1948) for a fuller and more detailed picture of what was intended, we should find a simple hedonism in which everyone gets what he wants because the behaviour managers have adjusted wants to what people are in fact going to get (ibid, chapter 32). Skinner calls that condition one of freedom and happiness.

One way in which Skinner fudges the issue is by pretending that the controllers are as much affected as are the controlled: 'the relation between controller and controlled is reciprocal' (Skinner,

1972, p. 169). The grain of truth in this is that in any project there will be objective conditions for success to which the agent has to submit. For example, you cannot travel from A to B without taking time and using energy, no matter how powerful you are. But there is also the question of who gets what he wants, whose is the initiative and whose intentions are being carried out. Generally speaking, behaviour modifiers in education have addressed themselves to teachers in their dealings with children. Would it make no difference if, instead, they addressed themselves to administrators at local or national level in their dealings with teachers?

It would be thoroughly in keeping with the 'technology' power fantasy for behaviour modifiers to express dismissive impatience with the problems of choosing and balancing educational ends. But, if ends do conflict, as indeed they do, then there is no alternative to the exercise of judgement in balancing one against another. Questions will regularly need to be asked, such as whether an adequate range of ends is envisaged, whose interest is at stake and how far consent is necessary.

If justifiable ends are being pursued, is it then simply a matter of choosing the most effective means, in which case the behaviour modifier's preoccupation with technique might be given full play? Not quite, for ends may not justify means. If we have good political ends, may we use torture and terrorism to achieve them? If we have good educational ends, may we use electro-convulsive shock, bellow down a megaphone at a child standing next to us, medicate perhaps a million 'hyperactive' children, or subject someone to a programme of sustained and vicious verbal abuse, to choose four actual examples from the field?

There is an ethical debate here, between those who think that certain values must be adhered to regardless of the consequences and those who think that circumstances and consequences may justify exceptions to otherwise binding principles. The position that we take concerning objectionable means to good ends will therefore reflect an option and not a necessity. However, two general points can perhaps be validly made about means and ends in behaviour modification programmes.

First, in education the means that may be chosen are typically constrained by the ends pursued. If a certain kind of understanding is aimed at, then the means chosen must be compatible with the emergence of such an end-state. This is why a theory of cognitive learning must be determined at least in part by the nature of the subject matter or topic to be learned (see Sockett, 1972). The 'reinforcers' typically envisaged are extrinsic to such ends and, therefore, at best what we shall then be offered is a theory that explains how you can motivate learning but not what (cognitive) learning is. But, secondly, it is not entirely satisfactory to concentrate on extrinsic motivation if we are concerned to educate. Behaviour modifiers do sometimes recognize this and speak of a transition from extrinsic to intrinsic motivation when the stage-managed reinforcers are withdrawn. But the nature of this transition is invariably left thoroughly obscure, probably because it would reintroduce such despised 'mentalistic' concepts as satisfaction, enjoyment, pleasure, and a sense of mastery (see Clark, 1979).

Whether the concern is with ends or means, a major presupposition in both cases would be that it is the child who has to change, and that presupposition may in particular circumstances be quite unjustified. What is really called for may be a political fight for more resources, or changes in the teachers, or a review of the curriculum, or an institutional re-organization. In this way, behaviour modification programmes may be as open to criticism as are some forms of pastoral care, for being strategies of defensive conservatism and hence politically biased or ideologically committed. Certainly it is to oversell behaviour modification to present it as the single answer to all of the educational ills that have caught the headlines in recent years.

Conclusions

In conclusion, I would like to identify some features of merit in the behaviour modification movement. My primary criticism has been the philosophically familiar one that there is a central and damaging confusion about what 'behaviour' is. I have also suggested that more specific criticisms should distinguish between essential deficiencies of the theory and contingent deficiencies of a particular behaviour modifier as a person. But together with these deficiencies come some things of value too. There are some pertinent criticisms of traditional approaches to motivation, such as that reinforcement is characteristically too exclusively negative, too infrequent and often too long delayed, as when a few negative criticisms are all that is to be found on an essay returned six months after it was handed in. Furthermore, this movement is helping to restore classroom management to a place of proper importance in teacher training. And frustrated or demoralized teachers, who face nothing but disruption and non-cooperation in their classes, are at least being made to feel that someone has seen their plight and cares. In that last sad situation, it nevertheless has to be said that some care still needs to be exercised in choosing one's friends.

References

Clark, C. (1979), 'Education and behaviour modification', *Journal of Philosophy of Education*, vol. 13, pp. 73–81.

Dearden, R. F. (1976), *Problems in Primary Education* (London: Routledge & Kegan Paul).

Dearden, R. F. (1979), 'The assessment of learning', *British Journal of Educational Studies*, vol. 27, pp. 111–24.

Ingleby, D. (1972), 'Ideology and the human sciences', in Pateman, D. (ed.) *Counter Course* (Harmondsworth: Penguin).

Poteet, J. A. (1973), *Behaviour Modification: A Practical Guide for Teachers* (London: University of London Press).

Skinner, B. F. (1948), *Walden Two* (New York: Macmillan).

Skinner, B. F. (1968), *The Technology of Teaching* (New York: Appleton–Century–Crofts).

Skinner, B. F. (1972), *Beyond Freedom and Dignity* (London: Jonathan Cape).

Skinner, B. F. (1974), *About Behaviourism* (London: Jonathan Cape).

Sockett, H. (1972), 'Curriculum aims and objectives', *Proceedings of the Philosophy of Education Society*, vol. 6, pp. 30–61.

Wilson, P. S. (1971), *Interest and Discipline in Education* (London: Routledge & Kegan Paul).

9

Explanations and the Behavioural Approach in Teaching

NIGEL HASTINGS and JOSHUA SCHWIESO

Several years ago we carried out a survey of initial teacher training courses, the results from which suggested that less than half of the teachers in training in 1978 would have encountered even the slightest mention of behaviour modification in their one, three or four years of training (Schwieso and Hastings, 1981). Since then the picture has surely changed. If the spate of books written for teachers on the subject is anything to go by, we suspect that the attention paid to behaviour modification in both initial and in-service teacher education has increased considerably.

Our 1978 survey sought to discover not only the extent to which behaviour modification was taught but also how it was taught. Was it presented as a last resort, as an example of American educational excess, as a subversive form of social control, as a general framework for considering and managing classroom behaviour, or what? From the limited response we received the answer was clear. As one respondent expressed it, 'Behaviour modification techniques are discussed to illustrate the extension of models of conditioning in educational practice'. While books and courses may introduce behaviour modification in any one of a variety of contexts, such as classroom management, coping with behaviour problems or the education of children with special needs, the explicit linking of behaviour modification to behaviourism, conditioning or learning theory is almost universal. For O'Leary and O'Leary (1977), their book, *Classroom Management*, might 'be used with basic experimental texts utilizing an operant learning framework since it well exemplifies many of the operant principles' (p. xvi). For Poteet (1973), whose book *Behaviour Modification: A Practical Guide for Teachers* was among the earliest on the British market, behaviour modification is 'the application of knowledge from experimental psychology with animals applied to humans and mixed up with a lot of scientifically stated common sense' (p.23). Common sense is not enough, however, as: 'A thorough knowledge of the theory is necessary in order for us to be able to decide how we, as teachers, are to behave when we are dealing with the target student' (ibid, p.22). For Docking (1980) also, 'The techniques are derived from the learning theory developed and applied to teaching by B. F. Skinner' (p.145). Saunders (1979) sees the origins slightly differently: 'As a clinical strategy it derives from social learning theory ...' (p.66). The clearest statement of the general proposition is perhaps made by Rettig and Paulson:

Behaviour modification represents the application of the principles of learning theory to actual, everyday-life problems. These learning principles have been derived from and tested in psychological research during the past seventy-five years. Pavlov, Thorndike, Watson, Guthrie, Hull and especially B. F. Skinner are learning theorists who have contributed greatly to our understanding of how people learn (Rettig and Paulson, 1975, p. 9).

Although one or two recent British books written for teachers make no explicit reference to the origins of behaviour modification (e.g. Harrop, 1983; Wheldall and Merrett, 1984), it is generally the case that behaviour modification is described, by friend and foe alike, as having a close historical and logical relationship to behaviourist accounts of learning. In short, behaviour modification is presented as the dependent offspring of behaviourism. This association of behaviour modification and behaviourism is a practice that seems to us to be widespread, wrong and unnecessary. In the following pages we aim to explain why we believe this and to offer an alternative way of conceptualizing behaviour modification.

Behaviour modification and behaviourism

Readers of these DIY books might form the impression that Watson, Pavlov, Thorndike, Guthrie, Hull and Skinner all worked on, and contributed to, the development of one coherent theory, and that behaviour modification, being one outcome of the collective endeavours of these psychologists, can only be understood and employed within the terms of this theory. Such a view would be mistaken. The idea that behaviourism is a unity is simply wrong: any two of these psychologists would disagree almost as much with each other as with any non-behaviourist. To examine the differences between behaviourists it is helpful to use Mace's (1949) distinction between methodological behaviourism and metaphysical behaviourism. Methodological behaviourism embodies the idea that, in the end, psychology must deal with the observable, as must any science. Whatever we think about thought, it cannot be directly studied and hypotheses about thinking must be tested by reference to the observable manifestations of thought, in other words, behaviour. Just as a teacher has to infer a child's understanding of a concept from his or her answers to questions or from his or her approach to a new problem, so psychology must test out ideas about what goes on 'inside' by examining what happens 'outside'. In this methodological sense, most contemporary psychologists are behaviourists. As Blackman points out:

Methodological behaviourism characterised all the competitors in the noisy battles between the opposing learning theories that dominated experimental psychology in the 1930s and 1940s, for Guthrie, Tolman, Hull and Skinner all constructed their interpretative accounts or theories on detailed studies of *behaviour*. The same is largely true of contemporary psychology. (Blackman, 1984, p. 4).

However, even though 'we are all behaviourists now' in this methodological sense, that is about as far as such general agreement extends, for, as Blackman continues, 'the data obtained from this methodological behaviourism are of course open to interpretation in many different ways' (ibid).

Metaphysical behaviourism, however, would not allow that the data of behaviour are open to interpretations that in any way involve unobservable states – such as thoughts, intentions or understanding. For metaphysical behaviourism denies the existence of mental life. It is, as Eysenck (1972) expresses it, 'little but a disguise for a very ancient philosophical belief, namely old-fashioned materialism' (p.288). So, while methodological behaviourism urges that psychology must deal with the observable, even as a means of studying such non-observables as reasoning and attention, metaphysical behaviourism argues that that which is not observable does not exist; there is nothing but neural activity and behaviour; there is no mind; there are no intentions. Such a view sounds quite bizarre to the layman, and it seems fairly odd to most psychologists, too. Watson, however, wandered up this relatively sterile avenue in some of his writing, urging consideration of thought as simply very quiet speech. Skinner's admiration for Watson has led him, too, a little way in this direction, with the result that his views on the nature of mental life are often confusing and sometimes untenable. As Robert Dearden has pointed out in the preceding chapter, when Skinner writes, 'mental life and the world in which it is lived are inventions' (Skinner, 1974, p.104), it is difficult not to interpret him as expressing a metaphysical behaviourist view, even though it is not actually the existence of mental life, so much as its role in human affairs, that Skinner disputes.

Although behaviour modification necessitates methodological behaviourism, does it entail metaphysical behaviourist views about mental states? We believe not, but what do the writers of DIY books make of it all? Here, we have to speculate a little, but it is our guess that few, if any, authors of these books actually believe that their own thoughts have no role in their behaviour, yet the way in which they write suggests that they might hold this view. Accounting for behaviour changing under conditions of reward and punishment is one area in which the concern to stick to the methodological principle of dealing with the observable gets confused with the metaphysical principle of dealing *only* with the observable, and thus results in most tortuous language. For example, most of these books define reinforcement as any event that follows a behaviour and results in an increase in the frequency of that behaviour occurring. In other words, if we give children a smile each time they ask for something without shouting and child A's frequency of 'asking without shouting' increases while B's does not, then the smile has been a 'reinforcer' for child A and not for B.

This is fine as a stipulative definition. What then tends to happen, however, is that the reinforcing smile is held to be the *explanation* for the behaviour change, so it is said that child A's 'asking without shouting' increased *because* it was reinforced. This argument is initially appealing, as it appears that we have explained the behaviour change entirely without reference to internal states. We have dealt only with the observable. But is this an explanation? Not really, because reinforcement is defined in terms of an increase in behaviour and is then held to cause that increase in behaviour. The trouble is that it is never defined independently of the changes for which it is held to be responsible. As Clark (1979) puts it, 'What one needs is some criterion for identifying a reinforcer which is logically independent of what it is supposed to cause' (p.75). Without this we are left with the tautological proposition that 'that-which-increases-behaviour increases behaviour', which is much like saying, 'things-which-float-on-water float on water'. Both statements are true, but neither gets us very far in understanding the way things work.

Now this sort of problem of defining reinforcement in terms of the effects it is held to cause is not exclusive to our DIY authors. It bedevils the writing of many. Blackman (1984), for instance, writes, 'Radical behaviourists *define* reinforcers and punishers in terms of their effects on behaviour ...' (p.5), but six lines later he writes, 'the concepts of reinforcement and punishment, supported as they are by empirical investigations of their effects ...' (ibid). Here again, reinforcement is defined in terms of behaviour change, which it is subsequently held to cause. Definitions are not the same as explanations.

There is reason to believe that it is simply not possible to explain most human learning or behaviour change without reference to perceptions, understandings, expectations and so on. To return to our two children A and B, an explanation for why child A's behaviour changed and B's did not seems difficult to construct without some reference to internal states – to the children's perceptions, understandings, feelings and so on. Indeed, what a person believes is going on *is* demonstrably related to the way in which he behaves. Extinction of an operant, for instance, is affected by the subjects' interpretations of the cause of an outcome. Rotter (1966) has demonstrated that when (human) subjects believe that the rate of reward delivery has been dependent on their own skill at a task, extinction is faster after a 50 per cent reward condition than after continuous reinforcement. This is the reverse of what is usually predicted on the basis of the hypothesized relationship between reward schedules and extinction. In aversion therapy, if the person perceives an association between a stimulus and the aversive stimulus, contingency is not always necessary. As reported by Meichenbaum (1976), aversion therapy can work as well with *non-contingent* shock as when the shock is contingent on the inappropriate stimulus or behaviour. Brewer (1974) goes so far as to conclude that there is no evidence of conditioning of adult humans without consciousness of the S–R relationship while it has been suggested more recently (Macintosh, 1984) that the learning of animals can only be explained by reference to their understanding.

Now here we seem to have grounds for total confusion! It seems that behaviour modification developed from the work undertaken within psychology, in the interwar years, on the study of learning. It is described by many as the application of the knowledge and theory generated in those years. The procedures of behaviour modification are evidently extremely successful in the work of many in the 'social professions' of teaching, social work, child care, etc., yet it now appears that the very theory that behaviour modification embodies, and of which it is held to be 'the application', is not only under question but is actually thought to be wrong by apparently increasing numbers of psychologists. Where does this leave behaviour modification? Is it the application of discredited or mistaken theoretical principles?

Here we need to pause for a moment or two in order to consider a little more carefully the relationship between practices and theories. Theories are employed within scientific disciplines in order to do several things. Any academic discipline needs explanatory theories, which can unify current knowledge within the subject, provide insight into the basic mechanisms generating the observed phenomena and give direction to fresh research. In psychology, theories are directed towards explaining human behaviour, and any general psychological theory must be able to account for any human behaviour. Now, in the last resort, behaviour modification is a thing, or a set of things, that people do; it is a sub-set of human behaviour, just as is train-driving, shopping or teaching, and each must be explicable by any theory that claims to explain human behaviour. Consequently, any theory that is represented as being able to explain human behaviour must be able to explain what 'behaviour modifiers' do and to explain why this has whatever effects it does have on others. Explaining why behaviour modification procedures work, when they do, is therefore not the prerogative of one particular approach. The only sense in which there can be said to be 'the theory of behaviour modification' is that there is a tendency for writers, and particularly, as Clark (1979) points out, for writers of do-it-yourself books for teachers, to couch their accounts of behaviour modification procedures within a causal theory and to proclaim such procedures as exemplifying behaviouristic learning theory. Were it the case that any one theory did provide a more adequate explanation of behaviour modification than any other theory, then there would be a *de facto* but not an *a priori* case for calling it 'the theory of behaviour modification'. As it is, however, there is no one theory that, by general agreement, does offer an adequate explanation.

Alternative (cognitive) theories for the explanation of behavioural change are emerging. Bandura (1977) has advanced a theory of 'self-efficacy', which recognizes that a person's cognitive and affective states are important in the regulation of behaviour, but that changes in these internal states, leading subsequently to changes in behaviour, are often best initiated by successful action. Even so, it is the person's own evaluation of the outcomes of his actions or of other sources of information, such as vicarious experience, verbal persuasion and physiological states, rather than the information *per se*, which changes self-efficacy. Again, Meichenbaum (1977), Mahoney (1974) and others explain behaviour modification in cognitive terms. Some clinicians (and this point is of considerable relevance to our own argument) adopt a deliberately eclectic approach to the issue of explanations and techniques (e.g. Lazarus 1976). London (1972) claims, in an amusing and insightful article, that the placing of behaviour modification techniques within a behaviourist theoretical explanation has more to do with the initiation rituals and collective mythologies of a developing field than with scientific advances.

Given the plethora of competing explanations available for the explanation of the effects of behaviour modification, we shall pursue a suggestion of London's and ask – do we need to present behaviour modification techniques within the context of any theory at all? Is it necessary to set the teaching of behaviour modification procedures within the framework of any explanatory theory, if the purpose of the teaching is to improve practice rather than to stimulate or satisfy intellectual curiosity? We believe not.

Now this may seem no more than a bowing to the current stampede to immediate applicability and relevance (if stampede is what lemmings do). However, our claim that theory and practice are separable is in no way intended as a sop to the prejudices of Secretaries of State against social science. We are challenging the supposition that psychological theory 'directs practice' in the way that it is often claimed to do and which is often understood to be the case in other areas of human endeavour. In questioning the relevance of the study of explanatory theory to the practice of teacher, we are urging a reappraisal of the relationships of such theory to practice in education.

Theory and practice

This reappraisal begins with the view that is often held of the development and history of the natural sciences and upon which claims for the relevance of theory to practice are often based, directly or indirectly. There is a common belief that behind the majority of useful artefacts that litter our lives lies 'science'. The belief is reflected in the term 'applied science'. In some areas it is true that the study of the material world has resulted in knowledge, which has then been employed in the design and development of machines and processes. However, it is only in relatively recent times that man has developed a good enough understanding, or theory, of parts of the material world to allow reliable prediction of the consequences of previously untried arrangements of materials and events, and it is only within the last century that 'science' has really taken the lead in solving certain types of practical problems. Bronowski (1951) has this to say of eighteenth-century Britain: 'Science did not bring about the Industrial Revolution. It did not even precipitate it, for science was quite out of touch with such work' (p. 54). The inventors, far from being 'boffins', were self-made 'untaught mechanics like James Brindley' (p. 43).

Again, in a more recent critique of the view that material progress results from the 'application' of science, Fores and Rey (1979) discuss the case of George Stephenson, pioneer of the steam engine. Although undoubtedly brilliant, he is known to have been virtually illiterate and hence very unlikely to have been abreast of developments in science at the time of his breakthrough. To describe the activities of Stephenson as the 'application of science' is clearly mistaken; he, like most inventors, 'used all the knowledge at his disposal to create useful artefacts – but through most of history, formal, written-down knowledge of natural science has not, as a rule, been directly useful in creating and improving these artificial products' (Fores and Rey, 1979, p. 48). The view within education that 'theory underpins and informs practice' is related to this mistaken view of the relationship of theory to practice and product in other areas. The 'application of science' is a relatively recent and restricted activity, even in the material sciences.

London makes exactly this point when discussing the relationship of theory to the practice of behaviour modification:

The status of theory comes largely from the belief that technique develops out of theory, that is, that science underlies engineering. But this is only partly true even among the very 'hard' sciences, less so among the 'soft' sciences like the social and behavioural sciences, and not at all true for many endeavours where the existence of technological capacity and the practical need is what produces the technical application and, indeed, what 'nourishes' much of the theoretical development itself (London, 1972, p. 917).

London argues that it is through the use of the metaphor or analogy of conditioning and from the desperate need for effective treatments for psychological disorders that the 'technology' of behaviour modification has developed. Its continued growth is not due to the power of any explanatory theory on which it is dependent, but to the fact that, particularly within the clinical field, it 'works'. It helps to solve problems that people face. Man has never felt restricted in the use of artefacts or procedures because he does not fully understand how they work; indeed it is through their use that understanding of how and why they work develops.

If behaviour modification is not the appliance of (behaviourist) science, then is it, as friends and foes have argued, scientifically (or scientistically) stated, common sense? What remains to bind the disparate practices and findings together, if the explanatory theory vanishes? Two things remain. First, the methodology of empirical science, which both guides the application and validates the utility of particular practices and, secondly, a set of effective strategies, some suggested by work in experimental psychology, but all tested in actual practice. In other words, behaviour modification is composed of two distinct and necessary components: a framework for guiding interventions (the methodological component) and a set of techniques for changing behaviour (the technical component).

The guiding framework comprises three general procedures. The first is the measurement of behaviour before and after intervention in order to provide an objective index of change. The second is the implementation of a 'sequence analysis' or 'A–B–C analysis'. In this the antecedent or setting condition for the behaviour to be changed (A), the exact form of behaviour (B), and the consequences of the behaviour for the child or others (C) are all carefully identified. The third general procedure is the specification of clear goals, which may include preferred alternative behaviours to the one that is causing concern. The techniques by which behaviour change is achieved can be described as serving one of three functions, those of increasing a behaviour, of reducing a behaviour and of maintaining a behaviour. Techniques for increasing a behaviour include the use of discriminative stimuli and reinforcement. Methods for reducing the rate of behaviour include extinction and punishment. Maintenance of behaviour can be effected through teaching, generalization and the management of schedules of reinforcement.

To use terms such as reinforcement, extinction and discriminative stimuli in this account may seem inconsistent with our claim that behaviour modification is a technology that is independent of any particular theory, because these terms carry not only descriptive but also explanatory responsibility in some behavioural theories. In our account, they function only to describe. Ironically, our case here seems to coincide with that of some leading contemporary behaviourists. 'Catania said that "reinforcement" names a functional relationship, a fact to be explained rather than an explanatory concept' (Lee, 1981, p. 43).

Behaviour modification, then, entails a commitment to a scientific or methodological behaviourist approach – but no more. Indeed, it may be that it is from the practices of behaviour modification that progress in theorizing about human behaviour may occur, rather than vice versa, just as it was from technology that scientific theory learned much in the last century.

Mindless technology or technik

In suggesting that possession of an explanatory theory is not necessary for the effective and efficient use of those practices that are appropriate to the classroom, we do not intend to suggest that teachers pursuing degree-level academic work should not be taught about and encouraged to explore explanations of those practices. Honours and postgraduate work is in part characterized by the appraisal of such theories. The point is simply that such study is not a necessary condition for the effective practice of behaviour modification and that the presentation of behaviour modification as the 'application of learning theory' or of 'conditioning' is not only unnecessary, but may be wrong, both factually and pedagogically. This view is not widely held, however. Berger (1979) for instance, cautions against the dangers of a 'mindless technology' which he defines as 'the use of techniques divorced from their theoretical framework' (p. 418). He continues, 'it is when the techniques are taught or used with little or no regard to the theory and system of application that the dangers arise' (p. 419). Among the dangers that he is concerned about are teachers employing 'inappropriately implemented token systems' and 'time-out procedures when the conditions likely to justify their use are not satisfied' (ibid). Blackman (1980) expresses similar concern.

We would share Berger's concern here, but it is not at all clear why he feels that greater knowledge of 'the theory' or of the 'theoretical framework' (if by this he means explanatory theories such as radical behaviourism or social learning theory) would avoid such dangers. What would certainly be of value is a greater regard for and knowledge of a 'system of application', by which we take Berger to mean the sorts of methodological guidelines outlined above. The 'mindless' use of any technology is not to be commended. Berger goes on, however, to reject the view of behaviour modification as 'technology'. He writes: 'Behaviour modification is not, and never has been, simply a technology' (p.

418). His rejection of this view is based on the claim that behaviour modification 'has always had associated with it some theoretical position, or at least a set of assumptions about behaviour and behaviour change' (ibid). Berger's qualification here is important. He is right to say that behaviour modification has always been associated with a set of assumptions about behaviour and behaviour change. The problem, as we have said, is to discover what the assumptions actually are. In practice, they seem to boil down to what London (1972) calls 'a principle and a half, that is, that learning depends on the conditions in time, space and attention between what you do and what happens to you subsequently' (p. 913). Incidentally, we should note that London does regard behaviour modification as a technology.

These two views of technology – as appliance of theory or as an independent body of practices – relate to our earlier discussions of the relationship of theory to practice and of the concept of 'applied science'. For it is as 'applied science', we suspect, that Berger and many others, see behaviour modification. Fores and Rey (1979), whose work we discussed earlier, argue that discussion of theory and practice, science and production of technique, is severely handicapped by the absence within English of a counterpart to the German word *technik*, and by the British use of the word 'technology' to mean something rather less grand than, yet dependent on, 'applied science'. As Fores and Rey point out, 'Those who use the Technik conception concentrate...on the product, its utility, its specification and the methods used in making it. Those who use the "applied science" conception concentrate on inputs of knowledge which are allegedly important to the manufacturing process' (Fores and Rey, 1979, p. 50). While Fores and Rey are discussing the way in which the production of material artefacts is considered, we find their distinction quite appropriate to and helpful in consideration of behaviour modification. If we construe behaviour modification as technik, then, as with all technik education, learning the 'systems of application' and the principles that the practices embody are of much greater immediate importance than learning about a number of competing accounts of why those practices work. (For a fuller discussion of technik in social science, see Hastings and Schwieso, 1981.)

Conclusion

Behaviour modification is generally presented and understood within education as the application of a particular body of psychological theory, namely, behaviourism. We have argued that this view of the development of behaviour modification is mistaken in the same way that regarding technology as the application of science is mistaken; technology generally precedes scientific understanding. It is our view that viewing behaviour modification as a technology, or as social technik, will enable it to be separated from the metaphysical trappings of behaviourism and its place and value within education to be more dispassionately appraised.

References

Bandura, A. (1977), *Social Learning Theory* (Englewood Cliffs, NJ: Prentice-Hall).

Berger, M. (1979), 'Behaviour modification in education and professional practice: the danger of mindless technology', *Bulletin of British Psychological Society*, vol. 32, pp. 418-19.

Blackman, D. (1980), 'Images of man in contemporary behaviourism', in Chapman, A. J. and Jones, D. M. (eds) *Models of Man* (London: Macmillan).

Blackman, D. (1984), 'The current status of behaviourism and learning theory in psychology', in Fontana, D. (ed.) (1984) *Behaviourism and Learning Theory in Education* (Edinburgh: Scottish Academic Press).

Brewer, W. F. (1974), 'There is no convincing evidence for operant or classical conditioning in adult humans', in Palermo, D. (ed.), *Cognition and the Symbolic Processes* (New York: Halstead Press).

Bronowski, J. (1951), *The Common Sense of Science* (London: Heinemann).

Clark, C. (1979), 'Education and behaviour modification', *Journal of Philosophy of Education*, vol. 13, pp. 73-81.

Docking, J. W. (1980), *Control and Discipline in Schools* (New York: Harper & Row).

Eysenck, H. J. (1972), *Psychology is about People* (Harmondsworth: Allen Lane).

Fores, M. and Rey, L. (1979), 'Technik: the relevance of a missing concept', *Higher Education Review*, vol. 11, pp. 43-57.

Harrop, A. (1983), *Behaviour Modification in the Classroom* (London: Hodder & Stoughton).

Hastings, N. and Schwieso, J. (1981), 'Social technik: reconstruing the relationship between psychological theory and professional training and practice', *Oxford Review of Education*, vol. 17, pp. 223-30.

Lazarus, A. A. (1976), *Multimodal Behavior Therapy* (New York: Springer).

Lee, V. (1981), 'Terminological and conceptual revision in the experimental analysis of language development: why?', *Behaviourism*, vol. 9, pp. 25-53.

London, P., (1972), 'The end of ideology in behavior modification', *American Psychologist*, vol. 27, pp. 913–20.

Macintosh, N. (1984), 'In search of a new theory of conditioning, in Ferry, G. (ed.) *The Understanding of Animals* (Oxford: Basil Blackwell and New Scientist).

Mace, C. E., (1949), 'Some implications of analytical behaviourism, *Proceedings of the Aristotelian Society*, vol. XL1X, pp. 1–16.

Mahoney, M. J. (1974), *Cognition and Behaviour Modification* (Cambridge: Ballinger).

Meichenbaum, D. (1976), 'Cognitive behavior modification', in Spence, J. T., Carson, R. C. and Thibaut, J. W. (eds) *Behavioral Approaches to Therapy* (Morriston, NJ: General Learning Press).

Meichenbaum, D. (1977), *Cognitive Behavior Modification* (New York: Plenum Press).

O'Leary, K. and O'Leary, S. G. (1977), *Classroom Management: The Successful Use of Behaviour Modification* (Oxford: Pergamon Press).

Poteet, J. A. (1973), *Behaviour Modification: A Practical Guide for Teachers* (London: University of London Press).

Rettig, E. B. and Paulson, T. L. (1975), *ABC's for Teachers* (Van Nuys, Calif.: Associates for Behaviour Change).

Rotter, J. B. (1966), 'General expectations for internal versus external control of reinforcement', *Psychological Monographs*, vol. 30, pp. 1–26.

Saunders, M. (1979), *Classroom Control and Behaviour Problems* (Maidenhead: McGraw Hill).

Schwieso, J. and Hastings, N. (1981), 'The role of theory in the teaching of behaviour modification to teachers, in Wheldall, K. (ed.) *The Behaviourist in the Classroom: Aspects of Applied Behavioural Analysis in British Educational Contexts* (Birmingham: Educational Review Publications).

Skinner, B. F. (1974), *About Behaviourism* (London: Jonathan Cape).

Wheldall, K. and Merrett, F. (1984), *Positive Teaching: The Behavioural Approach* (London: Allen & Unwin).

Index

Note: For citations and references, only the first-named author is indexed. Within a chapter no citations to the author's own works are indexed.

For Product Safety Concerns and Information please contact our EU representative GPSR@taylorandfrancis.com Taylor & Francis Verlag GmbH, Kaufingerstraße 24, 80331 München, Germany

Batch number: 08165901

Printed by Printforce, the Netherlands